R e v i s i o n   f o r

HISTORY

GCSE Modern World History

To Julia and Helen for their patience and understanding

Revision for HISTORY

GCSE Modern World History

BEN WALSH
is a former Head of History
and History Project Officer, NCET

WAYNE BIRKS
is Deputy Principal at
Casterton Community College

JOHN MURRAY

In the same series:

Revision for English	Key Stage 3 *with answers*	0 7195 7025 5
Revision for Maths	Levels 3-8 Key Stage 3 and GCSE *with answers*	0 7195 7083 2
Revision for Science	Key Stage 3 *Revised National Curriculum Edition with answers*	0 7195 7249 5
Revision for Science	Key Stage 4 *with answers*	0 7195 5394 6

Also available:

History Revision	GCSE Modern World History	0 7195 7055 7

First published in 1996
by John Murray (Publishers) Ltd
50 Albemarle Street, London W1X 4BD

Layouts by Ann Samuel
Illustrations by Chartwell Illustrations and Karen Donnelly
Typeset in 11/13pt Rockwell
Printed and bound in Great Britain by St Edmundsbury Press, Bury St Edmunds

A CIP catalogue entry for this title can be obtained from the British Library

ISBN 0 7195 7229 0

CONTENTS

Acknowledgements

While every effort has been made to trace copyright holders the publishers apologise for any inadvertent omissions. The publishers gratefully acknowledge the contribution made by the following sources:

The Centre for the Study of Cartoons and Caricature, University of Kent, Canterbury, for the cartoons by David Low, *Evening Standard*, 23 May 1934 and 20 September 1939, **pp.23** and **182**; Daily Mirror Newspaper Group, **p.23**; Hulton Deutsch Collection Limited, **p.49**; St Helens Local History and Archive Library, **p.121**; The Aldous Archive and FDR Library, **p.139**; S. Lorant, *Sieg Heil! An Illustrated History of Germany from Bismark to Hitler*, **p.162**; David King Collection for The Murderer's Hygiene (1937) by Kukrinisky, **p. 183**.

INTRODUCTION

You will soon be taking your GCSE in Modern World History.
Your aim is to get the best grade that you can. Our aim in this book is to help you to get that grade.

To improve your grade you need to:
- get organised – this book will help you make a revision plan and stick to it
- know the content – the book will help you learn the core content for your course
- apply your knowledge – this book will help you apply what you know to actual examination questions.

How to revise

There is no single way to revise. But there are some golden rules everyone should follow:

1. *Know the objectives of your course:*
   Ask your teacher for full details of the course you are taking. This book uses examples from MEG Modern World syllabuses but the content sections are an excellent revision aid for any modern history course.
2. *Make a revision plan and stick to it:*
   Start your revision early – the earlier the better. Revise regularly – regular short spells are better than panicky six-hour slogs until 2 a.m.
3. *Revise actively* – be a scribbler; make notes as you learn. You will need an exercise book for most of the revision tasks but you can also write in this book.

The rest of this introduction is about how to apply these rules to your revision and make sure that you get the grade you are aiming for.

1 Know the objectives of your course

Assessment objectives for GCSE History

GCSE History has assessment objectives. These are similar in all GCSE History syllabuses. For example, in the MEG examination these objectives are:

1. To recall, select and deploy relevant knowledge and communicate in a clear and coherent form.

   This means
   - *using your knowledge of a topic to give examples to back up what you say in an answer*
   - *writing clearly and structuring your answers clearly.*

2. To demonstrate understanding of historical terminology and concepts (cause and consequence, change and continuity, similarity and difference).

   This means showing you understand
   - *why events happened*
   - *what happened as a result; for example, how a country changed between two dates*
   - *the definition of terms like Nazi, Depression etc.*

3. Empathy. You do not need to worry about this in your revision as it is only tested in coursework.

4. To interpret and evaluate a wide range of historical sources and their use as evidence.

   This means using photographs, diaries, books, recorded interviews – just about any kind of material from the time you are studying right up to modern history books. You are expected to:
   - *pull out important information*
   - *decide how far historians can rely on that information.*

Ask your teacher to show you the assessment objectives for your syllabus. The most important thing to remember is that the examiner is not just interested in finding out what you know but finding out *how far you understand and can apply your knowledge*: how far you can think for yourself about history.

2 Making a revision plan You will not only need to plan your revision for history. You will also need to fit in your history revision with your revision for all your other GCSE subjects.

You could use this kind of table to plan your overall revision:

Dates		Revision targets and deadlines			
Month	**Week**	**History**	**Science**	**English**	**Others**
Jan	4	Key points summary card for Russia			
Feb	2		Tests on metals		
Mar				Mock oral	

You could construct a table like the one below to plan your history revision. In your plan, aim to come back to each topic several times so that you revise in stages:
Stage 1: Put the date normal school-based work on a topic will be/was completed.
Stage 2: Put the target date for finishing your own summary of the key points for each topic.
Stage 3: Give yourself memory tests.
Stage 4: Fine tuning (e.g. final memorising and/or practice examination questions).

History topics	Date	Key points summary	Memory test	Fine tuning
1 Versailles		March	April	1993 Question–May
2 League of Nations				
3				

3 Revising actively Most students say when faced with revising for GCSE History:

The ideas in this book are all aimed at helping you to remember.

Use the revision tasks in this book

We believe the best way to remember information is to use it – to revise actively. To take an everyday example: to start with it is difficult to remember a new telephone number, but the more you use it the easier it is to remember it.
Throughout this book therefore we have provided revision tasks for you to do. Don't miss them out. If you do the tasks you will have to use the information in the book. If you use the information you will remember it better. The more you use the information the better you will remember it.

Use the key words method

Think of your brain as being like a computer. To read a file on a computer you need to know the name of the file. The file name is the key, and if you do not have this key you cannot get to the file, even though the computer has the file in its memory.

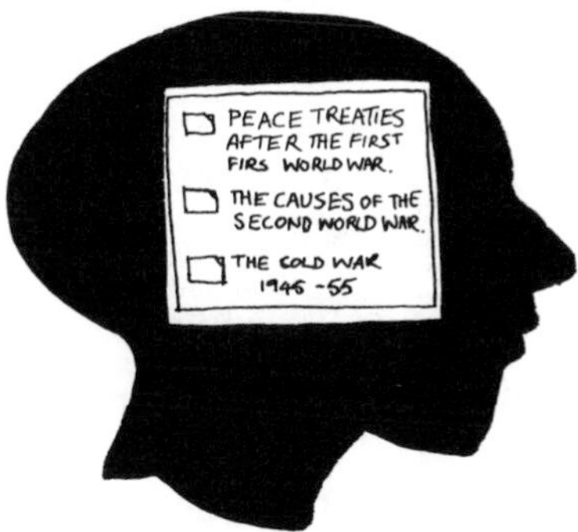

Your brain works rather like a computer. When you read something it goes in. But to get the information out again you have to have the keys to unlock your memory.

So one approach to jog your memory is to use a key words method. This is how it works.

1. As you read through each paragraph, highlight one or two key words. For example:
   What were the main political and economic features of the USA during the Cold War period?
   - It had a *democratic system*. The government of the USA was chosen in free democratic elections and the country was led by its President.
   - It had a *capitalist economy*. Business and property were privately owned. Individuals could make profits in business or move jobs if they wished. However, they might also go bankrupt or lose their jobs.
   - The USA was the world's wealthiest country, but under capitalism there were always *great contrasts* – some people were very rich, others very poor.
2. You can then use cue cards, or the revision plan at the end of each chapter to summarise your key words for each subheading. That way you can have a whole topic summarised on one sheet.
3. Later on, return to your revision plan and see if you can recall or rewrite important paragraphs using just the key words to jog your memory.

Other revision ideas

Different people revise in different ways and you may have your own ideas on how to work. Here are some other techniques which students have used.

- Summarising events in diagrams or pictures – see page 17 for an example
- Recording the text onto a cassette and playing it back
- Using acronyms or mnemonics – see page 47 for example
- Working with friends:
  - testing each other
  - comparing your answers to practice questions.

INTRODUCTION

How to use this book

Chapters 1–7 of this book cover part of the core content in Modern World History. You don't need to revise every topic, but the more topics you revise the more questions you will be able to answer in your examination – and the better chance you have of doing well.

Chapter 8 gives some general advice on answering source-based questions, and each of Chapters 9–12 covers one of the option units. Here again, you should concentrate on the topics you intend to answer in the examination.

Each chapter has the same features:

The opening page outlines the topic. It gives a summary of

- the KEY CONTENT which you need to know for that topic
- the KEY THEMES: the historical issues and themes which you need to understand and be aware of in order to tackle examination questions.

The Key Content

The next part is the largest section in each chapter. This is the part where the key content is described in detail. This is what you need to revise.

Important terms are highlighted in capital letters like this: APPEASEMENT. They are included in a glossary at the back of the book.

Analysis

At various points you will also see short paragraphs like this:

■ ***Self-determination sounds fine in theory but in practice it would be very difficult to give the peoples of Eastern Europe the chance to rule themselves because they were mixed and scattered across many countries. However the countries were reorganised, some people of one ethnic group were bound to end up being ruled by people from another.*** ■

These are to help you make your mind up about events. The examiner wants you to think for yourself about history. These paragraphs are supposed to help you do that. Sometimes they will give you ideas about how to interpret the events described in that part of the chapter. At other times they try to show how one event links with another, or to show the views of people involved in events at the time. These boxes will help you if you find it difficult to produce a balanced answer.

The following feature: ▲ will help you to prepare for answering source-based questions in particular. It highlights the reasons why particular sources might be useful in an enquiry and discusses the factors which affect the reliability of a source.

Revision tasks

These tasks help you revise actively. They help you to highlight important words, names, dates etc. and note them down. They also help you to think for yourself about the content.

Revision session

At the end of each chapter we take an examination question apart, and look at what should go into a good answer. We have called it a revision session because you can tackle it with another student or on your own. This feature will particularly help you if you find your answers sometimes miss the point, or if they are too long or too short.

Summary and Revision Plan This summarises the content covered in the chapter. Use this as a check list to make sure you are familiar with the content. Using the key word approach, this page could provide a complete summary of the chapter. You could also use it as a 'prompt sheet' when you are testing yourself.

The peace treaties after the First World War

The First World War was a disaster for Europe. Millions had been killed. Whole countries were devastated. The victorious leaders met in Paris in 1919 to try to work out how to stop a terrible war like this happening again.

To answer questions on the peace treaties at the end of the First World War you need to be familiar with both the key content and the key themes of the period.

KEY CONTENT

You will need to show that you have a good working knowledge of these areas:

A The background to the Treaty of Versailles
B The aims of the different leaders at the Paris Peace Conference
C The terms of the Treaty of Versailles
D German reactions to the Treaty of Versailles
E Criticisms of the Treaty of Versailles
F Other treaties at the end of the First World War

KEY THEMES

As with all examination questions, you will not be asked simply to learn this content and write it out again. You will need to show your understanding of some key themes from the period. These are:

- **Why the different leaders had different aims for the Treaty of Versailles**
- **Whether the Treaty of Versailles was really aiming to keep future peace or just to punish Germany**
- **How President Wilson's Fourteen Points affected the Treaty of Versailles**
- **The effects of the Treaty of Versailles on Germany**
- **How the German people and their leaders reacted to the Treaty of Versailles**
- **The problems of actually putting President Wilson's policy of self-determination into practice**

For example, look at the question below which is taken from MEG Paper I, 1993.

(a) (i) Name the President of the USA who signed the Treaty of Versailles. [*1 mark*]
(ii) Explain what is meant by 'reparations'. Briefly use your knowledge of the Treaty of Versailles to support your answer. [*3 marks*]

(b) In what ways were the Treaties of St Germain, Neuilly and Trianon similar to each other? [*6 marks*]

(c) To what extent were the terms of the Treaty of Versailles affected by the following?
I 'The Fourteen Points';
II The attitude of Prime Minister Clemenceau of France towards Germany;
III Lloyd George, the Prime Minister of Britain, promised to 'make Germany pay';
IV Germany was not involved in discussing the terms of the Treaty of Versailles.

Explain your answer fully by referring to I, II, III and IV. [*15 marks*]

This question is asking you to show your knowledge and understanding of this topic.

If you look carefully at the question you will see that you need to know about these important areas:

- *The leaders at the peace talks*
- *The terms of the Treaty of Versailles*
- *The other treaties at the end of the war*
- *The Fourteen Points.*

You will need to show your understanding of these themes:

- *How the attitudes of the different leaders affected the treaty*
- *How the Fourteen Points affected the treaty.*

We will look at this question in detail at the end of this chapter.

A The background to the Treaty of Versailles

1. Damage caused by the First World War The First World War was a shattering blow to Europe. Damage caused by the war had exceeded everyone's worst fears.

- Millions of soldiers on both sides had been killed or injured.
- Large areas of Belgium and France had been devastated and civilians had been killed.
- Two of Europe's most powerful countries, Germany and Austria-Hungary, were defeated and exhausted.
- Even the victorious powers were almost bankrupt from the cost of waging war for four years.

2. Germany was blamed for starting the war In France and Britain there was a strong feeling that Germany had been to blame for starting the war and that they should be made to pay for it.

Germans did not agree. They pointed out that other states should take a share of the blame for the war. But they were not invited to the Paris conference and so there was nobody to put their point of view.

3. The Paris Peace Conference The leaders of the victorious countries met in Paris in 1919 to try to settle the issues raised by the war. The biggest issue was how to prevent a war like this happening again. The old way of keeping peace, the ALLIANCES, had failed. In fact the alliance system helped to cause a small incident in the Balkans to turn into a world war. Everyone agreed that a new way of keeping peace was needed.

- The conference lasted from 1919–21.
- The most important outcome was the Treaty of Versailles. But there were other treaties agreed at Paris as well (see pages 8–9).

B The aims of the different leaders at the Paris Peace Conference

The most important and influential countries at the negotiations were France, Britain and the USA. Their leaders were known as the (victorious) allies. Even at the time it was clear that the different leaders had conflicting views of what a peace treaty should do. They could not all get what they wanted, so whose views would carry the most weight?

1. Georges Clemenceau: Prime Minister of France During the war France had suffered enormous damage. Large areas of land had been devastated and a lot of its factories had been destroyed. Millions of French people had been killed. Clemenceau was under pressure from his people to make Germany suffer.

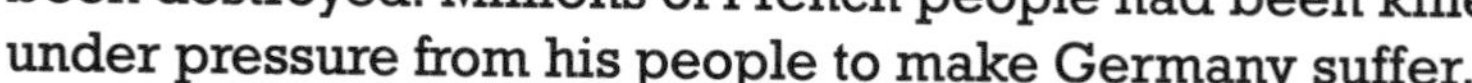

Clemenceau was also anxious about the future. He did not want Germany to recover its strength so that it could attack France again. So his aims were clear. He wanted a harsh treaty which would punish Germany and cripple it so that it could not threaten France again.

Some historians have criticised Clemenceau's attitude, but other historians can see his point of view.

2. Woodrow Wilson: President of the USA

The USA had only been in the war for its last few months. War damage was slight. American casualties were low in comparison with those of France or Britain.

Wilson did believe that Germany was to blame for the war but he believed that the treaty with Germany should not be too harsh. His view was that if Germany was treated harshly, some day it would recover and want revenge and another war would follow. Clemenceau was quite suspicious of Wilson.

The two most important ideas Wilson put forward at the peace conference were the ideas of:

- SELF-DETERMINATION (people ruling themselves, not being ruled by a foreign power)
- INTERNATIONAL COOPERATION (settling disputes by all countries working together).

His views on how to achieve these aims had been published in his 'Fourteen Points' in January 1918.

The Fourteen Points

1. No secret treaties between countries.
2. Free access to the seas for all countries.
3. Free trade between countries.
4. Disarmament by all countries.
5. Overseas colonies owned by European powers to have a say in their own future.
6. German troops to leave Russia.
7. Independence for Belgium.
8. France to regain Alsace Lorraine.
9. Frontier between Austria and Italy to be adjusted.
10. Self-determination for the peoples of Eastern Europe.
11. Serbia to have access to the sea.
12. Self-determination for the people in the Turkish Empire.
13. Poland to become an independent state with access to the sea.
14. A League of Nations to settle disputes between countries by peaceful means.

■ ***Self-determination sounds fine in theory but in practice it would be very difficult to give the peoples of Eastern Europe the chance to rule themselves because they were mixed and scattered across many countries. However the countries were reorganised, some people of one ethnic group were bound to end up being ruled by people from another.*** ■

3. David Lloyd George: British Prime Minister People in Britain were bitter towards Germany. They wanted a harsh peace treaty and Lloyd George had promised them that Germany would be punished. However, he wanted Germany to be justly punished. Like Wilson, he thought that Germany might want revenge in the future and possibly start another war. He also wanted Britain and Germany to begin trading with each other again.

Lloyd George was often in the middle ground between Clemenceau and Wilson at the peace talks. He did not agree with President Wilson about all the Fourteen Points – for example he did not support the idea of every country having free access to the seas.

REVISION TASKS

1. Use 4–6 key words to describe the damage caused by the First World War.

2. Complete the following table. Summarise each leader's view in no more than 5 words.

Leader	Country	Views on the Peace Treaty
Clemenceau		
Wilson		
Lloyd George		

3. Where would you put each of the leaders on this scale?

Moderate treaty → Harsh treaty

C The terms of the Treaty of Versailles

Each of the defeated countries had to sign a separate treaty with the victorious Allies. The most important treaty was the one which dealt with Germany. This was called the Treaty of Versailles. In the end this treaty was very severe. The main terms covered these areas:

1. **G**uilt for the war
2. **A**rmed forces
3. **R**eparations
4. **G**erman territories
5. **LE**ague of Nations.

1. Guilt for the war This clause was simple but harsh.
Germany had to agree that it was guilty of starting the war.

2. Armed forces of Germany The size of the German army worried all the Allies but especially France. The treaty therefore cut German armed forces to a level way below what they had been before the war.

- The army was limited to 100,000 men.
- Conscription (forced army service) was banned; soldiers had to be volunteers.
- Germany was not allowed armoured vehicles, submarines or aircraft.
- The navy could have only six battleships.
- The Rhineland (the area on the border between Germany and France) became a 'demilitarised zone'. No German troops were allowed into that area.

3. Reparations The Allies agreed (without consulting Germany, of course) that Germany had to pay compensation to France, Belgium and Britain for the damage caused by the war. These payments were called reparations. They were supposed to help the damaged countries to rebuild after the war. The exact figure (finally set in 1921) was £6,600 million, which was an enormous amount. If the terms of the treaty had not later been changed, Germany would not have finished paying this bill until 1984.

■ ***Clemenceau's influence can be seen in points 2 and 3. The limits on the armed forces were clearly designed to prevent Germany attacking France again and the demilitarisation of the Rhineland was an extra safety measure for the French against German aggression.***

The massive reparations figure was bound to cripple the German economy. ■

4. Loss of German territories The Allies agreed that lands and territories in Europe would be rearranged, and that Germany was going to lose out.

Germany's borders were very extensive, and the section dealing with territories was a complicated part of the treaty as the following map and table show.

Territory	From German control to:	Other points
1 Alsace Lorraine	France	–
2 Eupen, Moresnet, Malmedy	Belgium	–
3 North Schleswig	Denmark	After a vote (PLEBISCITE)
4 West Prussia and Posen	Poland	Free city controlled by League, to give Poland a port
5 Danzig	League of Nations	–
6 Memel	Lithuania	
7 Saar coalfields	France	A plebiscite would be held after 15 years
8 German colonies	France and Britain under League mandates	
9 Estonia, Latvia, Lithuania	Became independent states	Germany had taken these states from Russia in 1918

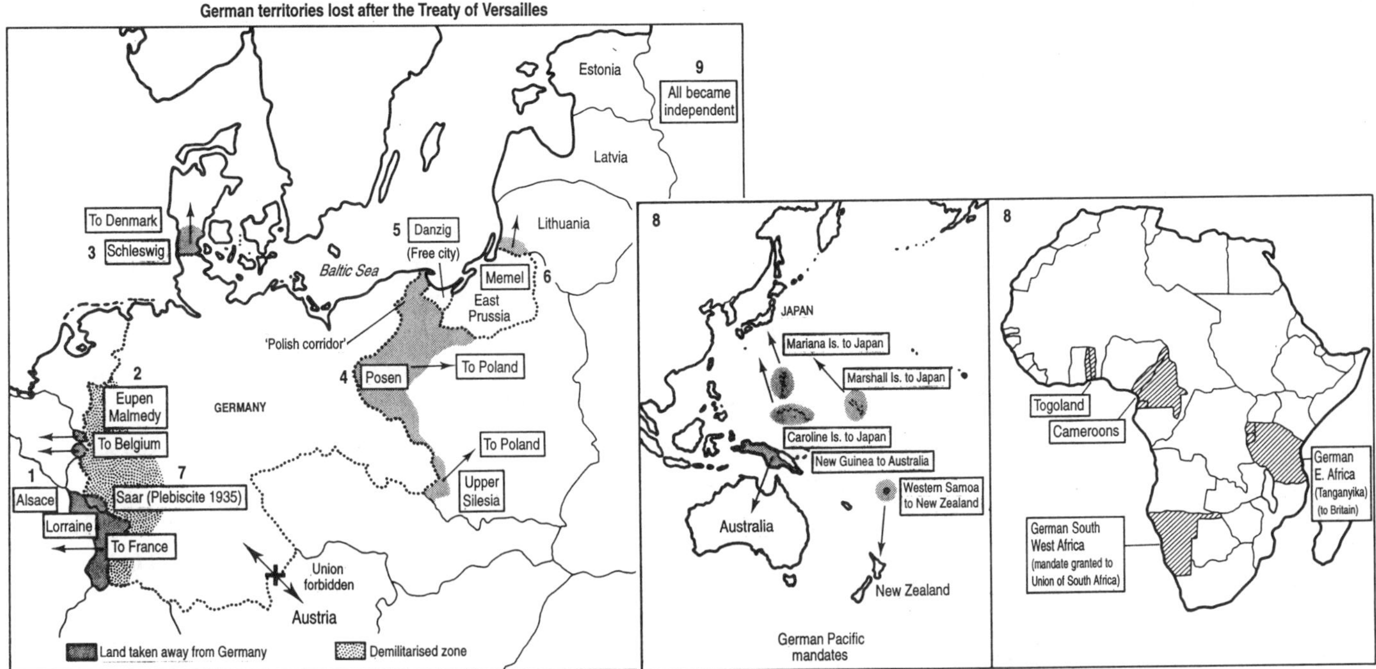

Other conditions

1. Anschluss (or joining together) between Austria and Germany was also forbidden. (Austria had always been a close ally of Germany and people in both countries were German-speaking.)
2. Along with the Treaty of St Germain (see page 8) a new country – Czechoslovakia – was created which included parts of Austria and Germany. Many of the people living in this new country were therefore German-speaking.

5. League of Nations Previous methods of keeping peace had failed and so the League of Nations was set up as an international 'police force'. The League was based on a covenant, or agreement (see page 14).

Germany was not invited to join the League until it had shown that it could be a peace-loving country.

■ ***In the treaty the spirit of revenge and harshness seemed to have triumphed over the desire for future peace. President Wilson's influence can be seen for example in that Estonia, Latvia and Lithuania became independent and the League of Nations was established, but his Fourteen Points did not influence the negotiations as much as he had hoped.***

Germany had been weakened and forced to accept a humiliating settlement which Germans saw as unjust. ■

REVISION TASKS

1. Did any state (except Germany) accept blame for the war?
2. Choose 5 key words to summarise the terms dealing with Germany's armed forces.
3. Explain why you think the reparations bill was so large.
4. Note 3 examples of territory lost by Germany.
5. Why was Germany not invited to join the League of Nations?
6. In your view which leader would have been most satisfied with the terms of the Treaty of Versailles? Explain your answer.

D German reactions to the Treaty of Versailles

The reactions of Germans were horror and outrage.

1. **Feelings of injustice** They felt the treaty was unjust on the following grounds:
   - *They did not feel they had caused the war*; yet they were forced to sign the war guilt clause.
   - *They did not even feel they had lost the war.* In 1918 they still had an army in the field. Many felt that Germany had not surrendered; they had simply agreed to stop fighting and seek peace. Yet they were being treated as the defeated side.
   - *They felt they should have been involved in the treaty discussions.* Yet their government was not represented at the talks and they were forced to accept the treaty without any choice or even a comment.

■ ***Whatever ordinary Germans may have believed, the German army could not realistically have fought on in 1918. Whether they liked it or not, they had lost the war.***

Most historians agree that other German reactions were valid; for example their point about not being consulted. However, others point out that German views would probably have been ignored in treaty negotiations. ■

2. **Feelings about war guilt** The Allies had to make Germany accept war guilt in order to justify the harsh terms of the treaty.

   The Germans were angry at this clause. At the very least the Germans thought that other countries should share the blame for the war.

3. **Feelings about disarmament** The disarmament terms angered Germans:
   - An army of 100,000 was very small for a country of Germany's size. Before the war it had been ten times this size.
   - The army was a symbol of German pride (just like Britain's navy).

   When the terms of the treaty were announced the German navy sank its own ships in the British Naval base of Scapa Flow in the Orkneys.

   As time went on German anger grew, particularly as none of the other countries disarmed during the 1920s, although disarmament was an aim of the League of Nations. When Hitler started to re-arm in the 1930s (secretly at first, then openly) it won him massive popular support in Germany.

4. **Feelings about reparations** The war was followed by economic chaos and crippling inflation in Germany which the Germans blamed on having to pay reparations. Most people agreed that the reparations figure was far too high. It was reduced in 1929.

5. **Feelings about loss of German territories** The loss of territories was deeply resented by the German people:
   - Some Germans would now be living in other countries ruled by foreign governments.
   - The Saar, an important industrial area, was taken over by France.
   - Their colonies in Africa (which had been a great source of pride) were to be run by Britain and France.

6. **Feelings about the League of Nations** Germany felt further insulted by not being invited to join the League.

7. **The contrast with the Fourteen Points** The Germans said that the treaty was not in keeping with Wilson's Fourteen Points. The Allies claimed they wanted to give self-determination to the peoples of Eastern Europe, yet the result of the treaty was that many Germans (e.g. in the Sudetenland which had become part of the new country of Czechoslovakia) were now part of a foreign country ruled by foreigners.

However, the Germans were not on strong ground in this respect. They had not previously shown much enthusiasm for the Fourteen Points. They did not pull their troops out of Russia, although the Fourteen Points demanded it. And even if Germans had ended up outside their own country, this was also true for many Poles, Russians, Romanians and Hungarians throughout Eastern Europe.

■ ***The bitter reaction of Germans to the Treaty of Versailles is a crucial theme in the history of the 1920s and 1930s. Partly as a result of the treaty, Germany had great problems in the 1920s. Hitler used these problems and German bitterness about the treaty to gain power in Germany. He promised the Germans that he would remove the injustices of the treaty.*** ■

REVISION TASKS

1. Produce your own key points summary of why Germans were outraged by the terms of the Treaty of Versailles. Mention:
   - War guilt
   - Army
   - Reparations
   - German territories
   - League of Nations
   - The Fourteen Points

E Criticisms of the Treaty of Versailles

The Treaty of Versailles was criticised by many people at the time and has also been criticised by historians since.

1. Views expressed at the time People at the time criticised the treaty for many different reasons.

- Some said it was too harsh on Germany. They predicted that Germany would want revenge and there would be another war.
- Some said it was not harsh enough – that it did not punish Germany enough.
- Some said the USSR should have been consulted.

The US Congress was very dissatisfied with the treaty and refused to sign it.

2. The views of historians Historians generally agree that the Treaty of Versailles failed, because in 1939 war broke out again in Europe.

They point out that it had two great weaknesses.

- Germany was punished and humiliated. Although this might have pleased people in the victorious countries at the time it was short-sighted because when Germany did recover many of its people wanted revenge.
- The treaty created some new countries which were weak and unstable.

However, it is important to realise how difficult a job the 'victorious allies' faced.

- The people in the victorious countries would not have accepted a fairer treaty. Clemenceau was criticised in France that the treaty *was not harsh enough.*
- In trying to ensure self-determination they faced the real problem that ethnic groups in Eastern Europe were so mixed up that it was impossible for each nation to rule itself.

REVISION TASKS

1. Use 3 key words to summarise why historians have criticised the Treaty of Versailles.
2. Use 6 words to summarise why people at the time criticised the Treaty of Versailles.
3. In your own words say why you believe (or do not believe) that the leaders at the Peace Conference had an impossible job.

F Other treaties at the end of the First World War

The Treaty of Versailles dealt only with Germany. Once it was settled 'The Big Three' left the conference and their assistants worked out the rest of the treaties dealing with Germany's allies. They used the Treaty of Versailles as a model.

1. Treaty of St Germain 1919: Austria This treaty separated Austria from Hungary. It forbade Austria from ever joining with Germany. It forced Austria to disarm. It also took territory from Austria as shown here:

Territory	From Austria to	Comments
1. Bohemia and Moravia	New state of Czechoslovakia	–
2. Bosnia and the new Herzegovina	New state of Yugoslavia	Also included the former kingdom of Serbia

Austria also lost territory to Poland, Romania and Italy. After this treaty, Austria was no longer a leading power in Europe.

However, the old Austrian empire had already collapsed by 1918. The Treaty of St Germain was really about sorting out a chaotic jumble of territories into new states rather than punishing Austria.

Italy was not happy with this treaty as it felt it should have received more land from Austria. On the other hand, many millions in Eastern Europe were given self-determination and freedom to rule themselves.

Austria suffered severe economic problems after the war, as much of its industry had gone to Czechoslovakia.

2. Treaty of Trianon 1920: Hungary This treaty was not signed until 1920 but like St Germain the main terms involved the transfer of territories:

Territory	From Hungary to
1. Ruthenia, Slovakia	Czechoslovakia
2. Slovenia, Croatia	Yugoslavia

Hungary was reduced in a similar way to Austria. It lost a lot of territory and population. Its industry suffered because it lost territories where its raw materials were found. Like Austria, Hungary had to disarm.

3. Treaty of Neuilly 1919: Bulgaria Bulgaria did well compared to Germany, Austria and Hungary. It lost lands to Greece, Romania and Yugoslavia and also lost its access to the sea. Like the other defeated countries, Bulgaria had to disarm.

Bulgaria had played a relatively small part in the war and was treated less harshly than its allies. Nevertheless, many Bulgarians were governed by foreign powers by 1920.

4. Treaty of Sèvres 1920: Turkey Turkey was important because of its strategic position and the size of its empire. Its territorial losses are shown here:

Territory	From Turkey to
1. Smyrna	Greece
2. Palestine, Iraq, Transjordan	League mandates under British control
3. Syria	League mandates under French control

Turkey also effectively lost control of the straits to the Black Sea. Turkey also had to formally accept that many of its former lands (e.g. Egypt, Tunisia, Morocco) were now independent or were under British or French MANDATE (control). In practice this was already true, but under this treaty, Turkey had to accept and agree to the arrangement.

Turks were outraged by this treaty. Turkish nationalists led by Mustafa Kemal challenged its terms by driving Greeks out of Smyrna. The result was the Treaty of Lausanne (1923) which returned Smyrna to Turkey.

Sèvres was not a successful treaty. The Turks successfully resisted part of it. The motives of Britain and France in taking control of former Turkish colonies were rather suspect. The Arabs who had helped the British in the war gained little. Palestine was also a controversial area and of course remains a troubled region to the present day.

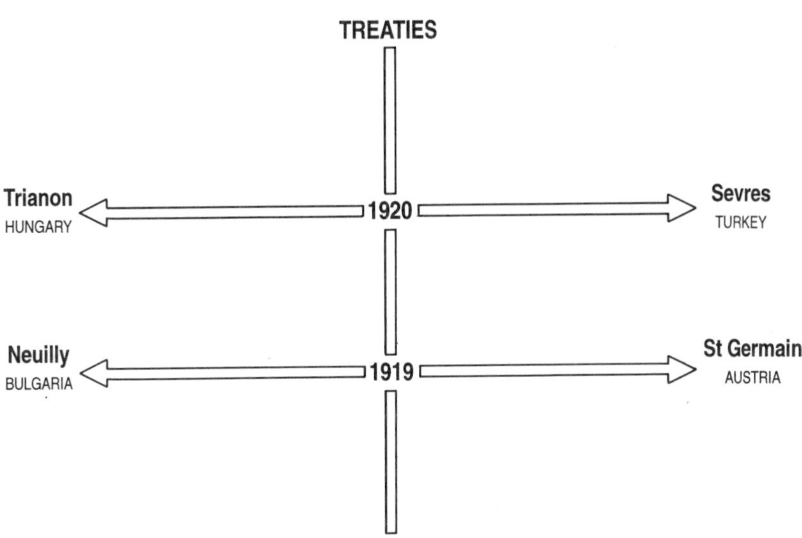

REVISION TASKS

1. Construct a summary table like the one below and use the information in this section to complete it.

Country	Treaty	Terms	Reactions
Bulgaria			
Turkey			
Hungary			
Austria			

The aim of this session is for you to see how you can apply your knowledge of the content in this chapter to the kind of questions you will face in your examination.

Examination questions

The peace treaties at the end of the war are very important and examiners usually set questions on this topic. Most of these questions concentrate on the Treaty of Versailles, but don't get caught out – the other treaties sometimes crop up too – as you can see from part (b) of this examination question from MEG Paper 1, 1993.

(a) (i) Name the President of the USA who signed the Treaty of Versailles. *[1 mark]*
(ii) Explain what is meant by 'reparations'. Briefly use your knowledge of the Treaty of Versailles to support your answer. *[3 marks]*

What is required?

Part (i) requires a simple factual answer.
Part (ii) is still testing your knowledge but is more demanding. An effective way to answer this would be to explain what reparations are and then provide examples from the Treaty of Versailles.

Ideas for your answer

1. For Part (i): Woodrow Wilson.
2. For Part (ii): Reparations were payments which had to be made by Germany to France, Belgium and Britain. The payments were supposed to help these countries to recover from the damage which had been caused by the fighting. The amount of reparations which Germany had to pay was £6,600 million. Germany had to pay because the Allies had forced her to accept the blame for the war.

(b) In what ways were the Treaties of St Germain, Neuilly and Trianon similar to each other? *[6 marks]*

What is required?

This is quite a complicated question. Obviously you need to know the terms of these treaties. You also need to show your understanding of the treaties by making clear which aspects are similar.

To aim for 2–3 marks you should identify and explain at least one similarity (e.g. all of them involve transfer of territories) and give details of which country gained or lost which territory. To aim for 4–6 marks you must pick out two or more similarities and explain the similarities, using examples.

Ideas for your answer

1. One similarity is that the three countries affected by the treaties all lost some of their territory. You should support this statement by giving examples of territories lost and who gained these lands (see pages 8–9).
2. You could then go on to point out that whilst Austria and Hungary lost a great deal of territory, Bulgaria was affected rather less. It would be a good idea to make the point that Bulgaria was far less involved in the war than Austria and Hungary and, as a result, lost less land.
3. Now go on to look at the effects on each country. Bulgaria lost land but Austria and Hungary lost large amounts of their populations and their economies were badly damaged. Also, all three countries were forced to disarm.
4. You could then reach a conclusion, pointing out that St Germain, Neuilly and Trianon worked in similar ways (taking away lands), but that the effects of Trianon and Saint Germain were greater than the effects of Neuilly.

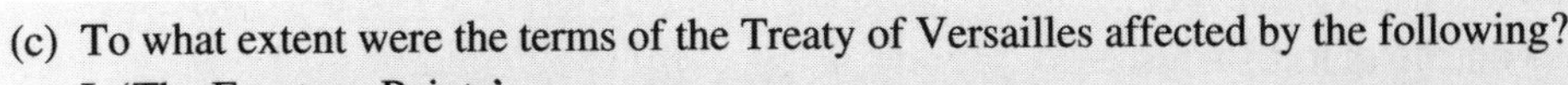

(c) To what extent were the terms of the Treaty of Versailles affected by the following?
I 'The Fourteen Points';
II The attitude of Prime Minister Clemenceau of France towards Germany;
III Lloyd George, the Prime Minister of Britain, promised to 'make Germany pay';
IV Germany was not involved in discussing the terms of the Treaty of Versailles.

Explain your answer fully by referring to I, II, III and IV. *[15 marks]*

What is required?

Although this is a challenging question, it is clear what the examiner wants from you. Your aim should be to show that you know the relevant details of points I–IV in relation to the Treaty of Versailles. In other words, you must:
- look at each of points I–IV
- explain how they are connected with the Treaty of Versailles
- explain whether these particular points had an important influence on what the treaty finally looked like when it was signed in 1919.

A low level answer will be a simple statement, for example: they all had some effect.

To aim for the next level (6–8 marks) you must describe points I–IV, saying how at least *one or two* of them did or did not affect the terms of the treaty.

To aim for the higher levels (10–15 marks) you must use examples to show how *each* of points I–IV did or did not affect the terms.

Ideas for your answer

1. It is usually a good idea to try to produce a balanced answer which shows that you can see that there are different ways of looking at events.

A good starting point might be to point out that very few of the original Fourteen Points were included in the final treaty. This would suggest at first that the Fourteen Points did not have much effect on the treaty. You could then give a brief explanation of the key aims of the Fourteen Points, and also say something about the beliefs and attitudes of President Wilson (see pages 2–3). From this, you could then go on to describe the unfavourable attitudes of Clemenceau or Lloyd George towards the Fourteen Points (and to Wilson himself) and why they felt the way they did (see Section B). These attitudes showed themselves in the final terms of the treaty.

So far you have shown how the Fourteen Points were not an important influence on the treaty. You could balance this up by pointing out which of the Fourteen Points were included in the treaty, and how important these particular points were, particularly the League of Nations (see Chapter 2).

2. The influence of Prime Minister Clemenceau is easier to demonstrate. A good approach would be to explain what Clemenceau's attitudes were to Germany before the treaty and why he held these views (see Section B).

You could then point out the terms in the Treaty of Versailles which affected Germany harshly (e.g. reparations) and those which brought advantages to France (e.g. the Saar region - see Section C for details). This would show how Clemenceau did influence the terms of the treaty, although he actually wanted a treaty which was even more harsh.

3. An important point to bring up when you look at Lloyd George is the question of reparations. This is obviously a case of 'making Germany pay'. You should also describe his attitudes to Germany before the peace talks began (see page 3). Again, to balance this picture you need to show that although he did want to make Germany pay, he did not want to go as far as Clemenceau in weakening Germany because he wanted to trade with her in the future. This would partly explain why Clemenceau did not get exactly what he wanted.

4. The fact that Germany was not consulted must be seen as important. Nobody was able to put the German case across at the talks and the other countries whose leaders were at the Paris Conference had all been at war with Germany. After the losses and destruction they were very unlikely to feel sorry for Germany without someone to argue the German point of view.

However, you must also make the point that Clemenceau and the others probably would not have listened to a German representative anyway, and that they had their own reasons for making the terms of the treaty the way they were.

SUMMARY AND REVISION PLAN

Below is a list of headings which you may find helpful. Use this as a check list to make sure that you are familiar with the material featured in this chapter. Record your key words alongside each heading.

A The background to the Treaty of Versailles

1. Damage caused by the First World War ____________ *millions dead*
2. Germany was blamed for starting the war
3. The Paris Peace Conference

B The aims of the different leaders at the Paris Peace Conference

1. Georges Clemenceau
2. President Wilson
3. Lloyd George

C The terms of the Treaty of Versailles

1. Guilt for the war
2. Armed forces
3. Reparations
4. German territories
5. League of Nations
   - aim
   - the Covenant

D German reactions to the Treaty of Versailles

1. Feelings of injustice
2. Feelings about war guilt
3. Feelings about disarmament
4. Feelings about reparations
5. Feelings about loss of German territories
6. Feelings about the League of Nations
7. The contrast with the Fourteen Points

E Criticisms of the Treaty of Versailles

1. Views expressed at the time
2. The views of historians

F The other treaties at the end of the First World War

1. St Germain 1919: Austria
2. Trianon 1920: Hungary
3. Neuilly 1919: Bulgaria
4. Sèvres 1920: Turkey

CHAPTER 2

The League of Nations and the search for international order in the 1920s

The First World War showed that the old ways of keeping peace had failed – the world's leaders now had to find another way to prevent war. The 1920s saw the setting up of the League of Nations and many other individual agreements between countries.

To answer questions on the League of Nations and the search for international order in the 1920s you will need to be familiar with both the key content and the key themes of the period.

KEY CONTENT

You will need to show that you have a good working knowledge of these areas:

A The aims of the League of Nations
B The roles of the various bodies within the League
C The strengths and weaknesses of the League
D The League's successes in the 1920s
E The League's failures in the 1920s
F The aims, terms and results of international agreements in the 1920s

KEY THEMES

As with all examination questions you will not be asked simply to learn this content and write it out again. You will be asked to show your understanding of some key themes from the period. These are:

- **The attitudes of the major powers to the League of Nations**
- **How the League made decisions**
- **The importance of the work of the League's agencies**
- **Why the major powers sometimes acted without the League**
- **How far the League was responsible for the relative peace in international affairs in the 1920s**

For example, look at the question below which is taken from MEG Paper I, 1994.

(a) (i) Name the 1928 Pact which was signed by sixty-five countries. [*1 mark*]
(ii) Explain what is meant by the phrase 'right of veto'. Briefly use your knowledge of the structure of the League of Nations to support your answer. [*3 marks*]

(b) How similar were the following to each other?
I The Dawes Plan;
II The Young Plan. [*6 marks*]

(c) Which one of the following statements is the more correct view of the work of the League of Nations in the 1920s?
– The work of the League of Nations greatly helped to keep peace in the world in the 1920s.
– The League of Nations was weak from the start and had more failures than successes in the 1920s.

Explain your answer fully by referring to I and II. [*15 marks*]

This question is asking you to show your knowledge and understanding of this topic.

If you look closely you will see that you need to know about these important areas:

- The terms of the Kellogg Briand Pact
- The structure of the League and how it made decisions
- The terms of the Dawes and Young Plans.

You will need to show your understanding of these themes:

- What the Dawes and Young Plans were trying to achieve
- The importance of the League's peace-keeping work
- The importance of the other work which the League did.

We will look at this question in detail at the end of this chapter.

THE LEAGUE OF NATIONS

A The aims of the League of Nations

The idea of a League of Nations had been around for many years, but it was the First World War which put the issue to the top of the agenda. People thought this was one way of preventing another war.

The League of Nations had a COVENANT or a set of rules which determined how it worked. The covenant had 26 articles (or sections).

The covenant also laid out the aims of the League. These were:

- To prevent aggression by any nation
- To encourage cooperation between nations
- To work towards international disarmament
- To improve the living and working conditions of all peoples.

The League was built around the idea of COLLECTIVE SECURITY. This meant that the members of the League could prevent war by acting together to protect and defend the interests of all nations.

■ ***The aim above all else was to prevent war. However, careful reading of the covenant shows that the League was setting itself a very ambitious task. As well as trying to prevent war, the League was planning to try to remove the factors (such as economic hardship) which made war more likely.*** ■

B The roles of the various bodies within the League

The League was made up of a number of different organisations or bodies. Each body dealt with different issues and had different powers and responsibilities.

The main bodies of the League of Nations

The Assembly

The Council

The Disarmament Commission

The Secretariat

Report

The Permanent Court of Justice

The Mandates Commission

Special Committees

The International Labour Organisation

1. The assembly

The assembly was the debating chamber of the League and was located at the League's headquarters in Geneva, Switzerland. When the League of Nations began work in January 1920, it had a total membership of 42 countries. Each of these countries had a single vote in the assembly. The assembly met once a year. It could

- admit new members to the League
- elect permanent members to the council

– vote on the League's budget
– suggest revisions or changes to existing peace treaties.

Any decisions made by the assembly had to be unanimous (agreed to by all members) and it could only recommend action to the League council. It could not carry it out.

2. The council The League council met up to three times a year and in times of emergency. The council had five permanent and four temporary members.

– The five permanent members were the major powers: Britain, France, Italy, Japan and (from 1926) Germany. The permanent members could VETO (stop) any action proposed by the council.
– The four temporary members were elected for three years at a time.

■ ***The USA should have been one of the permanent members. The idea of setting up a League was strongly supported by the US President, Woodrow Wilson. But the League was dealt a body blow right from the start: the US Senate voted against Wilson and refused to let America join (see page 18), so the most powerful country in the world was absent.*** ■

■ ***The council faced problems almost from the beginning. The creators of the League had hoped that the major powers would be able to dominate the council. But the absence of the USA meant that until 1926 the number of temporary members was equal to the number of permanent members. This in turn meant that the major powers could not always be sure of getting their way.*** ■

3. The Permanent Court of International Justice This court was based at the Hague in the Netherlands. It was made up of judges who represented the different legal systems of member countries. The court's two main functions were

- to give a decision on a dispute between two countries, if asked
- to give legal advice to the assembly or council (e.g. on treaties).

However, the court had no way of making sure that its decisions were put into action.

4. The International Labour Organisation (ILO) The aim of the ILO was to improve the conditions of working people throughout the world.

- It was made up of employers, governments and workers' representatives who met once a year.
- It collected statistics and information about working conditions.
- It tried to persuade member counties to adopt its suggestions and ideas for improvement.

Particularly important issues for the ILO were wage rates, hours of work, safety, health at work, unemployment and employment of women and children.

5. The League of Nations Commissions As well as dealing with disputes between its members the League also attempted to tackle other major problems. This was done through the creation of commissions or committees which looked into a wide range of issues.

- The Mandates Commission was set up to make sure that if a country controlled a territory under the terms of a League MANDATE, it acted in the interests of the people of that territory (not in its own interests).
- The World Health Organisation (WHO) attempted to deal with the problem of dangerous diseases.
- The Refugee Organisation helped to return people to their original homes at the end of the First World War.
- A Slavery Commission was set up to work for the abolition of slavery.

The League also made recommendations on the marking of shipping waters and produced an international highway code for road users.

6. The secretariat The secretariat was a sort of civil service which carried out the work and administration of the League.

- It kept records of League meetings and prepared reports for the different organisations within the League.
- The secretariat was also divided into many different sections (e.g. health, armaments, economic and financial matters).

■ ***The League seemed to be a large and prestigious organisation when it was first set up in the 1920s. Many powerful nations were members and its bodies had clear aims. The framework clearly existed in theory for the League to become an international 'police force'.***

However, from the start, there were doubts about whether it would work in practice, particularly without the USA. And the way the assembly and the council were set up meant that making a decision was a slow and complicated process. ■

REVISION TASKS

1. Produce a key words list (4–6 words) to summarise the aims of the League of Nations.
2. Use the text in this section to make notes on the diagram of the League on page 17.
   Note
   – what each body was for
   – how it worked and what problems it faced.

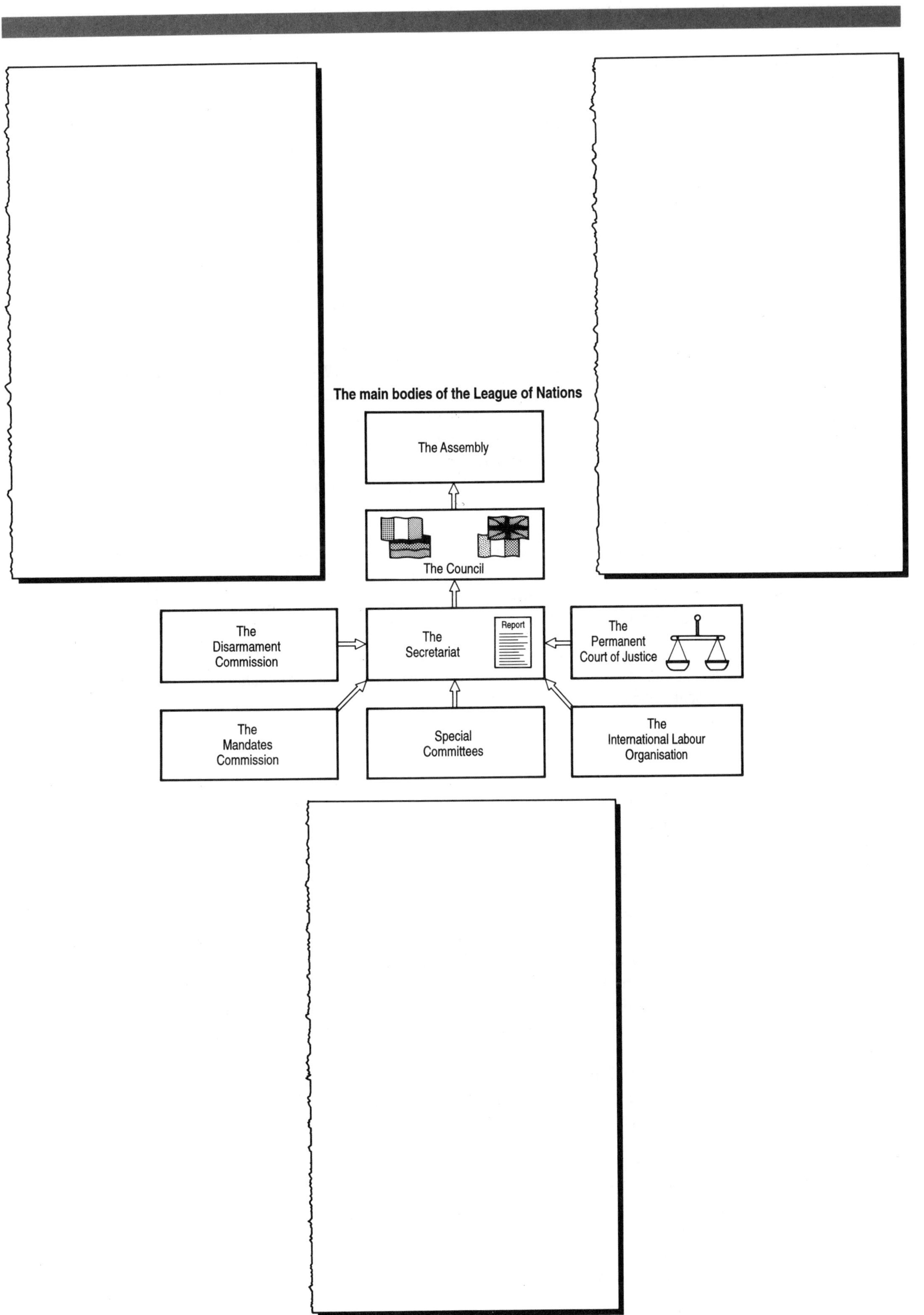
The main bodies of the League of Nations
The Assembly
The Council
The Disarmament Commission
The Secretariat
Report
The Permanent Court of Justice
The Mandates Commission
Special Committees
The International Labour Organisation

C The strengths and weaknesses of the League

1. **The League's powers in theory** Article 16 of the Covenant of the League spelt out its powers. If any member of the League committed acts of aggression against another member country, then the League could
   - say that it disapproved of the action by the aggressor
   - impose ECONOMIC SANCTIONS (stop members of the League trading with the aggressor)
   - use military force against an aggressor.

2. **The League's powers in practice** The powers sound considerable in theory. In practice, however, the League was weakened by the following:
   - *It had no armed forces of its own.* It relied entirely upon the cooperation of its members to carry out any of its decisions. Without the USA this meant it relied on its two principal members, Britain and France, to act. If it was not in their interests to take action, the League was powerless.
   - *Military force would always be a last resort because of the cost.* In the 1920s Britain and France were still recovering from the dreadful effects of the First World War and it was very hard to convince them to send troops to settle a dispute. Armed force was not used by the League even when Japan invaded Manchuria in 1931 (see page 46).
   - *Economic sanctions were difficult to enforce.* Member countries were unwilling to stop trading with an aggressor because it would harm their own trade as much as an aggressor's. When economic sanctions were imposed against Italy in 1935–6, they were not very effective.

   ■ ***The problems facing the League can be summed up as the conflict between the self-interest of the member countries and the interests of the League. If the two conflicted there was little chance of the League taking effective action.*** ■

3. **Membership of the League** When the League of Nations was created in 1920 there were 42 original member countries. By 1930 membership had risen to nearly 60. Unfortunately, at any one time, several of the biggest and most powerful countries in the world were not members of the League.

4. **Non-membership of the League**

The USA

The USA never joined the League of Nations despite the wishes of President Wilson in 1919. He was one of the original architects of the League of Nations and wanted his country to take a leading role in helping to maintain world peace. Many of his countrymen, however, did not agree with him. They wanted to keep the USA out of European affairs. This isolationist tendency was partly a result of the high human cost in the First World War and also because there was a feeling of self-sufficiency in the USA.

Historians have suggested that if the British government had known in advance that the USA would not join the League of Nations then Britain would have also refused to join.

The USSR (Russia)

In 1917 a communist government took power in Russia and made its own peace treaty with the Germans. This government was very suspicious of countries in the west and the countries in the west were suspicious of it. There were several reasons for this:

- The USSR saw the League of Nations as a club dominated by rich countries opposed to communism.

- The communists (Reds) were also fighting a desperate civil war against 'White' Russian forces who were supported by western countries.
- The USSR was encouraging revolution in other countries in the early 1920s – this would not have made it very welcome in the League.

The USSR did not join the League until 1934.

Germany

As the defeated enemy in 1918, Germany was forced to accept the Treaty of Versailles drawn up by the victorious powers (see Chapter 1). There was still much bitterness against Germany after the First World War. Under the terms of the treaty, Germany was not allowed to join the League of Nations.

German membership of the League was only considered after seven years of steadily improving relations. Germany was finally admitted to the League in 1926.

■ ***The success of the League depended on the right membership. The fact that the USA never joined badly weakened the League. Germany and Russia were members for a limited time only. The absence of major powers at various times meant that the British and French governments had to supply the necessary leadership to enable the League to operate effectively. The British and French governments were not really prepared to use force to help support the League. They were not the great powers they had once been.*** ■

REVISION TASKS

1. Make a list of the powers of the League.
2. Alongside each one explain why the League was not as powerful as it seemed.
3. For each of the USA, Russia and Germany, explain the following:
   a) why it was not a member of the League from the start
   b) when and why it joined the League (Russia and Germany only)
   c) the importance of this country to the League.
4. If you were the leader of a small country thinking of joining the League in 1920, what advantages do you think membership would give you and what disadvantages? Construct a table like the one below and list them under these headings:

Advantages	Disadvantages

Look at your list and decide whether you would join.

D The successes of the League in the 1920s

Although it had its problems and its critics, the League did also have its successes. However, the reputation of the League suffered because these successes were either small-scale or were only partial successes.

1. Solving international problems The major purpose of the League was to try to solve disputes between nations without them ending in war. In the 1920s the League became involved in trying to sort out many disputes in different parts of the world.

1920-1 The Aaland Islands
The League successfully intervened to prevent a conflict between Finland and Sweden over which state owned these islands. The League decided that the islanders should remain under Finnish control. However, the rights of the Swedish minority in the islands were to be protected.

1920 Upper Silesia
This area was on the border between Germany and Poland and contained both Germans and Poles. When conflict threatened the League organised a PLEBISCITE (people's vote) on whether they should become part of Poland or part of Germany. Based on the result of the vote the League decided to divide the area up. One third went to Poland and two thirds to Germany in a peaceful settlement.

1922 Austria
The Austrian government was facing economic disaster after the losses from the First World War and the Treaty of Versailles which followed (see Chapter 1). The League sent a team of financial experts to help the Austrian government. They managed to prevent the collapse of the Austrian economy by reorganising Austria's finances and it's currency.

1925 Greece/Bulgaria
In October 1925 Greek troops invaded Bulgaria. The League appealed to both countries to stop fighting, which they did. The League's commission of enquiry found in favour of the Bulgarians and the Greeks had to pay compensation.

■ ***These successes have often been forgotten. They all involved small nations rather than great powers. Even so the League showed that it was capable of successfully preventing disputes and in some cases it was even able to stop fighting once it had already broken out.*** ■

2. The International Labour Organisation (ILO) Some of the League's greatest successes came in its work to improve the lives of ordinary people throughout the world.

The ILO made several important contributions to improving people's working conditions. The ILO got its member countries to agree to the following principles:

- A target working day of 8 hours maximum and a working week of 48 hours maximum.
- All workers should have the right to join a trade union and have annual paid holidays.
- No one should be in full time work under fifteen years of age.

The ILO regularly published its findings and recommendations in order to increase pressure on governments throughout the world.

3. Other areas of success The League was also successful in other areas of work.

- It had some success in fighting three different but very unpleasant activities – slavery, gun-running and drug trafficking.
- The League's Minorities Commission put pressure on governments which did not respect the rights of minority groups.
- The World Health Organisation enjoyed some success in helping countries to control outbreaks of life-threatening diseases.
- The League helped to repatriate (return to their own countries) approximately 400,000 First World War prisoners.

■ ***The greatest success for the League tended to be in its work as an agency, helping people and tackling problems such as disease.*** ■

REVISION TASKS

1. Construct a table like the one below and use it to summarise the League's 'track record' in solving disputes in the 1920s.

Area	Reason for dispute	League action	Success?

2. Create a key word list to summarise the successes of the League's agencies in the 1920s.
3. Which of the League's successes do you think are more important – those in task 1 or those in task 2? Explain your choice.

E The failures of the League in the 1920s

The League of Nations has had a 'bad press' from historians. They often say it was a failure. This is not entirely fair. As you have seen, the League had its successes. However, these successes tended to be small-scale, whereas its failures were more high-profile (and they got worse in the 1930s).

1. International disputes in the 1920s

1919/20 Vilna

Vilna was the former capital of Lithuania, but contained many Poles. It was seized by the Polish army in 1919 and so the new government of Lithuania appealed to the League of Nations. The League protested against the Polish action, but Vilna remained under Polish occupation. France, a key member of League, supported Poland's claim to Vilna in return for Polish support in the event of a future attack by Germany.

1923 Corfu

In 1923 an Italian General named Tellini who was working for the League of Nations boundary Commission was murdered in Greece. Mussolini, the leader of Italy, demanded 50 million lira compensation from the Greek government, ordered his guns to bombard the Greek island of Corfu and demanded that the killers be handed over.

The Greek government did not know who the killers were and appealed to the League. The League Council suggested that the Greeks pay compensation to the League which would hand back the money once the murderers had been found.

However, Mussolini had other ideas. He said the Conference of Ambassadors (a group outside the League which was made up of the ambassadors of France, Japan and Italy) should judge the case rather than the League. Mussolini got his way and the Conference judged that Greece should pay Italy what it was demanding.

■ ***This was the first real sign of the limited power of the League of Nations when dealing with a powerful country such as Italy. The authority of the League was undermined by its own permanent members.*** ■

2. Disarmament By the mid 1920s it was accepted that an arms race had helped to cause the First World War. The major powers (UK, France, Italy, Japan and the USA) had met at the Washington Conference in 1922 and agreed some limits on naval power.

Then in 1925 there were plans for the League to organise a world disarmament conference. However, League members failed to agree on this – most were worried that disarming might leave them vulnerable.

■ ***League members were looking after their own self-interests as well as trying to be members of the League. In many cases there was no conflict, but there were other cases such as Corfu and the disarmament conference where the self-interest of a country clashed with the aims of the League.*** ■

BRITAIN HOLDS THE RING —PAGE 12

WIRELESS AND AMUSEMENTS: SEE "ON OTHER PAGES" ON PAGE 2

Daily Mirror

THE DAILY PICTURE NEWSPAPER WITH THE LARGEST NET SALE

No. 9,327 Registered at the G.P.O. as a Newspaper. MONDAY, OCTOBER 16, 1933 One Penny

ARMS CONFERENCE TO STOP —First Result

Germany's Action—

DOWNING STREET TALK TO-DAY

Swift developments have followed Germany's decision to cut herself loose from the League of Nations and the Disarmament Conference.

The first serious repercussion was felt last night, when British, French and Italian representatives met in Geneva to consider the future of the Disarmament Conference.

Mr. Henderson will recommend to-day that the General Commission on Disarmament shall adjourn for a brief period to enable Governments to take stock of the situation.

Signor Mussolini, apparently, is seeking to intervene in the crisis. It was reported last night that he wants to negotiate with Germany and to call a Four-Power Conference.

"The Utmost Gravity"

The French Government regards the situation as of the utmost gravity. Reuter was told in Paris last night, but talk of the application of sanctions and reoccupation of the Ruhr at this juncture was described as being "as mischievous as it is ridiculous."

Germany's decision may bring about the fall of M. Daladier's Government, which was already adversely affected by its decision to make a further cut in arms in support of the proposed Arms Convention.

Now M. Daladier's opponents will rally against him. Germany's action has provoked less evidence of alarm in authoritative quarters in London than appears to exist in some other capitals.

While her decision to leave the League of Nations caused profound surprise, the possibility of a refusal to accept the two main points of the proposed Arms Convention was foreseen.

But no one was prepared for the dramatic and spectacular method of rejection.

The Prime Minister returned to 10, Downing-street, last night from Chequers, and was in consultation there with Mr. Baldwin. They also spoke at length on the telephone to Sir John Simon in Geneva.

Several members of the Cabinet, it is understood, will meet in Downing-street to-day to discuss future developments, but there will be no official Cabinet meeting.

LAST EFFORT TO AVOID AN ARMS CRASH

GENEVA, Sunday.

The small committee of the Powers which discussed the future of the Disarmament Conference under the presidency of Mr. Henderson this evening was apparently not willing to make a cut-and-dried recommendation, but compromised on a suggestion for a brief adjournment to enable delegates to consult their Governments.

A week's adjournment is mentioned, but as the principal delegates will leave Geneva after the meeting it is doubtful whether proceedings will really be resumed a week hence.

The meeting this evening examined the situation from every angle, and realised that a recommendation to adjourn sine die might provoke strong opposition.

It was felt that it would be preferable to examine the grounds very thoroughly to avoid a crash in the General Commission. The Italian Government has openly come out for a complete adjournment and the Americans are known to favour it, but Dr. Benes was strongly opposed to it.

The meeting to-night also agreed upon the terms of the letter to be sent to Baron von Neurath in reply to his telegram to Mr. Henderson, accusing the Powers of refusing to disarm.

The latter will submit a draft to the General Commission to-morrow afternoon and it will probably be adopted without modification. It

(Continued on page 3)

Herr Hitler deliverin[illegible]

Herr von Keller, who was the last official German representative at the League of Nations.

Grave faces as [illegible]

THE CONFERENCE EXCUSES ITSELF.

REVISION TASKS

1. Use the two examples of Vilna and Corfu to explain the weaknesses of the League of Nations.
2. Why was disarmament such a sensitive issue?
3. In task 4 on page 19 you put yourself in the position of a leader in 1920. Do you think the views of that leader would have changed by the late 1920s?

F The aims, terms and results of international agreements in the 1920s

1. Concerns of the major powers Each of the major powers had different interests and concerns in the 1920s:

- France was most worried about protecting itself from attack by Germany.
- Germany was most concerned about getting a stable government and economy at home and regaining its position as a peaceful and respectable state.
- Britain was most concerned about rebuilding its empire and trade which had suffered badly in the war.
- The USA was most concerned with staying well out of European affairs.

Sometimes these aims could be achieved through the League of Nations – sometimes they could not. As a result, the 1920s was a period which saw a large number of international agreements. Some of these aimed to strengthen the League of Nations. Some of them were completely separate from it.

2. France's treaties Despite the damage done to Germany by war and by the Treaty of Versailles, France's main concern in the 1920s was still how to protect itself from possible future attacks by Germany.

France felt very isolated in this because the USA and Britain did not share France's fear of Germany.

- Neither Britain nor the USA shared a border with Germany.
- Britain was mostly concerned with its empire.
- The USA was keen to stay out of European affairs.

So throughout the 1920s French governments tried to create a network of alliances with other countries in Europe which could help her against Germany if war broke out. The result was a series of military or friendship treaties with countries which surrounded Germany. These included agreements with the following:

– Belgium (1920)
– Poland (1921)
– Czechoslovakia (1924)
– Romania (1926)
– Yugoslavia (1927).

■ ***Although France was enthusiastic about many of the League of Nations agreements, it was clear from her other alliances that she did not have complete faith in the League's ability to protect her from Germany.*** ■

3. The Geneva Protocol, 1924

Background

The Corfu incident in 1923 (see page 22) showed that the League of Nations had serious weaknesses when it was challenged by a powerful country. Britain and France drew up the Geneva Protocol **to strengthen the position of the League** in case of future disputes.

Terms

If two members of the League were in dispute they would have to ask the League to sort out the dispute. The two countries had to accept the decision of the League's council. The protocol meant that the armed forces of the League's member countries could be used against an aggressor.

Results

The French government hoped that the protocol would help to secure the peace treaties signed at the end of the First World War. However, the Geneva Protocol was unsuccessful.

Before the plan could be put into effect, the Labour government in Britain fell from power and early in 1925 the new Conservative government announced it would not agree the protocol and refused to sign it.

The new British government was worried by the protocol. They were concerned that Britain would be forced to agree to something which was not in her interests.

■ ***The failure of the Geneva Protocol showed that the League of Nations had serious weaknesses. The Geneva Protocol had been designed to strengthen the League, but it had to be abandoned because of the self-interests of one of its members (in this case, Britain). This problem was to appear again over the coming years.*** ■

4. The Dawes Plan, 1924

Background

In 1923 Germany was in chaos.

- There had been no stable government since 1918. Extreme groups of Nazis and communists were threatening to take over the government.
- The economy was on the verge of collapse.
- There was the huge reparations bill.
- Massive inflation had made the German currency worthless (see page 36).

In 1923 Germany announced that it simply could not pay its reparations instalment. French and Belgian troops moved in to the Ruhr (Germany's main industrial area). German workers resisted the occupying troops by refusing to work.

To resolve the problem, the British government asked the United States to intervene **to sort out the German economy**.

Terms

In January 1924 a committee led by General Charles Dawes began to look into ways of making sure that Germany continued to pay her large reparations bill without bankrupting her economy.

In April 1924 Dawes produced his proposals:

- Germany's reparations bill would be paid over a longer period.
- American loans would be made available to help rebuild German industry and to help them pay the reparations bill.
- The German currency would be reorganised.

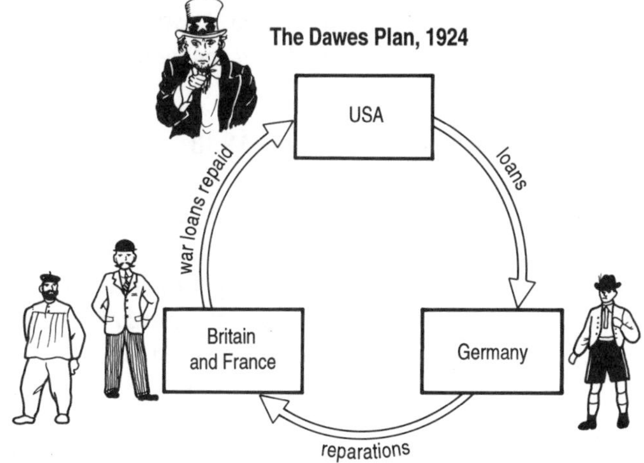

Results

The Dawes Plan had something for everyone. The proposals were accepted by Britain, France and Germany. By November 1924 French and Belgian troops finally pulled out of the Ruhr.

By 1926 the German economy was strong again and its government was stable. It was invited to join the League of Nations. Most neutral observers were happy to see Germany 'back in the fold'. They felt that a stronger Germany was much less of a problem than a weak one had been in 1919.

■ ***The acceptance of the Dawes Plan was a sign that tensions in Europe were beginning to ease after the First World War. Germany was on the verge of being accepted once again as a fellow European country rather than being treated as an enemy.***

However, it was not the League of Nations which sorted out this problem. Only the American economy was strong enough to offer the financial help Europe needed to avert a major crisis. ■

5. The Locarno Treaties, 1925

Background

In 1925, there were signs that international relations were improving. However, France was still wary of Germany and Germany was anxious to re-establish itself as a 'respectable' country. Therefore, in October 1925, representatives of Germany, Britain, France, Italy, Belgium, Czechoslovakia and Poland met at Locarno in Switzerland. Here they signed a series of agreements **to settle disputes between them** that became known as the Locarno Treaties. These agreements were reached independently of the League of Nations.

Terms

The main features of the agreements were:
- Belgium, France and Germany agreed to accept the borders drawn up by the Treaty of Versailles. These borders would be guaranteed by Britain and Italy.
- The Rhineland was to remain demilitarised.
- France guaranteed to support Poland and Czechoslovakia if they were attacked by Germany.
- Germany agreed not to use force to settle disputes with her neighbours.

Results

The Locarno Treaties were seen as an important improvement in international relations in the 1920s. Germany was treated as an equal partner after years of being on the outside of international affairs. In 1926 Germany was invited to become a member of the League of Nations.

■ ***At first sight the Locarno Treaties seemed to suggest that Europe was entering a new phase of 'peace and security'.***

However, some historians suggest the Locarno treaties actually undermined the Treaty of Versailles. Britain and Italy guaranteed Germany's western frontiers, but there was no guarantee about her eastern frontiers. This gave the impression that the Polish and Czech borders with Germany were not permanent and in the future Germany might change them.

At the time, however, the treaties signed at Locarno began a short but welcome phase of international cooperation between the major European powers. ■

6. The Kellogg Briand Pact, 1928

Background

The Locarno Treaties of 1925 and the generally prosperous world economy created a spirit of optimism in world affairs. In 1928 the Foreign Ministers of France (Briand) and the United States (Kellogg) drew up an agreement **not to go to war** which was signed by 65 other nations.

The Kellogg Briand Pact (also known as the Pact of Paris) was greeted enthusiastically by people throughout the world.

Terms

The terms of the agreement were fairly simple.
- The countries who signed the pact agreed to reject war as a way of solving international disputes.
- They also agreed not to go to war for five years (except in self defence).

Results

The signing of the Kellogg Briand Pact can be seen as the high point of friendly international relations during the 1920s. The 65 nations who signed the pact included Germany, the USSR, Italy and Japan. They seemed to be rejecting war.

However, nothing was said about how the pact would be enforced if one country broke the rules. This meant the agreement would only work if members kept their word. In 1931 when Japan invaded Manchuria, the Japanese government claimed that it was not at war with China over Manchuria but merely dealing with an 'incident', and thus had not broken the terms of the Kellogg Briand Pact.

■ *The League of Nations was involved in drawing up this plan. It could be seen as a great success. But the problem rears its head again of how the League of Nations would be able to enforce the agreement.* ■

7. The Young Plan, 1929

Background

In 1929 the terms of the Dawes Plan were due to run out. Owen Young, an American financier, drew up a plan **to reorganise Germany's reparations payments** when the Dawes Plan came to an end.

Terms

There were two major changes in the new agreement:
- It reduced the size of the reparations bill by about 75 per cent.
- Germany was given 59 years to pay the bill.

Results

The Young Plan never had a chance to work. It was accepted by Germany, but in October 1929 a world economic crisis began (see page 31). Suddenly American loans to Germany dried up, and Germany was once again plunged into crisis. As the economic depression deepened, Germany stopped paying reparations (and they were effectively cancelled by the Lausanne Conference in 1932).

■ *It was the Great Depression (see Chapter 3) which marked the end of the period of improving international relations. As countries began to suffer they (not surprisingly) put their own interests first. Money to help Germany came low on the list of priorities.* ■

REVISION TASKS

1. Make a list of key words to summarise the concerns of each of these major powers in the 1920s.
   - Germany
   - France
   - Britain
   - USA
2. Construct a table like the one below and use the information in this section to summarise the major international agreements in the 1920s.

Agreement	Date(s)	Issue(s) to be resolved	Countries involved	Terms	Success?

3. Do you think that the world was a more secure place in 1928 than in 1920?

REVISION SESSION

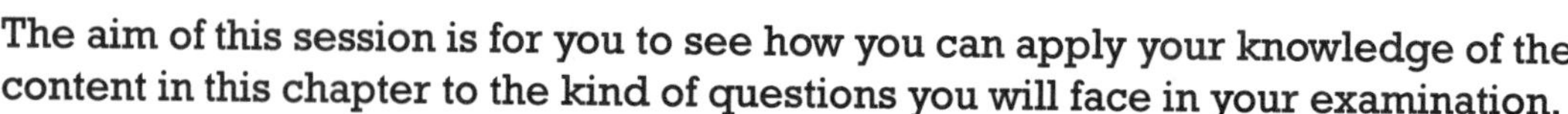

The aim of this session is for you to see how you can apply your knowledge of the content in this chapter to the kind of questions you will face in your examination.

Examination questions

Examination questions on this topic vary from year to year. Examiners generally set questions on how successful the League was (or was not) in the 1920s, but this issue is often mixed in with questions on the international agreements of the period.
In this example we will look at a question from MEG Paper I, 1994.

The League of Nations was set up after the First World War in order to keep peace and to attempt to settle disputes between countries. In the 1920s there were also attempts to improve the working of the world economy and trade.
The following questions are about the working of the League and other international agreements.

(a)(i) Name the 1928 Pact which was signed by sixty-five countries. *[1 mark]*

(ii) Explain what is meant by the phrase 'right of veto'. Briefly use your knowledge of the structure of the League of Nations to support your answer. *[3 marks]*

What is required?

Part (i) is a simple test of your knowledge and memory. A simple factual answer will do.
Part (ii) is asking you to show your understanding of important historical terms. To aim for the top level here (2–3 marks) you need to give a clear definition of the term and an example of how it can be used.

Ideas for your answer

1. For Part (i): The Kellogg Briand Pact.
2. For Part (ii): Try to keep your answer simple, for example: the right of veto meant that certain countries had the right to stop the League of Nations taking action even if the majority of members was in favour.
   You should then explain that this was a key feature of how the League's council worked and use an example such as the Geneva Protocol to show how the veto could be used.

(b) How similar were the following to each other?

I The Dawes Plan;

II The Young Plan. *[6 marks]*

What is required?

For this question you must show your understanding of similarity and difference.
A low level answer (1 mark) will be a very general statement, for example: they both helped with reparations.
To reach the next level (2–3 marks) you must identify a similarity or a difference and support it with an example.
Top level answers (4–6 marks) must identify a number of similarities and differences and provide examples.

Ideas for your answer

1. The easiest way to answer the question is probably to take the similarities and differences in turn. There were some clear *similarities* between the two plans:
   - Both plans were centred on the problem of Germany's reparations bill. You should give details of the bill and why it was a problem for Germany.
   - Both plans were put together by the USA.
2. You could then point out the important *differences* between the plans.
   - The Dawes Plan was an emergency plan to get Germany out of a crisis (see page 25) while the Young Plan was meant to be more long-term.

- The two plans also worked differently. The Dawes Plan made large loans to pay the reparations bill while the Young Plan actually cut the bill and made it more manageable (see page 27).

(c) Which one of the following statements is the more correct view of the work of the League of Nations in the 1920s?

I The work of the League of Nations greatly helped to keep peace in the world in the 1920s.

II The League of Nations was weak from the start and had more failures than successes in the 1920s.

Explain your answer fully by referring to I and II. [*15 marks*]

What is required?

In this question, you are being asked to express your own opinion on the record of the League of Nations in the 1920s. You must look at each of statements I and II and produce a balanced answer.

Each of the statements is partially true. Your task is to analyse or explain how accurate you feel each of the statements is and then reach a conclusion.

For the lower levels it will be enough to tell what you know of the story of the League of Nations in the 1920s.

To reach the higher levels (7–9 marks) you need to analyse both statements and explain in outline why you agree or disagree with each one.

To aim for the top level (10–15 marks) you must analyse both statements in detail and reach a conclusion.

Ideas for your answer

If possible it is always best to take the points made in the statement in turn and produce a balanced response on each one.

1. There is some evidence to support statement I. You could make this point by bringing in evidence and examples of the League's successes in the 1920s – Upper Silesia, Aaland Islands, Austria, Mosul, Greece/Bulgaria (see section D).

   At the same time you should point out that these successes in keeping peace were fairly small scale. By doing this, you are showing the examiner that you can put together a balanced view.
2. You may wish to point out that the work of the League's agencies may have indirectly helped to keep the peace by improving economic and social conditions. However, you should not get too bogged down in this as you may run out of time to make you main points.
3. You can now move on to statement II. Your evidence to support statement I would suggest that statement II is wrong. However, there is evidence to support statement II as well. You could start by looking at the structure of the League. The League's structure made it difficult to make decisions and carry them out (see page 14). There was also the problem that its powers in theory were not really there in practice (see page 18). Added to these structural problems was the fact that the League never really represented world opinion because at one time or another one or more of the major powers was not a member (see page 18).
4. As well as these general problems it would be valuable to refer to the failures of the League in the 1920s. The two main events which showed the League's weaknesses were the Vilna and Corfu incidents (see page 22). You could also point out that the many international agreements in the 1920s which took place outside the influence of the League suggested that the powers did not have complete confidence in the League.
5. Finally, you must explain your conclusion. There is evidence to support both statements, so both have some truth in them. It is then up to you to say whether one is more correct or whether it is not possible to say.

SUMMARY AND REVISION PLAN

Below is a list of headings which you may find helpful. Use this as a check list to make sure that you are familiar with the material featured in this chapter. Record your key words alongside each heading.

A The aims of the League of Nations

– The Covenant

– collective security

B The roles of the various bodies within the League

1. The assembly
2. The council
3. The Permanent Court of International Justice
4. The International Labour Organisation
5. The League of Nations Commissions
6. The secretariat

C The strengths and weaknesses of the League

1. The League's powers in theory
2. The League's powers in practice
3. Membership of the League
4. Non-membership of the League

D The League's successes in the 1920s

1. Solving international disputes
2. The International Labour Organisation
3. Other areas of success

E The League's failures in the 1920s

1. International disputes
2. Disarmament

F The aims, terms and results of international agreements in the 1920s

1. Concerns of the major powers
2. France's treaties
3. The Geneva Protocol
4. The Dawes Plan
5. The Locarno Treaties
6. The Kellogg Briand Pact
7. The Young Plan

CHAPTER 3

The effects of the Great Depression

In the 1920s most countries' economies were booming. Then in 1929 the Wall Street Crash followed by the Great Depression caused economic disaster, particularly in the form of unemployment. This in turn led to political problems in many countries and growing tension between the great powers in the world.

To answer questions on the effect of the Great Depression you need to be familiar with both the key content and the key themes of the period.

KEY CONTENT

You will need to show that you have a good working knowledge of these areas:

A The importance of the US economy 1919–29 to world trade
B The events which led to the Wall Street Crash and the Depression
C The effects of the Depression on the USA and the rest of the world

KEY THEMES

As always, you should remember that in the examination you will not be asked to simply 'tell the story' of the Depression. The Depression is a particularly good historical topic for examining the historical concepts of cause and consequence, and examiners have used it this way in many past examination questions. The questions you face will be designed to show your understanding of the key themes from the period. These are:

- **How and why economic problems were linked to political problems**
- **Why and how the Depression led to the rise of extremist governments**
- **How different countries responded to the Depression**
- **How far the Depression was a cause of the Second World War**

For example, look at the question below which is from MEG Paper I, 1994.

(a) (i) Explain briefly what is meant by the 'Wall Street Crash'. [2 *marks*]
(ii) State two economic problems that were caused by the Wall Street Crash. [2 *marks*]

(b) Why did the Wall Street Crash cause financial problems in Germany, France and Britain? [6 *marks*]

(c) Which one of the following caused the most serious international tension between 1929 and 1935?
I The Wall Street Crash, 1929;
II Japan's invasion of Manchuria, 1931;
III Italy's invasion of Abyssinia, 1935.

Explain your answer fully by referring to I, II and III. [*15 marks*]

This question is asking you to show your knowledge and understanding of this topic.

If you look carefully at the question, you will see that you need to know about these important areas:

- The Wall Street Crash and its consequences
- The Japanese invasion of Manchuria
- The Italian invasion of Abyssinia

You will need to show your understanding of these themes:

- The impact of the Wall Street Crash on the economies of Europe
- The links between the Crash and the Depression
- How the Crash affected Japan and Italy, and whether it was the only reason (or one of several reasons) why they invaded other territories
- How the rest of the world reacted to these invasions.

We will look at this question in detail at the end of this chapter.

THE EFFECTS OF THE GREAT DEPRESSION

A The importance of the US economy to world trade

1. **How international trade worked in the 1920s and 1930s** Trade means the process of buying and selling goods between people or countries. By the 1930s the economies and industries of many countries depended on international trade (imports and exports). For example, the USA produced many motor cars and sold them all around the world. Similarly, France provided a lot of wine and sold it all over the world.

Problems in one country could cause disruption in another. For example, unemployment in the USA might mean that people cut back on their spending and stopped buying French wine. This might mean job losses in France and French people would cut back on their spending. This in turn might cause problems for other countries which tried to sell goods to France.

In the 1930s the USA was the world's biggest economy and the richest country, so problems there could seriously affect the whole of the world's trade.

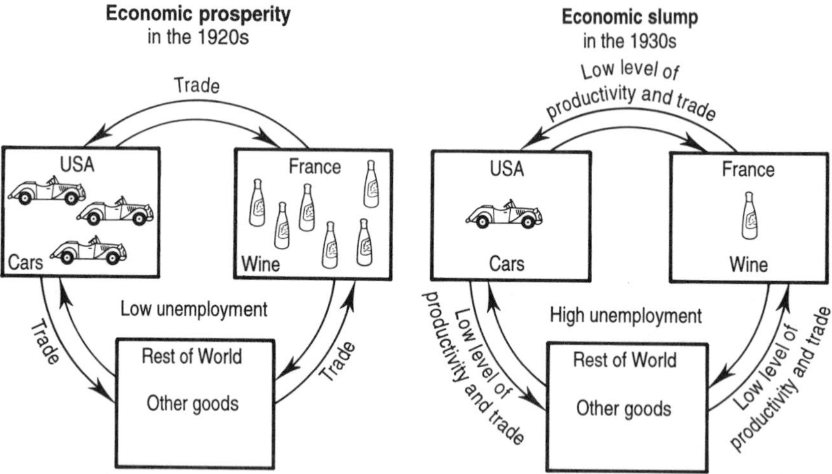

2. **The economic effects of the First World War** As you have seen in Chapter 1 the First World War devastated Europe's economies as well as causing death and destruction.

- Germany was exhausted by war and lost important industrial areas to France in the Treaty of Versailles (see pages 4–5). By the mid 1920s it was in crisis.
- France had suffered enormous damage.
- Both France and Britain owed huge war debts, mainly to the USA.

The Americans helped out with loans (see page 25). By the late 1920s all of Europe's economies were showing signs of prosperity. At the same time Japan's trade and industry was growing rapidly.

■ ***By the late 1920s the world economy seemed to be recovering. Europe's prosperity depended heavily on the USA, but this was not seen as a cause for concern. In the 1920s nobody really expected the USA to experience economic troubles.*** ■

B The events which led to the Wall Street Crash and the Depression

1. **US prosperity 1919–29** The 1920s was a boom time for the USA. It had grown steadily richer since the 1860s and had been helped by a number of factors:

- Vast natural resources (especially oil and coal)
- Cheap labour
- Selling goods to Europe during the war
- The war had also allowed American businesses to take over much of Europe's export trade.

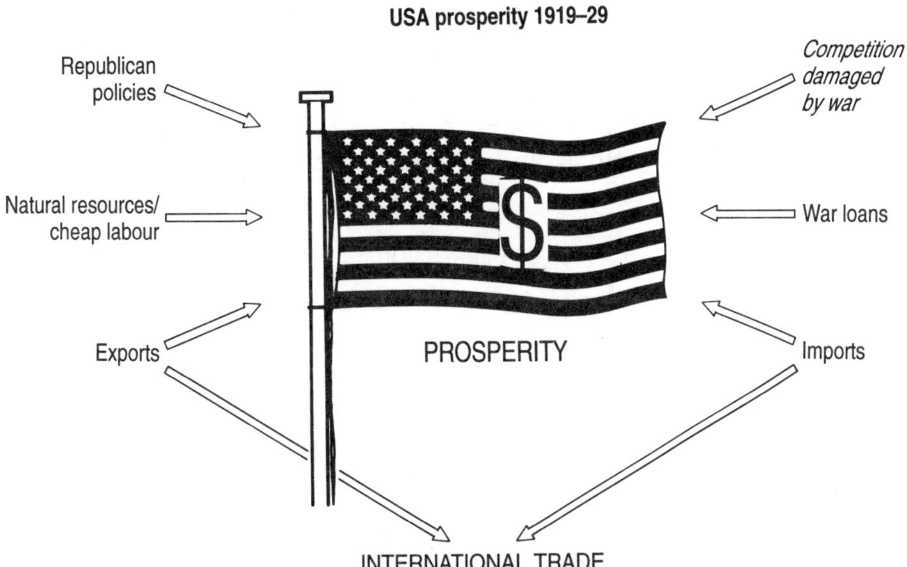

After the war, America grew richer still. The policies of the Republican party (low taxes and protective trade tariffs or duties) helped. America was also receiving repayment of its war loans to the European powers, particularly Britain.

American companies began to make large profits. They introduced new ideas, such as production lines, credit and hire purchase.

2. Danger signs in the 1920s There were some weaknesses in the American economy.

- *American agriculture struggled in the 1920s.* Farmers produced more than they could sell, so prices stayed low.
- *Ordinary people did not have much money to spend.* Many groups in society such as black people and low-paid workers did not share in the country's prosperity. Wages stayed low because companies wanted to keep their profits high.
- *Foreign trade was restricted.* As other countries tried to sell goods to the USA the USA placed duties on foreign goods to protect its own businesses. This was known as PROTECTIONISM. By the late 1920s foreign countries were also placing duties on American goods.
- *Borrowing increased.* The value of shares in successful companies went up and up – so ordinary people began to trade them on the Wall Street stock market. They borrowed the money to buy shares, then watched the value go up. It seemed such an easy way of making money. No-one really thought that the values of these could go down. However, if they did it would be disastrous, because people had borrowed so much money.

Together these factors were a threat to the American economy. If the American government had tried to solve at least some of these problems then the Crash might have been avoided. However, at the time there was a strong feeling in America that it was not the job of governments to interfere with business or with the actions of individuals.

REVISION TASKS

1. Draw your own diagram to show how goods were traded back and forth between countries.
2. Use 6–8 key words to explain why the American economy was important to economic recovery in Europe.
3. Create two key word lists to explain
   a) why the USA was prosperous in the 1920s
   b) the weakness in the US economy.

3. The Wall Street Crash The combination of factors meant that some big investors began to worry about how safe their money was in the shares of American companies. As a result they sold their shares in these companies. The price of shares began to go down, and in October 1929 some shares lost all their value. Investors lost all their money. This set off a vicious circle of problems.

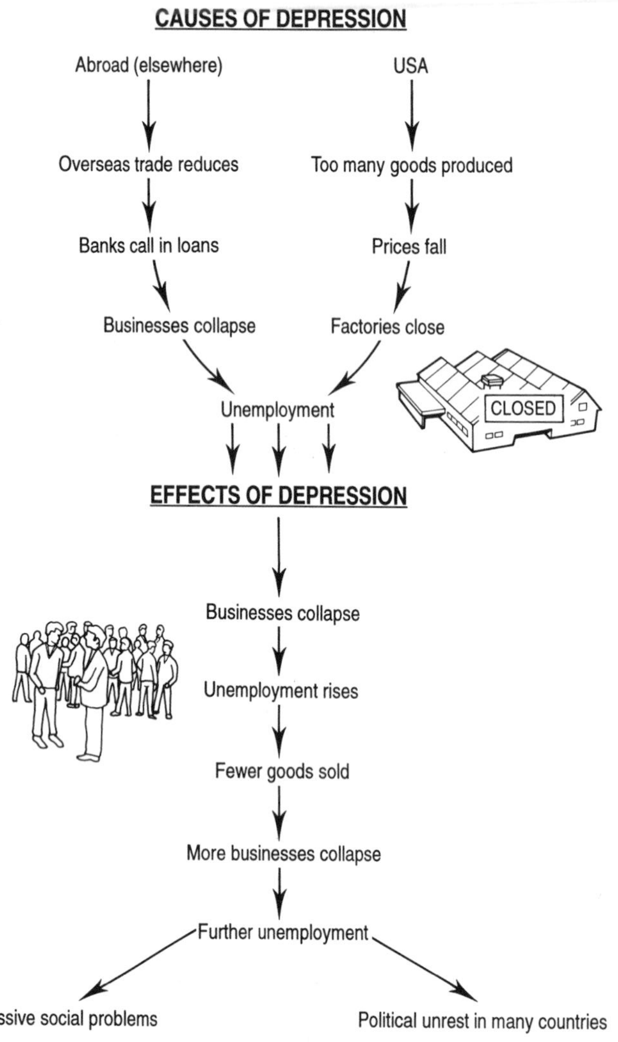

4. The Depression The Crash plunged America into economic depression and social upheaval.

- Banks and companies went bankrupt. Thousands of people who had invested their savings in shares were ruined.
- As companies closed, unemployment rocketed from 5 per cent to 25 per cent.
- Enormous social problems (unemployment, homelessness) developed.

C The effects of the Depression on the USA and the rest of the world

1. The USA The Depression hit America very hard. Industrial production fell by a half. Agriculture also suffered. Unemployment remained high throughout the 1930s. Less money was spent – people were unemployed or were cutting back. This meant that companies could not sell their goods and their workers were laid off. It was a downward spiral.

2. The wider effects of the Depression The USA was a market for many companies in Europe. As the USA stopped buying, companies which exported to the USA began to suffer. Industrial production in Europe fell by a third. Britain, Germany and the rest of Europe began to suffer unemployment and depression as well.

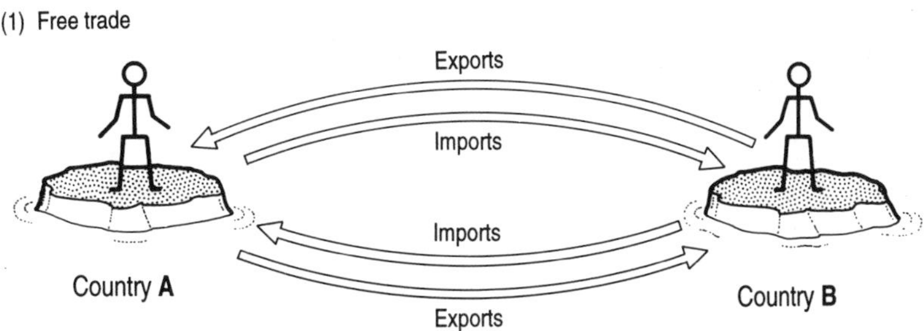

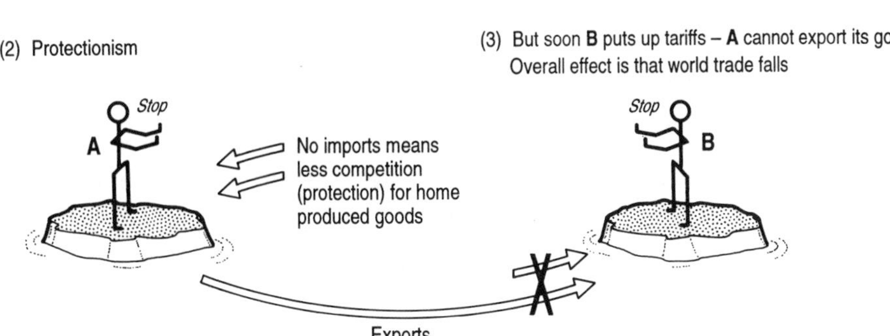

The USA also stopped lending money to other countries which made matters worse. The Depression was an economic problem but it caused political problems in many countries.

As trade declined, many countries tried PROTECTIONISM. They charged tariffs and duties on goods coming from foreign countries. The aim was that these duties made foreign goods more expensive and so made home-produced goods more attractive. The idea was to protect industries and jobs from foreign competition.

Although protectionism worked in some cases, protectionist policies simply reduced the amount of world trade. In the long run it made the effects of the Depression worse; it actually slowed down recovery.

■ ***The Depression had very severe economic effects. However, these economic effects (especially unemployment) in turn caused political problems and tensions between countries. As a result, it is very difficult to separate the economic from the political impact of the Depression.*** ■

REVISION TASKS

1. Why and how did the Depression in the USA cause economic problems in Europe? Try to answer this using 4–6 key words.
2. Why did unemployment continue to be such a problem through the 1930s?
3. Use 6 key words to explain why countries adopted protectionist policies.
4. Explain why you feel these policies were or were not a good idea.

THE EFFECTS OF THE GREAT DEPRESSION

3. The effects of the Depression on particular countries

Germany

The Crash and Depression were disastrous for Germany. In 1924 Germany's economy had collapsed because it could not pay its reparations. Germany was rescued by American loans in the Dawes Plan (see page 25) and was promised further help in the Young Plan.

However, when America went into depression, American banks began to call in their loans – this meant that they wanted the money paid back straight away. Germany simply could not pay – banks and industries failed and unemployment rose.

The government was in chaos in the years 1929–33. The people turned to the extremist Nazis and Hitler became Chancellor in 1933 (see Chapter 4). Hitler blamed the Treaty of Versailles for Germany's troubles. He promised to reverse it, even if it meant war.

Japan

Protectionist policies made some states (particularly Japan) feel that they were simply being abandoned, which put a real strain on international relations (see page 44). The USA was the main importer of Japanese goods such as silk. The Depression in the USA meant that Japan faced economic ruin.

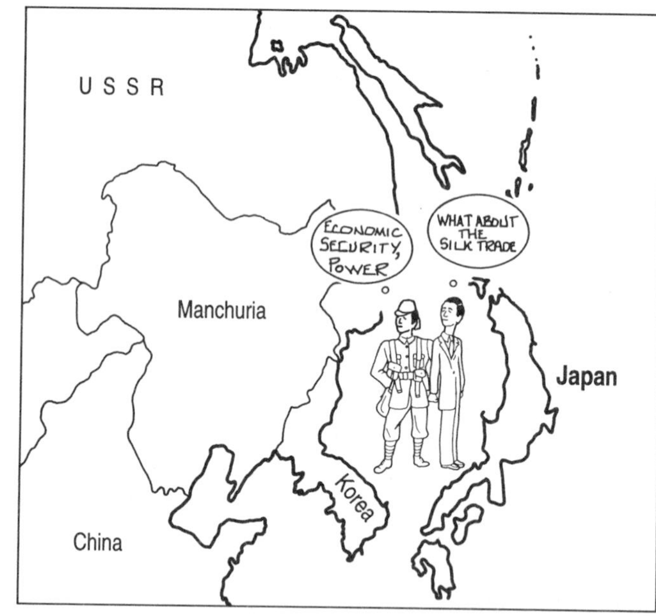

The country's military leaders believed that Japan needed an empire to be economically secure. The League of Nations certainly showed no sympathy for Japan's economic troubles, and Britain and France seemed to be interested only in their own problems.

Japan began to build its empire by invading Manchuria in 1931. Manchuria could provide Japan with the raw materials it needed. Historians disagree as to whether Japan was driven to invade Manchuria or whether it would have done so anyway.

Italy

Italy had been under the control of the Fascists, led by Mussolini, since 1922. He had made it clear that he wanted to restore Italy as a great power and talked about restoring at least some of the Roman Empire. The unemployment and other problems caused by the Depression almost certainly influenced Mussolini's decision to invade Abyssinia in 1935. This openly broke international law, but Mussolini simply ignored the League of Nations.

■ ***These examples show how the economic problems led to political problems in some countries. The two cannot really be separated. Economic problems led governments to become more selfish which caused international tension. These problems got worse during the 1930s and eventually led to the Second World War.*** ■

Britain

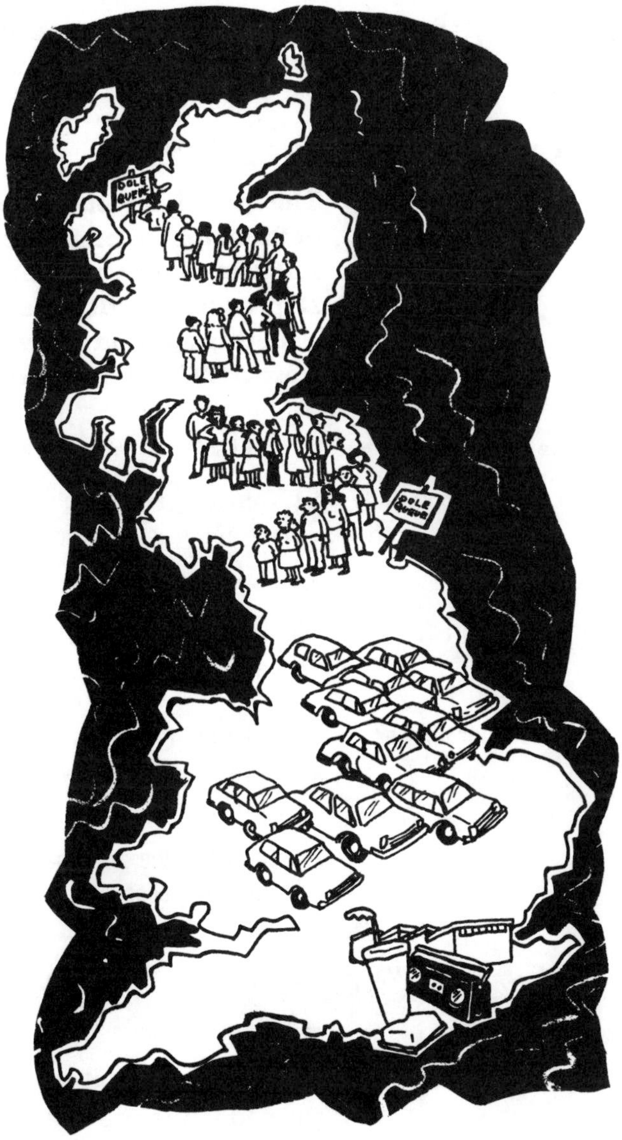

Britain had also borrowed heavily from the USA and its businesses therefore suffered as the USA called in its loans. Unemployment was desperate in some regions, especially in the traditional industries such as coal, shipbuilding, cotton. But Britain was not as badly affected as Germany. Some areas of Britain recovered quickly and south-east England and the Midlands were fairly prosperous by the late 1930s. Although extreme parties did grow in the 1930s, they never posed a serious political threat, and gained little support in elections.

France

France did not feel the full effects of the Depression until 1931. However, by then France could not sell its luxury goods and jobs were being lost because of cheap imports. Production fell and over one million jobs were lost. The government adopted a protectionist policy but France did not really start to recover until 1935.

The Depression caused very great political disruption in France. There were many extreme groups called 'leagues'. However, they had little real support so France was not in danger of going the same way as Germany.

REVISION TASKS

1. How did the Depression help Hitler?
2. Why did the Japanese attack Manchuria?
3. Did the Depression lead Mussolini to invade Abyssinia?
4. Use 6 key words to summarise the effects of the Depression on
   a) Britain
   b) France.
5. Construct a table like the one below and use the information in this section to complete it. You can do this instead of, or in addition to, tasks 1–4.

Country	Economic effects of Depression	Political effects of Depression	Impact on international relations

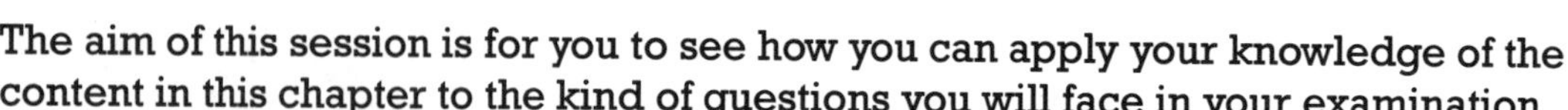

The aim of this session is for you to see how you can apply your knowledge of the content in this chapter to the kind of questions you will face in your examination.

Examination questions

The questions on this topic vary. Sometimes you need to use your knowledge of this topic in one part of a different question, for example on the League of Nations. However, there are often examination questions which focus on the Depression itself. The key theme is the effects of the Depression.

In this session we will look at an example of a past examination question from MEG Paper 1, 1993.

Between 1929 and 1935 the world suffered from many serious economic and political problems.

(a) (i) Explain briefly what is meant by the Wall Street Crash [*2 marks*]

(ii) State two economic problems that were caused by the Wall Street Crash [*2 marks*]

What is required?

These are starter questions to see whether you have a basic knowledge of the topic and also to test your understanding of concepts like economic problems.

Ideas for your answer

1. For Part (i) begin by stating that Wall Street was the site of the New York Stock Exchange. You could then explain how and why confidence in shares collapsed in 1929 and the value of shares 'crashed' as a result.
2. For Part (ii) there are many problems which you could refer to, e.g. unemployment, the collapse of banks, the collapse of American farming, falling wage levels.

(b) Why did the Wall Street Crash cause financial problems in Germany, France and Britain? [*6 marks*]

What is required?

This question is asking you to extend the knowledge and understanding which you showed in the previous question. It is testing your understanding of historical terms (like financial problems) and also whether you can describe the consequences of the Wall Street Crash for these countries. A low level answer (1 mark) would be a simple statement such as 'business was bad'. To reach higher levels you need to give convincing examples of reasons why there were financial problems (e.g. calling in loans). To reach the top level you should provide 2 or 3 examples.

Ideas for your answer

1. Make sure you stick to the point – in other words make sure your answer concentrates on Germany, France and Britain. You will probably find it helpful to take each one in turn. Remember also to concentrate on financial rather than political problems.
2. Germany: The first major consequence of the Crash was the withdrawal of loans. In this first section you should explain how and why the Crash led to this withdrawal (see pages 34–35). You could then explain why this problem caused banks and other business to go bankrupt and then point out that the result of this was unemployment (use the statistics from the diagram on page 36).
3. France: You could point out that France was affected in different ways compared with Germany – France took some time to feel the effects of the Crash and the Depression (see page 37) – and explain that this was because France had a different type of economy compared to Germany.

   However, it is also important to explain why and how France also suffered from economic problems in the 1930s (see page 32).
4. Britain: It is worth pointing out how Britain was affected in a similar way to Germany by the Crash (loans being called in, bankruptcies, unemployment) - this is quite an important point and does need to be made clearly (see page 36).

However, it is just as important to explain why Britain was not affected as badly as Germany, and was affected in different ways.

(c) Which one of the following caused the most serious international tensions between 1929 and 1935?
I The Wall Street Crash, 1929;
II Japan's invasion of Manchuria, 1931;
III Italy's invasion of Abyssinia, 1935.
Explain your answer fully by referring to I, II and III. *[15 marks]*

What is required?

This is quite a tricky question. You clearly need to bring in your knowledge of other topics, particularly the League of Nations in the 1930s covered in Chapter 4. However, the most important aspect of this question is the links between events (cause and consequence).

You must certainly look at each of these events and how they caused serious international tension. However, you must also look at how these events are linked. In other words, you must explain how the Wall Street Crash caused tension, but also how it was partly a cause of the other two events. Therefore, in a good answer you should point out that it is very difficult to say which one event caused the most serious tension because the three events were closely linked to each other.

A low level answer (1–3 marks) will give very general comments, for example: they were all important. To score more highly you need to describe at least one of events I, II, III in detail and explain why it was important.

To reach the next level (7–9 marks) you must explain (using examples) why you believe one event is particularly important and why you have chosen this event.

To aim for the top level of answer (10–15 marks) you must do this for all three events, and then reach a conclusion on which was the most important.

Ideas for your answer

1. To show your understanding of cause and consequence you need to point out that the Wall Street Crash was a key economic problem which contributed to the Depression (see page 34). It was the Depression which caused economic problems across the world – this is described in Section C. In turn, these economic problems caused political problems (e.g. the rise of Hitler – see page 42) and these led to international tension.

   You could then conclude that the Wall Street Crash was an indirect cause of much of the tension in the world in the years 1929 to 1935. You would need to back this up by referring to the calling in of loans; the protectionist policies, rising unemployment and the economic threat to countries like Japan.

   Remember, the Wall Street Crash on its own was not really a cause of serious tension.

2. When you write about Japan's invasion of Manchuria it is important to point out how the economic situation in the USA after 1929 threatened Japan (see page 36).

   You must also explain that Japan wanted an empire anyway, and economic problems were not the only reason for the invasion. You need to look at the fact that the invasion worried France and Britain (who had interests in this area) and that many states opposed the invasion. You must also point out that if France, Britain and the USA had continued trading with Japan (instead of putting up duties) then Japan might not have taken such a drastic step. Therefore, the invasion caused very serious international tension (see Chapter 4 Section B), but the invasion itself was partly a result of world economic problems, and so events I and II are closely linked.

3. As with event II, Italy's invasion of Abyssinia caused great tension. It resulted in arguments in the League of Nations and sanctions against Italy (see Chapter 4 Section B). Soon after, several states actually left the League of Nations.

   As with I and II above, there are connections between these events. Mussolini was under pressure at home because of economic problems – he believed that invading Abyssinia would distract his people (see page 36). He was also encouraged by the fact that Japan had invaded Manchuria in 1931 and the League of Nations had not been able to prevent this. Again, it is difficult to separate these events out.

4. In conclusion, you should make it clear which event you believe was the most important. You could also point out that each of the events I–II caused international tension. However, because they were closely connected to each other, it is very difficult to say which one caused the most serious tension.

SUMMARY AND REVISION PLAN

Below is list of headings which you may find helpful. Use this as a checklist to make sure that you are familiar with the material featured in this chapter. Record your key words alongside each heading.

A The importance of the US economy to world trade

1. **How international trade worked in the 1920s and 1930s**
2. **The economic effects of the First World War**

B The events which led to the Wall Street Crash and the Depression

1. **US prosperity 1919–29**
2. **Danger signs in the 1920s**
3. **The Wall Street Crash**
4. **The Depression**

C The effects of the Depression on the USA and the rest of the world

1. **The USA**
2. **The wider effects of the Depression**
3. **The effects of the Depression on particular countries**

- **Germany**
- **Japan**
- **Italy**
- **Britain**
- **France**

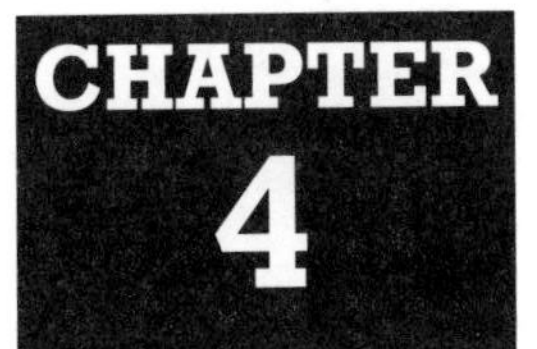

The causes of the Second World War

In 1928 the world was celebrating the Kellogg Briand Pact. It seemed to guarantee lasting peace. Ten years later the world was at war again. How did this happen?

To answer questions on the causes of the Second World War you need to be familiar with both the key content and the key themes of the period.

KEY CONTENT

You will need to show that you have a good working knowledge of these areas:

A The foreign policies of the major powers in the 1930s
B The failure of the League of Nations
C The steps towards war

KEY THEMES

In your examination there is a good chance that an entire question will be devoted to the causes of the Second World War. However, as with other topics you will not be asked simply to list the facts. You will be asked to show your understanding of the events that led to war and how they are related. This will mean thinking through the key themes of the period. These are:

- **Why Italy, Germany and Japan pursued aggressive foreign policies in the 1930s**
- **The ways in which the policies of Germany, Italy and Japan were similar or different**
- **Why the League of Nations was unable to resist these policies**
- **The importance of these aggressive policies as a cause of the Second World War**
- **The importance of the Depression as a cause of the Second World War**
- **The importance of the Treaty of Versailles as a cause of the Second World War**
- **Why Britain and France adopted the policy of appeasement**
- **The differing views of historians about appeasement**

For example, look at this examination question from MEG Paper I, 1994.

(a) (i) Name the British Prime Minister who signed the Munich Agreement with Germany in 1938. [*1 mark*]

(ii) Explain what is meant by the term 'plebiscite'. Briefly use your knowledge of events in Austria in 1938 to support your answer. [*3 marks*]

(b) How similar were the following to each other:
I Japan's foreign policy in the 1930s
II Italy's foreign policy in the 1930s? [*6 marks*]

(c) The following linked together caused the outbreak of war in 1939:
I Britain's foreign policy from 1936 to 1939;
II Weakness of the League of Nations in the 1930s;
III Germany's foreign policy from 1936 to 1939.

Do you agree with this statement? Explain your answer fully by referring to I, II and III. [*15 marks*]

This question is asking you to show your knowledge and understanding of some important events of the time.

If you look carefully at the question you will see that you need to know about these important areas:

- The Anschluss between Germany and Austria in 1938
- The Munich Agreement of 1938
- The Manchurian crisis
- The Abyssinian crisis
- Hitler's plans to reverse the Treaty of Versailles in the 1930s.

You will need to show your understanding of these themes:

- The reasons behind Italian, German and Japanese aggression in the 1930s
- Why the League of Nations was unable to stop their aggression
- Why Britain and France chose the policy of appeasement and the consequences of that policy.

We will look at this question in more detail at the end of the chapter.

THE CAUSES OF THE SECOND WORLD WAR

A The foreign policies of the major powers in the 1930s

Foreign policy is the term used for the way in which a country deals with other countries. The 1930s saw international relations get steadily worse until the Second World War broke out in 1939. To understand why this happened you must first understand the position of each of the major powers in the 1930s and why they acted the way they did. You also need to see how the events of the 1930s had their roots in earlier events, particularly the Treaty of Versailles (see pages 4–5) and the Depression (see pages 34–37).

1. Germany's foreign policy in the 1930s Between 1924 and 1929 relations between Germany and the other major powers had been steadily improving. However, the economic depression caused chaos in Germany and Adolf Hitler, leader of the Nazis, took advantage of the situation to take power in 1933. From 1933, German foreign policy was controlled by Hitler.

- He immediately left the League of Nations.
- Hitler saw the Treaty of Versailles as one of the major causes of Germany's problems. He promised the German people he would reverse the treaty and get back the territory Germany had lost. This he steadily did from 1936 onwards (see page 48).
- In the longer term he also planned to expand into Eastern Europe to give the German people the LEBENSRAUM (living space) which Hitler believed they needed.
- Each time he took over some more territory he managed to convince many European leaders – including Britain – that once Germany had obtained territory lost at Versailles, no further demands would be made.

■ ***There is still controversy about Hitler's foreign policy. Some historians argue that he planned for war from the beginning. Others see Hitler as an opportunist who took chances. If he was given what he wanted then he demanded more.*** ■

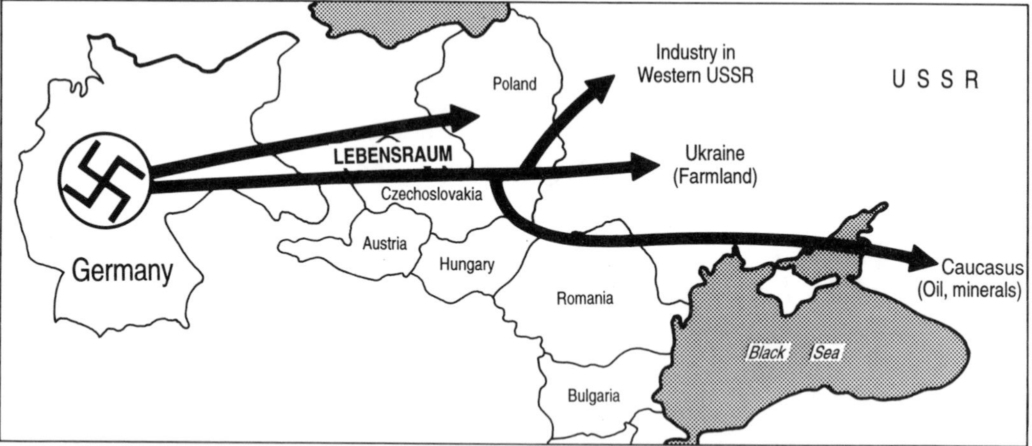

2. Italy's foreign policy in the 1930s From 1922–43 Italy was a dictatorship led by Benito Mussolini, the leader of the Fascist party. Mussolini's aim was to increase the prestige of Italy as a major power. He signed the Locarno and Kellogg Briand treaties because he thought Italy should be playing a key role in world affairs. He did not particularly believe in peaceful solutions to disputes.

In the early 1930s Mussolini was very suspicious of his main rival, Adolf Hitler.

- He opposed Hitler's attempted take over of Austria in 1934 and seemed to be drawing closer to Britain and France.
- Mussolini even joined Britain and France in the Stresa Front, an agreement aimed at supporting the terms of the Treaty of Versailles.

From 1935, however, Italy's foreign policy changed. Mussolini began to look for ways to increase Italian territory overseas. He had always planned this but he also wanted a distraction from the economic problems being caused by the Depression. In 1935 he decided to attack Abyssinia to extend the Italian colonies in Africa.

Italian expansion, 1934–36

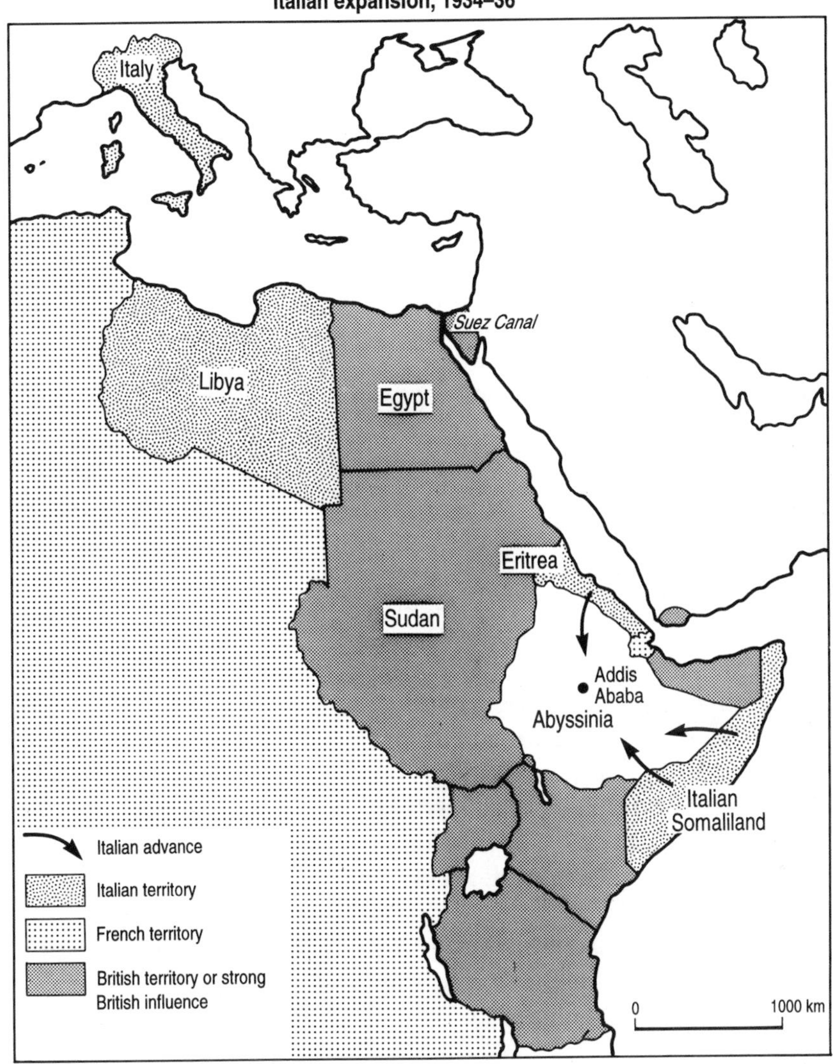

Mussolini's invasion of Abyssinia upset Italy's relationship with Britain and France and undermined the Stresa agreement. From this point onwards, Italy drew closer to Germany as the following record of events shows:

- When the League of Nations imposed sanctions against Italy over its invasion of Abyssinia, Hitler did not comply.
- In 1937 Mussolini signed the Rome Berlin Axis with Hitler.
- In 1939 ties between Germany and Italy were strengthened with the signing of the Pact of Steel.

Mussolini began the 1920s with plans to be the most powerful leader in Europe. By 1939 Mussolini seemed to have fallen under the spell of Hitler and allied himself with the Nazis.

REVISION TASKS

1. Why was the Depression helpful to Hitler?
2. Use 6–8 key words to summarise Hitler's foreign policy aims.
3. Was Hitler planning another world war?
4. Why did Mussolini join the Stresa Front and why did he leave?
5. Why did his invasion of Abyssinia bring him closer to Hitler?

3. Japan's foreign policy in the 1930s Japan was a rising power in Asia and the Pacific and played an important role in the First World War. During the early twentieth century Japan developed very quickly into a modern trading nation.

There were powerful groups in Japan (especially in the army) which wanted Japan to expand and build an empire, although moderates within the government did not agree.

The Wall Street Crash and Depression had a major impact on the Japanese economy. PROTECTIONIST policies by the USA and others meant its trade was reduced. Japan began to look for other ways to expand.

In 1931 the Japanese invaded Manchuria, to the north of Korea. Manchuria was rich in natural resources and raw materials (particularly coal and iron) which Japanese industry needed. The area also provided a new market for Japanese goods. The Japanese successfully conquered Manchuria and renamed it Manchukuo (see page 46 for details).

Japanese expansion, 1931–40

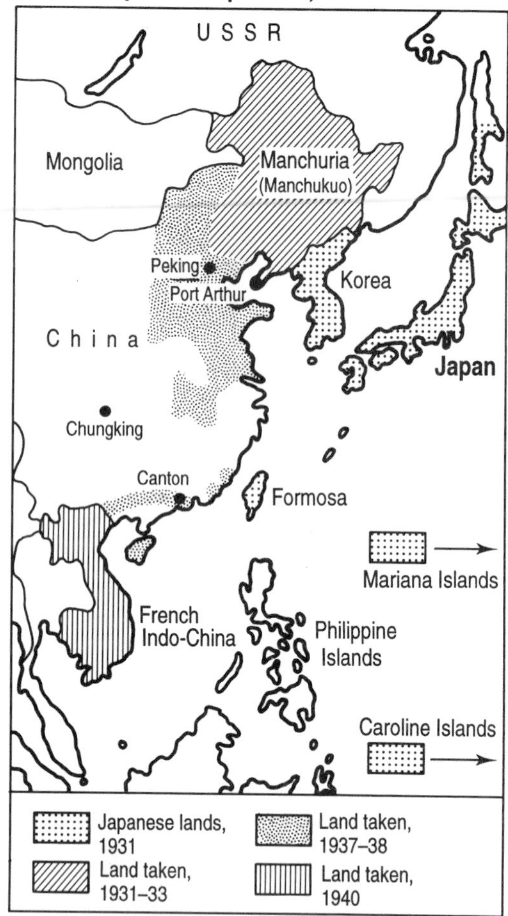

Japan's EXPANSIONIST foreign policy continued in 1937 when Japanese forces attacked China. It was the beginning of a long struggle which finally led to war with Britain and the attack on the US naval base at Pearl Harbor in December 1941.

4. France's foreign policy in the 1930s French foreign policy in the 1920s and 1930s was dominated by its desire to defend itself against Germany. France felt unsupported and isolated in the fear of German attack.

- Agreements were signed with Germany's neighbours, Belgium, Poland, Czechoslovakia, Romania and Yugoslavia in the 1920s.
- From 1929–34 the French built a series of strong defensive fortifications all along the German border from Switzerland to Belgium. This was known as the Maginot Line.
- In the late 1930s French policy towards Germany was closely linked to British policy. Both the French Prime Minister Daladier and British Prime Minister Neville Chamberlain were supporters of the APPEASEMENT policy (see pages 48–51). This meant giving Hitler what he wanted on condition he did not try to expand further.

5. Britain's foreign policy in the 1930s After the First World War the main interest of British foreign policy was to deal with its empire. Britain hoped that peace in Europe could be maintained by the League of Nations.

However, by the mid 1930s Britain had lost some of its confidence in the League of Nations and started to make its policy in Europe.

- In 1935 Britain signed the Stresa Front with France and Italy (see page 43).
- Also in 1935 Britain signed a naval agreement with Germany (which was against the terms of the Treaty of Versailles).
- In 1936 Britain refused to intervene when Hitler re-occupied the Rhineland.
- In 1938 Britain and France together agreed to give Germany the Sudetenland (part of Czechoslovakia).

However, by 1939 it was clear that appeasement had failed. Hitler kept on wanting more. Poland was the next country in Hitler's eye, so Britain guaranteed to protect Poland against a German attack. When Hitler did attack Poland in September 1939, France and Britain declared war on Germany.

REVISION TASKS

1. Was the Depression the only reason why Japan invaded Manchuria or were there others?
2. Why was France so nervous of standing up to Germany in the 1930s?
3. Choose two examples from Britain's foreign policy in the 1930s which could be described as appeasement.
4. Construct a table like the one below and complete it with the relevant information from this section.

Country	**Aims of foreign policy (e.g. security, expansion)**	**Important influences (e.g. Depression)**	**Other points**
Germany			
Italy			
Japan			
France			
Britain			

B The failure of the League of Nations

Technically, the League of Nations was still active until the end of the Second World War. However, by 1935 it was clear it could no longer perform its main role – that of keeping peace. Two major international incidents saw to this.

1. **The Manchurian crisis, 1931** In 1931 Japan invaded the Chinese province of Manchuria (see page 44). China was in the middle of a civil war and was not able to defend Manchuria. China appealed to the League of Nations for support against Japan. After much delay, the League condemned the Japanese and called for Japan to leave Manchuria.

However, instead of leaving Manchuria, Japan left the League of Nations. Japan remained in control of Manchuria and the League of Nations did not try to stop the Japanese occupation there.

This event marked the beginning of the end for the League of Nations. Britain and France were not willing to support the League in taking action against Japan. The Manchurian crisis seemed to signal that aggression would not be punished by the League.

2. **The Italian invasion of Abyssinia, 1935** Abyssinia was one of the few countries in Africa not under the control of a European power. It had defeated a previous attempt by Italy to invade in 1896.

- In 1935 a well-equipped Italian force invaded Abyssinia again.
- Haile Selassie, the leader of Abyssinia, appealed to the League of Nations for assistance.
- The League condemned Italian aggression and imposed ECONOMIC SANCTIONS against Italy. However, they were not effective. Italy was still allowed to buy oil and other essential supplies.
- Mussolini completed his invasion of Abyssinia and then left the League of Nations just as Japan had done.

Why did the League not act more decisively? You will recall (see Chapter 2) how the League depended on leadership by Britain and France. In 1935 France and Britain did not want to offend Mussolini in case he joined forces with Hitler. The British Foreign Secretary even worked out a plan with the French (called the Hoare Laval pact) to offer Mussolini most of Abyssinia. However, he was forced to resign when the plan became public.

The effects of the Abyssinian crisis were very serious for the League. It marked the end of the League of Nations as a peacekeeping organisation. It could no longer be taken seriously:

- It showed that its members were not willing to use force to stop aggression.
- The secret deal – the Hoare Laval Pact – had also shown Britain and France undermining the League.

■ ***No one, it seemed, was prepared to go to war in order to keep the peace. The League's credibility as a peacekeeper was damaged beyond repair. Force and aggression had clearly triumphed again. The world now seemed a much less secure place and certain states were encouraged to pursue aggressive policies to achieve their aims. This weakened the determination of Britain and France to resist them.*** ■

3. **Reasons for the League's failure** Examination questions often ask you to explain why the League of Nations was so ineffective in the 1930s. There were several reasons for this and the memory aid opposite will help you to remember them.

French and British self-interest
Absent powers
Ineffectiveness of sanctions
Lack of armed forces
Unfair treaty
REaching decisions too slowly

- **The self-interest of leading members:** The League depended for its success on the willingness of its two key members (France and Britain) to provide firm support in times of crisis. When conflicts occurred, however, neither the British nor French governments were prepared to abandon its own self-interest in support of the League.
- **America and other important countries were absent:** Membership was a key problem for the League. Germany was not a member until 1926 and left in 1933. The USSR did not join until 1934 whilst Japan left in 1933 and Italy left two years later. Most important, the USA was never a member. Without such major powers the League lacked authority.
- **Economic sanctions did not work:** They were easily broken. The League lacked the muscle to enforce the decisions of its assembly and council.
- **Lack of troops:** The League had no armed forces of its own and relied upon the cooperation of its members. But Britain and France were not willing to commit troops. At no time did troops ever fight on behalf of the League.
- **The treaties it had to uphold were seen as unfair:** The League of Nations was set up as part of the peace treaties signed at the end of the First World War. It was seen by some as an organisation dominated by the victorious powers. The League was also bound to uphold the peace treaties which had created it. In time, however, it became apparent that some of the terms of those peace treaties were harsh and unjust and needed amending. This further undermined the League.
- **Decisions were slow:** When a crisis occurred, the League was supposed to act quickly and with determination. In many cases, however, the League met too infrequently and decisions took too long to make. The need for all members to agree on a course of action undermined the strength of the League.

REVISION TASKS

1. Make a key word summary of Japan's reasons for invading Manchuria. Use 6–8 words.
2. Find 4 key words to summarise Italy's reasons for invading Abyssinia.
3. Why did the League of Nations fail in each of these incidents?
4. What else could the League have done?
5. Produce your own key word list of the reasons why the League of Nations failed.

C The steps towards war, 1936–39

From 1936–39 relations in Europe became increasingly tense.

Civil War in Spain
Re-occupation of Rhineland
Anschluss with Austria
Sudetenland crisis – Munich Agreement
Hitler takes remainder of Czechoslavakia
Italy and Germany form pact of steel
Nazi-Soviet pact
Germany invades Poland

1. The Spanish Civil War, 1936–39 In 1936 Civil War broke out in Spain between the Nationalists and Republicans. The Nationalists (led by General Franco) were supported by the Catholic Church, wealthy landowners and fascists (Falange). The Republicans (the democratically elected government) were supported by communists, socialists and most of the peasants and urban workers.

Britain and France urged that no aid should be given to either side. However, other countries reacted differently:

- Franco received troops (they were called volunteers), supplies and air power from Italy and Germany.
- The Republicans received a lot less help from other countries. However, the USSR sent some supplies and many volunteers joined up to serve in the International Brigade.

The support of Italy and Germany was vital to the Nationalists. By 1939 Franco had captured key cities such as Barcelona and laid seige to Madrid. The Spanish capital finally fell to the Nationalists in March 1939 and in April the Spanish Civil War was over. Franco became a dictator.

■ ***The Spanish Civil War represented another blow to peace in Europe. A democratic government had been removed and replaced by a dictator. Hitler and Mussolini had been able to give their military forces practice of actual war. The League of Nations could do nothing and Britain and France appeared weak and helpless.*** ■

2. German re-occupation of the Rhineland, 1936 Hitler had made it clear that he intended to reverse the Treaty of Versailles. He began this process in 1936 by moving German troops back into the Rhineland.

The following reasons explain why this was a calculated risk for Hitler:

- The re-occupation of the Rhineland was a clear breach of the Versailles Treaty and Locarno agreements.
- German troops were in no position to stand up to the French army if it reacted (Hitler's troops were under strict orders to retreat if this happened).

However, in 1936 France was occupied with domestic problems and Britain was keen not to provoke Germany. In addition there was also doubt in Britain about the fairness of the Treaty of Versailles. The French were unwilling to act without the support of Britain, and so Hitler's gamble paid off.

This success convinced Hitler that Britain and France would not stop him achieving his other aims. To many smaller nations, particularly those in Eastern Europe, collective security seemed to have failed.

■ ***This was the beginning of the controversial policy of appeasement. Britain and France certainly did not want war. They felt that they were not strong enough to go to war. They were prepared to give Hitler what he wanted. However, at the same time Britain and France began to re-arm.*** ■

3. Anschluss: the annexation of Austria, 1938 Hitler had been born in Austria and one of his objectives was to see Germany and Austria as one country. By 1938, Hitler felt ready to try. This was the sequence of events:

- Hitler bullied the Austrian Chancellor, Schuschnigg, into accepting a Nazi, Seyss-Inquart, as Austrian Minister of the Interior.
- Schuschnigg ordered a PLEBISCITE (vote) to be held to find out if the Austrian people really wanted union with Germany.
- Hitler feared a 'no' vote, so he moved German troops to the Austrian border, and threatened to invade if Schuschnigg did not resign in favour of Seyss-Inquart.
- Seyss-Inquart became Chancellor and invited German troops into Austria. On 12 March 1938 the German army entered Vienna. The Anschluss was complete.
- The Nazis organised their own vote about union with Germany and of those who voted 99 per cent voted in favour. Austria immediately became a province of the new German Reich (empire).

The Anschluss with Austria was another clear breach of the Versailles and Locarno treaties. The British and French governments complained about the German violation of the Treaty of Versailles but took no action. Again, there was a feeling among some people in Britain that the treaty had been harsh and Britain should not defend it.

■ ***Appeasement had allowed Hitler's aggressive diplomacy to triumph again. The western powers had shown that they were unwilling to support the terms of the Versailles Treaty. By 1938 it also seemed that the League of Nations was completely irrelevant.*** ■

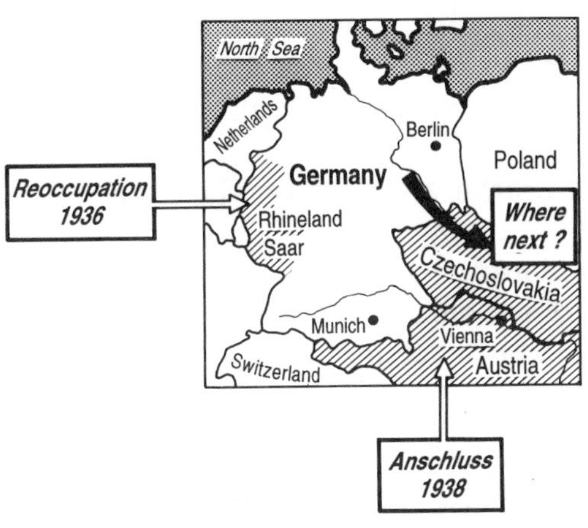

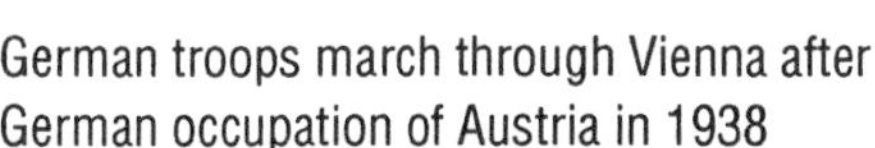

German troops march through Vienna after German occupation of Austria in 1938

REVISION TASKS

1. Explain the differences between the actions of
   a) Britain and France
   b) Germany and Italy
   c) Russia
   in the Spanish Civil War.
2. What were the effects of the Spanish Civil War?
3. Explain why Hitler was able to re-occupy the Rhineland without opposition.
4. How did Hitler achieve the Anschluss?
5. Look at the map. What would his next step be?

4. The Sudeten crisis and the Munich Agreement, 1938 Encouraged by his successes, Hitler took his plans a stage further and began to look at Czechoslovakia. Czechoslovakia was a new state set up after the First World War (see page 8). Part of the new state consisted of German-speaking peoples in the area known as the Sudetenland. It was this area which next received Hitler's attention.

- Hitler ordered Henlein (the leader of the Sudeten Germans) to stir up trouble in the Sudentenland.
- German newspapers produced allegations of crimes apparently committed by Czechs against Sudeten Germans.
- Hitler threatened war if a solution was not found.

The British Prime Minister Chamberlain believed that a peaceful solution could be worked out. He tried to persuade the Czech President Benes to accept self- government for the Sudetenland. Benes reluctantly agreed, but Hitler then produced new demands in which he claimed the Sudetenland should be part of the German Reich.

On 22 September at a meeting at Godesberg, Benes refused to accept the German demands. It seemed that war was a real possibility but Chamberlain appealed to Hitler to give him more time to find a settlement.

On 29 September, Chamberlain made one last effort to maintain peace:

- He met with the French Prime Minister Daladier, Hitler and Mussolini at Munich in a last bid to resolve the Sudeten crisis.
- The Czech representatives were not invited to the meeting.
- The Czechs were forced to hand over the Sudetenland to Germany and a commission was set up to decide which territory the Czechs would lose.

Chamberlain and Hitler had a further meeting at Munich in which both men agreed that Britain and Germany would not go to war. Hitler promised he did not want the rest of Czechoslovakia. Chamberlain returned to Britain a hero, apparently having saved Europe from war.

The results of the Munich Agreement were extremely serious for Czechoslovakia and Europe as a whole:

- The Czech government was completely humiliated.
- The vital area of the Sudetenland was lost and in October and November 1938 Hungary and Poland also occupied other parts of Czech territory.
- Britain and France had again given in to Hitler.

Although the Munich agreement was initially seen as a success, it actually marked the end of Chamberlain's appeasement policy. After Munich, few people believed that Hitler could be trusted again. Britain and France increased the pace of their rearmament programme.

5. Czechoslovakia, 1939 In March 1939, Czechoslovakia finally disappeared from the map of Europe.

- Hitler invaded what was left of Czechoslovakia.
- Bohemia and Moravia became German protectorates (controlled by Germany).
- Slovenia remained independent in theory but was dominated by Germany.
- Ruthenia was handed over to Hungary.

The destruction of Czechoslovakia

6. The end of appeasement The final occupation of Czechoslovakia suggested that war was on its way:

- Hitler's promises made at Munich were clearly worthless.
- Britain and France were rapidly re-arming and it was accepted that the policy of appeasement had failed.

■ ***Historians have disagreed about the policy of appeasement. Some simply see it as Britain and France's weakness. However, others see it as a deliberate policy which had plenty of backing from the British public. The losses of the First World War had been so great that governments were willing to look at all alternatives rather than risk the prospect of a second war against Germany within twenty years.***

It has also been argued by some historians that the British and French saw war as inevitable. Appeasement gave them vital months in which to prepare their forces for the inevitable war. ■

REVISION TASKS

1. Explain why Hitler felt he had a claim on the Sudetenland.
2. Describe the actions of Britain and France.
3. The Czechs felt they were betrayed. Do you agree?
4. What were the consequences of Munich:
   a) for Czechoslovakia?
   b) for the policy of appeasement?

7. The Pact of Steel, May 1939 In the spring of 1939 across Europe, the tide of events seemed to be favouring the dictators.

- March: Hitler forced the Lithuanians to hand over the Baltic town of Memel and a portion of land along their south-west border.
- April: Nationalist forces supported by Germany and Italy took power in Spain.
- May: Mussolini followed Hitler's example in Czechoslovakia by invading Albania.

In May 1939, Hitler and Mussolini signed the Pact of Steel in which they promised to act side by side in future events.

Europe was now firmly divided into two camps. Both Britain and Germany began to look towards the USSR as a way of helping their own security.

8. Poland, 1939 Poland was Hitler's next target. In the Treaty of Versailles, German territory had been handed over to the Poles to give them access to the Baltic Sea (the 'Polish Corridor') and the German city of Danzig was put under the control of the League of Nations.

Following his success with Czechoslovakia, Hitler now demanded the return of Danzig and the Polish corridor.

The Polish crisis, 1939

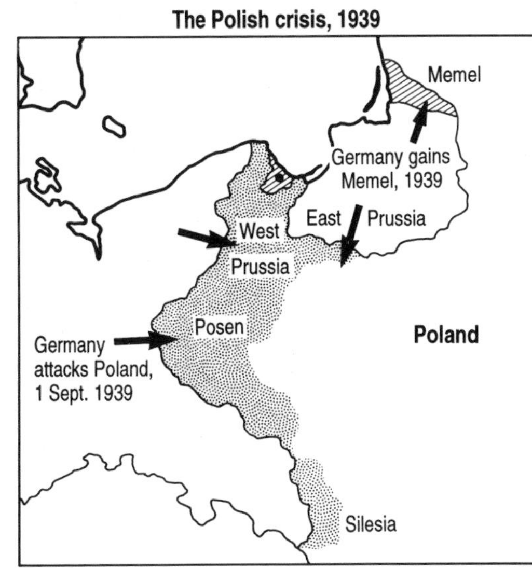

Humiliated by Munich and the events which followed, the French and British governments now acted decisively:

- They gave guarantees of support against German aggression to the Polish, Greek and Romanian governments.
- They increased production of arms and equipment.

The prospect of a future war over Poland now partly hinged on the attitude of the Soviet government, Poland's neighbour on its eastern side. Britain and France tried to reach an agreement with Stalin. They hoped to entice Stalin into an agreement to threaten Germany on her eastern frontier.

9. Nazi-Soviet Non-Aggression Pact, August 1939 On 23 August 1939 the German Foreign Minister Ribbentrop and Soviet Foreign Minister Molotov signed the Nazi-Soviet Non-Aggression Pact:

- The Soviets and Germans guaranteed not to fight each other in the event of war in Europe.
- In a secret agreement both powers agreed to divide up Polish territory should war occur.
- Hitler gave Stalin a free hand to occupy part of Romania and the Baltic States of Latvia, Estonia and Lithuania.

The news of the Nazi-Soviet pact stunned the world because Hitler and Stalin represented two totally opposing political systems (Communism and Nazism).

However, on closer inspection the Nazi-Soviet Pact comes as less of a surprise. Despite their different political beliefs, Hitler and Stalin had a lot to offer each other:

- For Hitler, the pact removed the threat of war on two fronts. It also gave him the opportunity he needed to deal with Poland despite the threats coming from Britain and France.
- Stalin had been suspicious of the British and French approaches – before the rise of Hitler they had shown little friendship to the USSR. Hitler on the other hand had more to offer the Soviets (e.g. territory in Eastern Europe).

10. The outbreak of war, September 1939 Soon after the signing of the Nazi-Soviet Pact, Hitler decided to invade Poland:

- He did not believe that Britain and France would go to war, just as they had not done so over Czechoslovakia.
- Even if war was declared, Poland was too far away for Britain and France to provide practical support. If war came, Hitler decided, it would all be over very quickly and he would have achieved another of his objectives.

On 1 September 1939, German troops invaded Poland. Britain and France declared war soon after. On 15 September, the USSR also invaded Poland and took the territory agreed in the Nazi-Soviet Pact. Within six weeks Poland had been defeated and like Czechoslovakia disappeared from the map of Europe.

In the years 1936–39 Hitler took a series of diplomatic risks and succeeded. However, in 1939 Britain and France made their position clear – they would declare war if Germany invaded Poland. What gave Hitler the confidence to go ahead?

- The British and French guarantees of support for Poland in April 1939 came too late to convince Hitler that they were willing to go to war.
- The policy of appeasement had given Hitler the impression that the British and French governments would agree to almost anything in order to prevent another war with Germany.
- The Nazi-Soviet Non-Aggression Pact gave Hitler the extra confidence he needed to deal with the Polish problem without having to worry about a possible Soviet attack.

REVISION TASKS

1. Use the information in this section to complete the diagram below. This task will probably work best if you work with a partner.

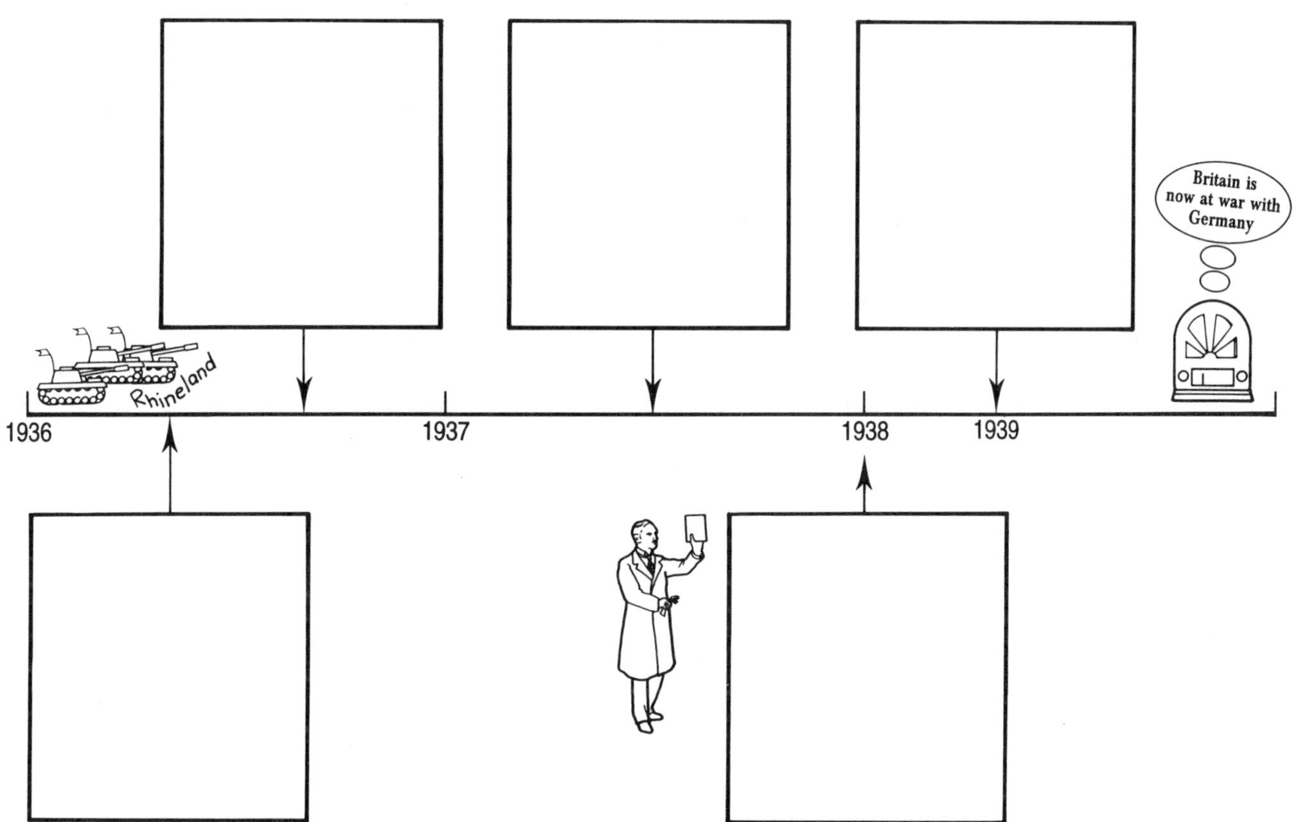

2. Now give each of these factors leading to war a 'mark' out of 100 which reflects your view of how important it was as a cause of the Second World War: for example, you may feel that the Depression is worth 20 per cent while the Treaty of Versailles is worth 25 per cent.

Remember there are no right answers – the world's leading historians all have different views. The important point about this task is that you express your opinion and provide evidence and examples which support your view.

REVISION SESSION

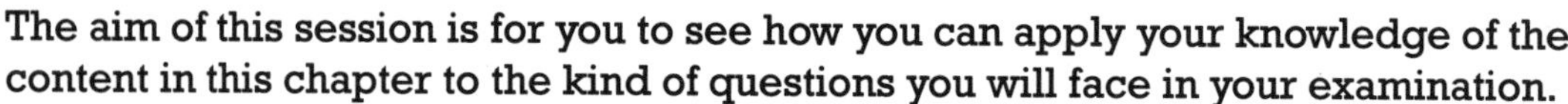

The aim of this session is for you to see how you can apply your knowledge of the content in this chapter to the kind of questions you will face in your examination.

Examination questions

The key theme of the examination questions on this topic is the outbreak of the Second World War. However, there are also some important sub topics on individual countries or events. Look at this examination question from MEG Paper I, 1994.

In the 1930s international problems became more and more serious until in September 1939 Britain declared war on Germany. The following questions are about the events of the 1930s which led up to the outbreak of war.

(a) (i) Name the British Prime Minister who signed the Munich Agreement with Germany in 1938. [*1 mark*]
(ii) Explain what is meant by the term 'plebiscite'. Briefly use your knowledge of events in Austria in 1938 to support your answer. [*3 marks*]

What is required?

This question is designed to test your factual knowledge and understanding of specific ideas and terms.

Ideas for your answer

1. For Part (i) you need to give a specific answer, for example: Neville Chamberlain was the British Prime Minister in 1938.
2. To score full marks for Part (ii) you need to show first of all that you understand the term, for example: a plebiscite is a vote by people to decide to which country they would like to belong. You then need to give an example – such as the Anschluss in 1938: Hitler called a plebiscite in Austria. Because of Nazi pressure and propaganda, 99 per cent of those who voted supported the joining of Austria with Germany.

(b) How similar were the following to each other:
I Japan's foreign policy in the 1930s
II Italy's foreign policy in the 1930s? [*6 marks*]

What is required?

This question tests your understanding of similarity and difference. In particular you need to show that you understand the ways in which Italian and Japanese foreign policies were *similar* and *different* and support your answer with examples. To aim for the lowest level (1 mark) you will need to produce a very general answer, for example: both were aggressive. To reach the next level (2-3 marks) you must identify a similarity or a difference and support it with an example. Top level answers (4–6 marks) must identify a number of similarities and differences and provide examples.

Ideas for you answer

1. You should show several ways in which Italian and Japanese foreign policies were similar.
   - Both used aggressive tactics on weaker countries.
   - Each one also wanted the prestige that an empire would bring (see pages 43–44 for details).
2. However, there were also differences:
   - Japan's motives were more influenced by the impact of the world economic depression.
   - Japan invaded Manchuria in order to expand her territory and take advantage of Manchuria's mineral resources.
   - Japan also saw the invasion of Manchuria as a way to increase the market for her goods in China.
   - Mussolini was motivated more by the desire for prestige and to establish Italy as an important power on the world stage.
   - He also wanted to distract the attention of the Italian people from the failures of his government (see page 43).

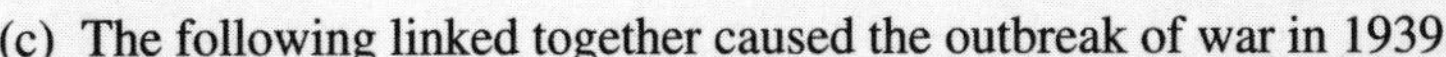

(c) The following linked together caused the outbreak of war in 1939:
I Britain's foreign policy from 1936 to 1939;
II Weakness of the League of Nations in the 1930s;
III Germany's foreign policy from 1936 to 1939.

Do you agree with this statement? Explain your answer fully by referring to I, II, and III. [*15 marks*]

What is required?

This question tests your understanding of causes and consequence. It is asking you to explain why the Second World War broke out in 1939. General and vague answers will score low level marks (1–3 marks or 4–6 marks). An example of this type of answer would be simply listing reasons without analysing their importance or connections.

To aim for the next level (7–9 marks) you will need to analyse several of the listed items and say how they contributed towards war.

To aim for the higher levels (10–15 marks) you will need to analyse the listed items, show how they contributed towards war and show that there was a link between them. To score a top mark (13–15) you must

- analyse the listed items in detail
- show how they are linked
- mention other factors which helped to cause the outbreak of war.

Ideas for your answer

There are several ways you may wish to approach this answer. One option is to examine the items listed in the question but also to point out that there were other factors which led to the outbreak of war.

1. The most important reason for the outbreak of war was Hitler's aggressive foreign policy between 1936 and 1939. Hitler wanted to create 'Lebensraum' in Eastern Europe and this led to the invasion of Poland in September 1939. Britain and France had guaranteed to defend Poland against German aggression and so the European part of the Second World War began.

2. Aggressive German foreign policy had been encouraged by the weakness of the League of Nations. The League failed to act decisively against Japanese aggression towards Manchuria and Italian aggression towards Abyssinia. This gave Hitler confidence that his policies would not be opposed. Britain and France had also shown themselves to be unwilling to support the League in a decisive way. The weakness of the League was not a direct reason for the outbreak of war in 1939 but it helped to create a climate which encouraged German and Japanese expansionist policies.

3. The British foreign policy of appeasement was an important factor in the outbreak of war particularly when linked to German expansionist policies. From 1936 onwards Britain and France allowed Hitler to break section after section of the Treaty of Versailles in the hope he would be appeased. This appeasement policy allowed Hitler to re-militarise the Rhineland in 1936, unite with Austria in 1938 and seize the Sudetenland from Czechoslovakia in 1938.

   Hitler's confidence grew throughout the 1930s as he saw Britain and France fail to act decisively against Japan over Manchuria, Italy over Abyssinia or in support of Republicans in the Spanish Civil War. When the Nazi-Soviet Non-Aggression Pact was signed in August 1939, Hitler was confident he could crush Poland and ignore the appeasers in Britain and France.

4. There are also other factors which created the climate for war: the isolationist policy of the USA, the resentment and bitterness caused by the terms of the Treaty of Versailles, the Great Depression and the failure of Britain and France to sign an agreement with Stalin.

5. In conclusion you could point out that German foreign policy, combined with the appeasement policies of Britain and France, were key reasons for the outbreak of war. Other factors combined, however, to help create the climate for war.

SUMMARY AND REVISION PLAN

Below is a list of headings which you may find helpful. Use this as a check list to make sure that you are familiar with the material featured in this chapter. Record your key words alongside each heading.

A The foreign policies of the major powers in the 1930s

1. **Germany**
2. **Italy**
3. **Japan**
4. **France**
5. **Britain**

B The failure of the League of Nations

1. **The Manchurian crisis, 1931**
2. **The Italian invasion of Abyssinia, 1935**
3. **Reasons for the League's failure**

C The steps towards war

1. **The Spanish Civil War, 1936–39**
2. **German re-occupation of the Rhineland, 1936**
3. **Anschluss: the annexation of Austria, 1938**
4. **The Sudeten crisis and the Munich Agreement, 1938**
5. **Czechoslovakia, 1939**
6. **The end of appeasement**
7. **The Pact of Steel**
8. **Poland, 1939**
9. **The Nazi-Soviet Non-Agression Pact, August 1939**
10. **The outbreak of war, September 1939**

CHAPTER 5

The Cold War, 1945–55

During the Second World War the USA and the USSR had fought together as allies against Germany and Japan. Once this war was won, relations between the two 'superpowers' quickly got worse. A new war began – it was a war of ideas. For this reason it was known as the Cold War.

To answer questions on the Cold War you need to be familiar with both the key content and the key themes of the period.

KEY CONTENT

You need to show that you have a good working knowledge of these areas:

A The background to the Cold War
B The Allied conferences at Yalta and Potsdam
C The differences between the superpowers
D The USSR's policy on Eastern Europe
E US policy on Eastern Europe
F Crisis points in the Cold War, 1948–53
G NATO, the Warsaw Pact and other alliances set up between 1945 and 1955

KEY THEMES

As with other topics you will be expected to do more than simply write out all the content you have learnt about the Cold War. The questions you face will be asking you to show your understanding of one or more of these themes from the period:

- **How the Second World War changed the world balance of power**
- **The meaning of the term 'superpower'**
- **The difference between the communist and capitalist systems**
- **Why the wartime allies so quickly became hostile to each other**
- **The 'domino theory' and 'containment'**
- **Why and how relations between the superpowers changed in this period**
- **The attitudes of each side towards the other**
- **Why Germany became a cause of tension**
- **Why war actually broke out in Korea**

For example, look at the question below, which comes from MEG Paper I, 1994.

(a) (i) Name the leader of the USSR who attended the Yalta Conference in 1945. *[1 mark]*

(ii) Explain what is meant by the 'Truman Doctrine'. Briefly use your knowledge of the USA's policy towards communism between 1945 and 1955 to support your answer. *[3 marks]*

(b) How similar were the following to each other?
I The Yalta Conference;
II The Potsdam Conference. *[6 marks]*

(c) Which one of the following was the most important reason why relations became very poor between the USSR and the USA by 1955?
I The 'Iron Curtain';
II the division of Germany;
III Marshall Aid.

Explain your answer fully by referring to I, II and III. *[15 marks]*

To answer this question you must show your knowledge and understanding of this period. If you look carefully at the question you will see that you need to know about these important areas:

- The Yalta and Potsdam conferences
- What happened to Germany at the end of the Second World War
- Stalin's policies in Eastern Europe after the war
- American policies in Europe (including Marshall Aid).

You will also need to show your understanding of these key themes:

- The Truman doctrine and the policy of containment
- Why the USA and its allies were so concerned about Stalin
- The attitudes of each side toward the other in the period 1945–55.

We will look at this question in more detail at the end of this chapter.

A The background to the Cold War

1. **Damage caused by the Second World War** Millions of lives were lost on all sides as the table below shows. This does not include the millions of people who were killed in the holocaust.

Houses, factories, shops, entire cities had been destroyed by bombing and by fighting on the ground. By 1945, there were millions of sick, hungry, homeless refugees around Europe and the world.

	Soldiers	Civilians
Australia	29,295	243
Britain	271,311	95,297
Canada	39,319	not known
France	205,000	173,000
Germany	3,300,000	800,000
India	36,092	79,498
Japan	1,380,000	933,000
Italy	279,820	93,000
USSR	13,600,000	7,720,000
USA	292,131	5,662

Because of the disruption to all countries at the end of the war it was very difficult to be sure about numbers of killed and wounded. What is certain is that the USSR lost millions of its people as a result of the war with Germany, and Stalin (the leader of the USSR) was determined to make the USSR secure in future. You will need to bear this in mind as you look at the events of this period.

2. **The rise of the superpowers** Perhaps the most important change brought about by the Second World War was the rise of the superpowers. Before the war there had been many countries in the world which could claim to be great powers, such as the USA, USSR, Britain, France, Germany and Japan.

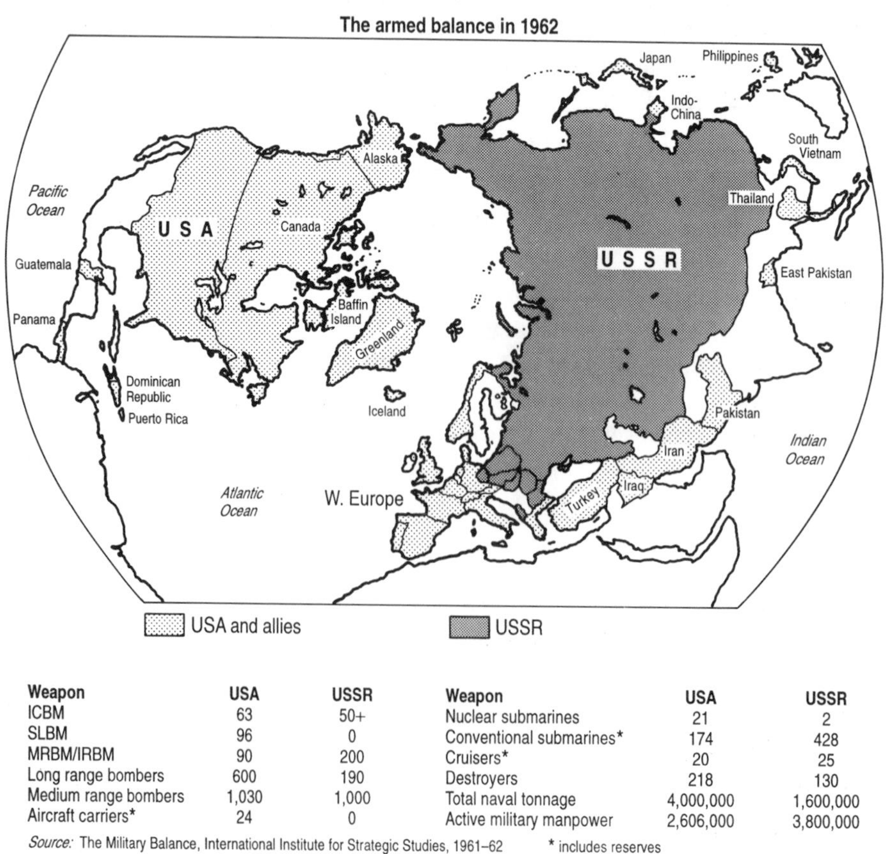

Weapon	USA	USSR
ICBM	63	50+
SLBM	96	0
MRBM/IRBM	90	200
Long range bombers	600	190
Medium range bombers	1,030	1,000
Aircraft carriers*	24	0

Weapon	USA	USSR
Nuclear submarines	21	2
Conventional submarines*	174	428
Cruisers*	20	25
Destroyers	218	130
Total naval tonnage	4,000,000	1,600,000
Active military manpower	2,606,000	3,800,000

Source: The Military Balance, International Institute for Strategic Studies, 1961–62 * includes reserves

By 1945 it had become clear that the USA and USSR were in a league of their own as superpowers. Their military strength and resources were far greater than any other country's, especially after the damage which the war had caused to other countries.

3. **Conflicting ideologies: communism and capitalism** During the war the communist superpower, the USSR, had united with the capitalist superpower, the USA, to defeat fascism.

However, communism and capitalism were very different economic systems strongly opposed to one another (see pages 62–63). With Germany and Japan defeated, the reason for this cooperation was gone. Differences of opinion soon began to emerge.

4. **Political changes in Europe: occupation, resistance and liberation** In Europe, most countries had been occupied by the German army, and run by German governors. When the Germans left, there was no government in place. The question was: who would take over?

New national leaders could possibly come from the resistance movements which had fought an undercover war against the Germans (e.g. sabotaging railways, helping servicemen to escape). However, there was sometimes more than one resistance movement in a country.

European resistance movements during the war

- In France the main resistance movement was organised by General Charles de Gaulle but there was also a communist resistance movement.
- In Greece and Yugoslavia there were also rival communist and non-communist movements. Whilst both movements fought the Germans, they were soon fighting each other once the Germans had gone, and the superpowers had strong views as to which of the resistance groups they wished to take over. The USSR favoured the communist groups, the USA the non-communists.

Defeating the Germans had been the main aim of all of the resistance movements. However, it was clear that once the Germans had gone it would not be a simple task to form new governments to run liberated countries. Where there were rival communist or non-communist groups major powers might get involved to support either the communists or non-communists. By 1947 this was the cause of great tension between the superpowers.

REVISION TASKS

1. The aim of the resistance movements was to defeat the Germans. Explain why their problems continued after their countries had been liberated.
2. Use 4 key words to describe two important differences between the superpowers.

B The Allied conferences at Yalta and Potsdam

By early 1945 it was clear that Germany would be defeated. The minds of the Allied leaders turned to the problems which peace would bring. To discuss these matters they held meetings or conferences at Yalta and Potsdam.

The aim of the conferences at Yalta and Potsdam was to discuss the challenges which the defeat of Germany would bring. These were:

- What to do with Germany and its leaders after surrender
- What was to happen to the occupied countries after they had been liberated, especially the countries of Eastern Europe
- How to bring the war with Japan to a speedy end
- How to create and maintain a peace which would last.

1. **The Yalta Conference, February 1945** At the Yalta Conference the Allied leaders (Churchill, Roosevelt and Stalin) got on well together. The following points were agreed at Yalta:

- Germany would be divided into four zones. These would be run by the USA, France, Britain and the USSR.
- Germany's capital city, Berlin (which was in the Soviet zone), would also be divided into four zones.

The division of Germany after the war

- The countries of Eastern Europe would be allowed to hold free elections to decide how they would be governed.
- The USSR would join in the war against Japan in return for territory in Manchuria and Sakhalin Island.

2. The Potsdam Conference, July–August 1945 In April 1945 President Roosevelt died, so by the time of the Potsdam Conference there was a new US President – Harry Truman. During the conference Churchill was replaced by Clement Attlee as British Prime Minister. The new leaders did not get on nearly so well with Stalin as the previous two.

Potsdam continued the discussions left over from the Yalta Conference. There were two points of agreement:

- The Nazi party was to be banned and its leaders would be tried as war criminals.
- The future border between Poland and Germany was agreed.

However, on other issues there were disagreements. There were clear signs that Stalin did not trust the USA and Britain and that they did not trust him.

Tensions at Potsdam

1. Britain and the USA denied Stalin a naval base in the Mediterranean:
   - They saw no need for Stalin to have such a base.
   - Stalin saw this as evidence that his allies mistrusted him.
2. Stalin wanted to take reparations from Germany but Britain and the USA opposed this:
   - America and Britain did not wish to cripple Germany; they had seen the results of reparations after the First World War.
   - Stalin was suspicious about why his allies seemed to want to protect Germany and even help it to recover.
3. Stalin had set up a communist government in Poland. Britain preferred the non-communist Polish government which had lived in exile in Britain throughout the war. Truman and Atlee were very suspicious of Stalin's motives in setting up a communist government in Poland based at Lublin.
4. President Truman did not tell Stalin about the atomic bomb before they first used it in 1945.

■ ***Even before the end of the war, disagreements were beginning to appear among the Allies. Britain and the USA represented one political system, the USSR another – each side was suspicious about the motives of the other.*** ■

REVISION TASKS

1. Construct a table like the one below on the Yalta and Potsdam Conferences and produce a key word summary to complete it.

Conference	Points agreed	Areas of disagreement
Yalta		
Potsdam		

2. What important changes had occurred by the time of the Potsdam Conference?

C The differences between the superpowers

To understand how and why tension built up in the years immediately after the war, it is important to understand the beliefs and ideas of each of the superpowers. This helps to explain the attitude of each side towards the other.

1. The USA

What were the main political and economic features of the USA?

- It had a democratic system. The government of the USA was chosen in free democratic elections and the country was led by its President.
- It had a capitalist economy. Business and property were privately owned. Individuals could make profits in business or move jobs if they wished. However, they might also go bankrupt or lose their jobs.
- The USA was the world's wealthiest country, but under capitalism there were always great contrasts – some people were very rich, others very poor.

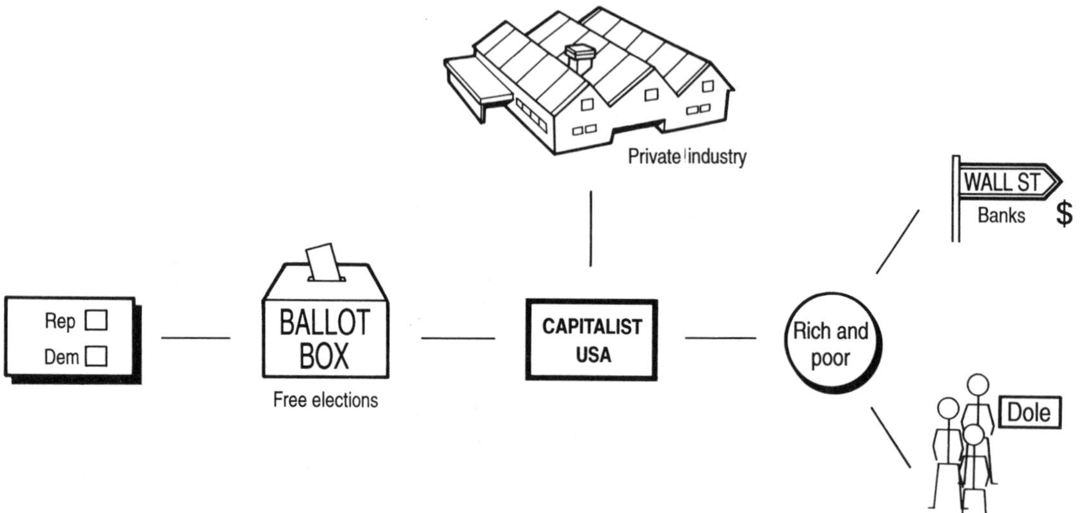

- Americans firmly believed that the American way of doing things was 'the right way'.
- President Truman was worried about the way Stalin seemed to be setting up communist governments in Eastern Europe.

In the 1920s and 1930s the USA followed a policy of ISOLATIONISM (staying out of world affairs). Now faced by communism extending into Eastern Europe the US government was prepared to help and support people and countries who wanted democratic states with capitalist economies. This was seen as simply the defence of people's freedom against a system they did not want.

2. The USSR

The USSR was a communist state. This meant that the rights of individuals were seen as less important than the good of society as a whole.

- In this system people could only vote for the communist party and their lives were closely controlled.
- It had a planned economy. The government owned all industry and planned what every factory should produce.
- The general standard of living in the USSR was much lower than in the USA, but unemployment and poverty were rare, and there were not the extremes of wealth seen in the USA.
- Unlike the USA, the USSR had been attacked many times in the past. Germany had invaded Russia in 1914 and Hitler's invasion in 1941 had been particularly vicious. Stalin was determined that this would never happen again. In his view, the USSR could only be safe if the countries on its borders were controlled by communist governments. He believed that if he did not set up communist governments the USA would set up hostile countries on his border.

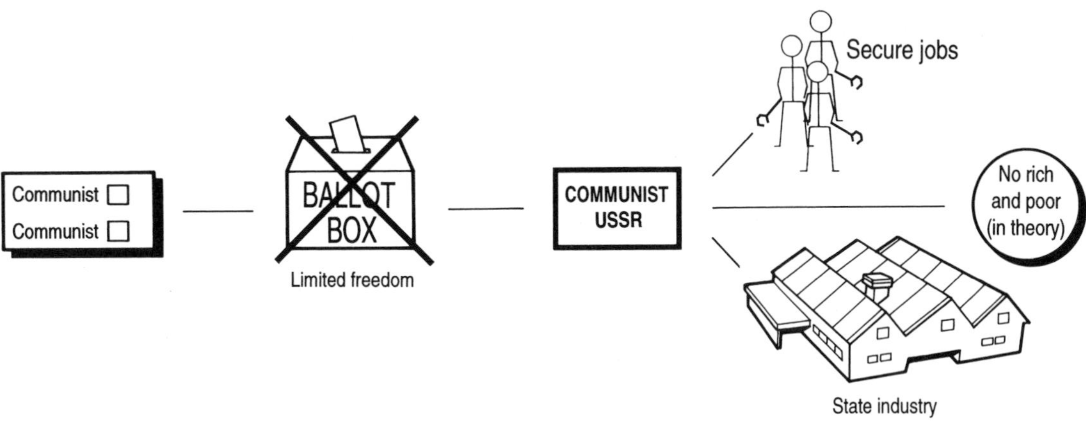

REVISION TASKS

1. Choose 6 key words to summarise the USA's system of government. Now choose 6 key words to summarise the USSR's system of government.
   Compare the two under the headings:

USA	USSR

2. Use 6–8 key words to explain why Stalin was determined to keep control of Eastern Europe.

D The USSR's policy on Eastern Europe

The Soviet Red Army advanced through large areas of Eastern Europe whilst driving back the Germans. One year after the war many troops remained in much of Eastern Europe, as the table below shows:

Troops in Europe (millions)	1945	1946
USA	3.1	0.4
UK	1.3	0.5
USSR	6.0	6.0

1. Creating satellites Elections were held in each East European country as promised in Yalta in 1945, but the evidence suggests that they were rigged to allow the USSR-backed communist parties to take control. In Bulgaria, Albania, Poland, Romania, Hungary opponents of the communists had been beaten, murdered or frightened into submission. By 1947 all Eastern European states except Czechoslovakia (see page 65) had communist governments.

Yugoslavia was also under communist rule, although the communist leader Tito was not controlled by Stalin like the other communist governments. Tito had refused to submit to Stalin's control and Yugoslavia was cut off from any type of support from the USSR.

Europe was now divided – East and West. In 1946 Churchill called this division the IRON CURTAIN.

Stalin created the Cominform and later Comecon – a trading alliance of communist countries (see page 68) – to help him keep a tight grip on his neighbours. These countries became known as SATELLITE countries because their governments and economies depended so heavily on the USSR.

■ ***Stalin was simply carrying out his policy of making sure he had friendly governments on his doorstep. However, to the British and Americans he seemed to be trying to build up a communist empire.*** ■

E US policy on Eastern Europe

1. Greece

You can see from the map below that Greece appeared to be next in line in the spread of communism. Greek resistance against the Germans had been divided into two movements – the royalists (who wanted the return of their king) and the communists. After the war, the royalists were in charge and had restored the king with the help of British troops. However, they were under attack from the communist forces and asked the USA for help early in 1947.

Truman was already very worried about the spread of communism. The USA supplied Greece with arms, supplies and money and the communists were defeated.

2. The Truman doctrine Events in Greece had convinced Truman that unless he acted, communism would continue to spread. He therefore explained his policy to the world. This became known as the Truman doctrine:

- Truman said:

> *I believe it must be the policy of the USA to support all free peoples who are resisting attempted subjugation by armed minorities or by outside pressure.*

- The USA would not return to isolationism – America would play a leading role in the world.
- The aim was to contain (stop the spread) of communism but not to push it back. This was the policy of CONTAINMENT.

At this point it became clear that a 'cold war' had started. The two sides believed in totally different political ideas. Each side feared the spread of the other idea. When one tried to extend its influence or support (e.g. the USSR in Eastern Europe), this was seen as a threat by the other side.

3. Marshall Aid, 1947 Truman believed that poverty and hardship provided a breeding ground for communism and so he wished to make Europe prosperous again. It was also important for American businesses to have someone to trade with in the future, yet Europe's economies were still in ruins after the war.

The American Secretary of State, George Marshall, therefore visited Europe and came up with a European Recovery Programme – usually known as the Marshall Plan or Marshall Aid.

This had two main aims:

- To stop the spread of communism (although Truman did not admit this at the time)
- To help the economies of Europe to recover (this would eventually provide a market for American exports).

Thirteen billion dollars poured into Europe in the years 1947–51, providing vital help for the recovery of Europe. However, Marshall Aid also caused tensions:

- Only sixteen European countries accepted it – and these were all Western European states.
- Stalin refused Marshall Aid for the USSR and banned the Eastern European countries from accepting it.

■ ***Marshall Aid was a generous gesture by the USA but it was not entirely an act of kindness. Stalin saw it as an attempt by American business to dominate Western Europe. If the USA was determined to 'buy' Western Europe with its dollars, then he was determined to control Eastern Europe with his communist allies and the Red Army.*** ■

4. The communists take over in Czechoslovakia, 1948 The only Eastern European country that considered accepting Marshall Aid was Czechoslovakia. Czechoslovakia was not fully part of Stalin's 'Eastern bloc' of countries – communists were not fully in control. In the spring of 1948 elections were due and it seemed likely that the communists (who were opposed to accepting Marshall Aid) would do badly, while the opposition (who were in favour) would do well.

Communists organised marches and protests. Non-communist ministers resigned and Foreign Minister Jan Masaryk was probably murdered. In May 1948 elections took place but only communists were allowed to stand. Czechoslovakia was now fully a part of the communist Eastern bloc.

■ ***East and West were now divided completely. Czechoslovakia had been a link between them. Although there is no definite proof, historians believe that Stalin did not want a link between East and West and that the USSR was behind the takeover in Czechoslovakia.*** ■

REVISION TASKS

1. Use 6 key words to explain why Truman was worried about Stalin's plans?
2. Write your own definition of Marshall Aid.
3. Why was the takeover in Czechoslovakia a cause of tension?
4. How far do you feel each side was to blame for the tension after the Second World War? Decide where you would put the USA and the USSR on the scale below:

Mostly to blame 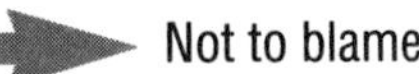 Not to blame

F Crisis points in the Cold War, 1948–53

1. **The Berlin blockade and airlift, 1948–49** At the end of the war the Allies divided Germany and Berlin into zones (see map on page 60). Germany's economy and government had been shattered by the war and the Allies were faced with a serious question: should they continue to occupy Germany or should they try to rebuild it?

- Britain and the USA wanted Germany to recover – they could not afford to keep feeding Germany and they felt that punishing Germany would not help future peace.
- The French were unsure about whether to get Germany back on its feet or to 'ram home its defeat'.
- The USSR did not want to rebuild Germany and Stalin was suspicious about why the USA and Britain did.

In 1948 the French, US and British zones merged to become West Germany. With the help of Marshall Aid, West Germany began to recover and prosper. It was a very different story in East Germany. In this area, controlled by the USSR, there was poverty and hunger. Many East Germans were leaving the East because West Germany seemed much more attractive.

In Stalin's eyes it seemed the Allies were building up West Germany in order to attack him. When they introduced a new West German currency (money) this was the last straw.

Stalin tried to blockade Berlin. Berlin, the capital of Germany, was in the middle of East Germany (see map on page 60). In a month he closed all road and rail connections from Berlin to West Germany hoping he could force the Western Allies out of Berlin. For many people at the time it seemed there was a real risk of war. The USA and Britain faced a choice:

- They could withdraw – but this would be humiliating and it might encourage Stalin to think he could invade West Germany.
- They could lift supplies into West Berlin by air – they had the planes but it would be risky – their planes might be shot down.

The Allies decided to airlift supplies. The airlift was a great success. The planes were not attacked. By May 1949 the USSR lifted the blockade. It was a victory for the West. Relations with the USSR hit rock bottom. Cooperation in Germany in the future was very unlikely. Germany would remain divided. The Federal Republic of Germany (West Germany) was decreed in August 1949. In October 1949 the Soviet zone became the German Democratic Republic (East Germany).

2. **The Korean War 1950–53** Europe was not the only part of the world where the USSR came into conflict with the USA. Stalin supported communists in Asia – in China, Malaya and Indonesia, Burma, Vietnam and the Philippines. Not surprisingly, the Americans thought they were seeing the Eastern Europe story repeated all over again in Asia. In 1949 China became a communist state. The Americans were determined to contain the further spread of communism.

The crisis came in Korea. At the end of the war the USSR took control of North Korea and set up a communist state. In the South, the Americans set up a democracy. The South Korean President (Syngman Rhee) and the North Korean President (Kim Il Sung) each claimed to be president of all Korea. Relations were tense. In June 1950 North Korea invaded South Korea.

Main events of the Korean War:

- First of all South Korean forces were pushed back. President Truman asked the United Nations Organisation to help.
- UN forces from many countries (but mainly American) drove the communists back to the Yalu River on the border with China (see map on page 67).

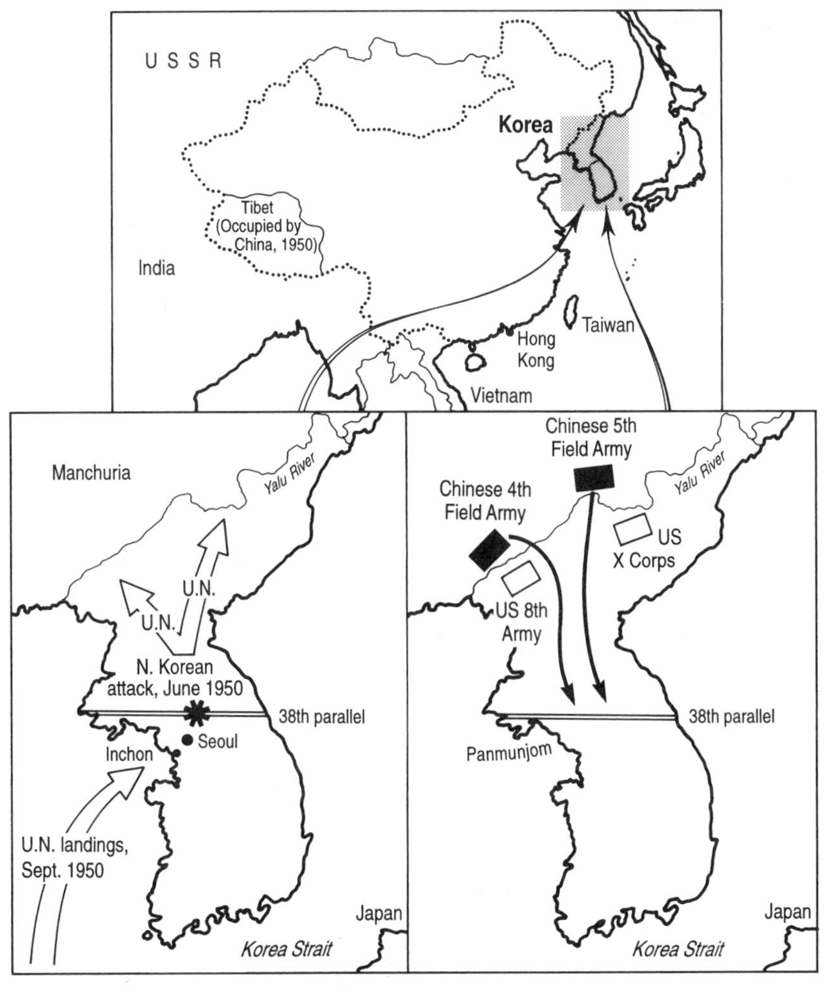

- This worried China who did not want a non-communist neighbour supported by US troops. China joined the war.
- The UN forces were driven back and the UN commander, General MacArthur, called for the use of the atomic bomb. US President Truman sacked MacArthur.
- Once again UN troops began to push the communists back. By June 1951 the fighting seemed to be settling roughly around the 38th parallel (see map above).
- In 1953 a truce was agreed at Panmunjon (on the 38th parallel).

To this day there are two states in Korea and relations can still sometimes be strained.

When China became a communist country in 1949 the USA was extremely worried. Chinese-US relations were strained for many years. President Truman was worried that the DOMINO EFFECT (see below) would work in Asia like it had in Europe. So the USA was pleased with the result. The Americans saw the Korean War as an example of successful containment.

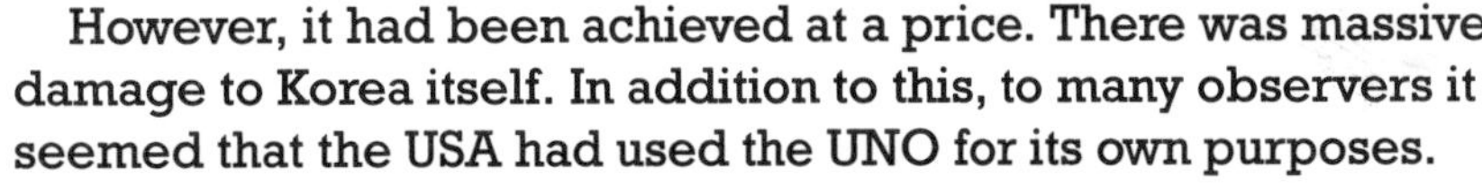

However, it had been achieved at a price. There was massive damage to Korea itself. In addition to this, to many observers it seemed that the USA had used the UNO for its own purposes.

■ ***The Berlin Blockade and the Korean War were extreme examples of Cold War relationships. The USA and USSR held totally different ideas and neither side trusted the other. Any attempt by one side to help another country was seen as a threat to the other side.*** ■

REVISION TASKS

Construct a table like the one below and use the information in this section to complete it. You should summarise the different views about the Berlin blockade and the Korean War. In each case use not more than 5 key words.

1. Berlin Blockade	**Causes**	**Effects**
US view		
USSR view		

2. Korean War	**Causes**	**Effects**
US view		
USSR view		

G NATO, the Warsaw Pact and other alliances set up 1945–55

1. **Cominform, 1947** Stalin set up the Cominform – an alliance of communist countries – in 1947, probably as a response to the Marshall Plan. Its aim was to spread Stalin's communist ideas. Cominform helped Stalin tighten his hold on his communist allies because it restricted their contact with the West.

   Only one communist leader, Marshall Tito of Yugoslavia, was not prepared to accept Stalin's total leadership and split with Moscow. However, Yugoslavia remained communist.

2. **Comecon, 1949** This was set up by Stalin to coordinate the production and trade of the Eastern European countries. It appeared rather like an early communist version of the European Community. However, Comecon favoured the USSR far more than any of its other members.

3. **NATO (North Atlantic Treaty Organisation), 1949** This military alliance contained most of the states in Western Europe as well as the USA and Canada. Its main purpose was to defend each of its members. If one member was attacked, all the others would help to defend this member. When the USSR developed its own atomic bomb in 1949, NATO seemed even more important to the defence of Western Europe, since at the time no European country had atomic weapons.

4. **The Warsaw Pact, 1955** In 1955 West Germany joined NATO. The Soviet response was to set up the Warsaw Pact – a communist version of NATO. The Soviets had not forgotten the damage which Germany had done to the USSR in the Second World War.

■ ***These alliances again demonstrated the fear and mistrust which brought about the Cold War. The Western democracies and the USSR both feared the rise of another state like Nazi Germany. However, each side saw the other side as this potential threat, certainly not themselves. The creation of alliances for self-defence on one side could very easily look like an alliance preparing for attack to the other side.*** ■

REVISION TASK

1. Construct a table like the one below and use the information in this section and the map opposite to complete it.

Organisation	Members	Purpose	Effects on East-West relations
Coniforn			

Iceland
Norway
Sweden
Finland
North Sea
Irish Rep.
U.K.
Denmark
USA & Canada
Netherlands
Belgium
West Germany
East Germany
Poland
U S S R
Atlantic Ocean
France
Czechoslovakia
Switz.
Austria
Hungary
Romania
Yugoslavia
(Associate member of Comecon 1964)
Portugal
Spain
Italy
Corsica
Sardinia
Albania
Bulgaria
Greece
Turkey
Mediterranean Sea
Comecom countries
NATO countries
Warsaw Pact

REVISION SESSION

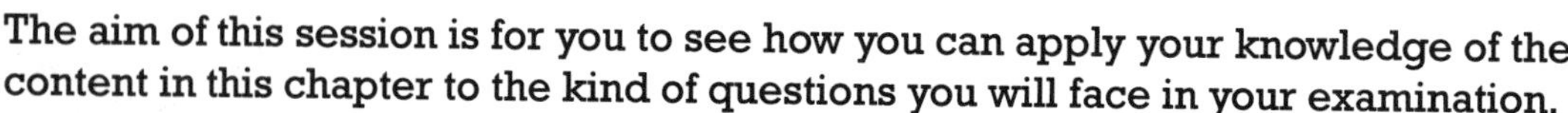

The aim of this session is for you to see how you can apply your knowledge of the content in this chapter to the kind of questions you will face in your examination.

Examination questions

The Cold War is an important examination topic. Questions usually concentrate on the following points:
- **why relations between the superpowers got worse**
- **the importance of particular events in this process.**

This question is from MEG Paper I, 1994.

(a) (i) Name the leader of the USSR who attended the Yalta Conference in 1945. [*1 mark*]

(ii) Explain what is meant by 'The Truman Doctrine'. Briefly use your knowledge of the USA's policy towards communism between 1945–55 to support your answer. [*3 marks*]

What is required?

The aim here is to test your knowledge of the topic and your understanding of important historical terms.

Part (i) requires a simple factual answer. Part (ii) is more demanding, but notice that your answer should be brief, so one example will be enough to support your answer.

Ideas for your answer

1. For Part (i) Stalin was the Soviet leader.
2. For Part (ii) you should explain that the Truman Doctrine was US President Truman's policy of containing or stopping the spread of communism. Good examples of this were his actions in Greece in 1947 and Korea in 1950–53.

(b) How similar were the following to each other:
I The Yalta Conference
II The Potsdam Conference? [*6 marks*]

What is required?

This question is looking for you to show your understanding of similarity and difference. General answers describing one conference will score only 1 mark.

To reach the next level (2–3 marks) you must concentrate on examples (e.g. new leaders) of what was similar or different between the conferences.

To reach the higher levels (4–6 marks) you must identify at least three important similarities or differences and provide details of them.

Ideas for your answer

1. There are some clear similarities which you could point out. For example, both discussed what would happen to Germany and other issues concerning territory (see page 60). Both conferences also looked at the question of Eastern Europe.
2. In some ways the differences between Yalta and Potsdam were more important. There were new leaders (except Stalin) and Japan was an extra subject of discussion. You could also point out that the mood of relations seemed to be changing (see page 61). By this time also the USA had the atomic bomb.

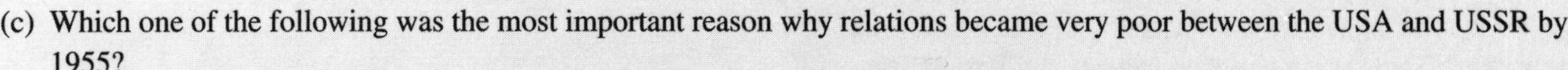

(c) Which one of the following was the most important reason why relations became very poor between the USA and USSR by 1955?
I The Iron Curtain;
II The division of Germany;
III Marshall Aid.

Explain your answer fully by referring to I, II and III. [*15 marks*]

What is required?

For this question you need to show that you understand the historical concept of cause and consequence. The important thing is to look at each of I-III and explain:

- how each one caused tension
- how serious that tension became
- how the events were linked.

A low level answer (1–3 marks) would simply be a general statement. To reach the next level (4–6 marks) you must look at how at least one of the events caused poor relations.

If you choose one item and explain briefly why you rejected the others then you will reach the next level (7–9 marks). To reach the top level (10-15 marks) you must look at each event in detail and explain how each one caused problems. You must also reach a conclusion.

Ideas for your answer

It is a good idea to take each point in turn:

1. You need to define the Iron Curtain as the barrier which appeared in Europe between the communist East and the non-communist West. This was clearly a source of poor relations after 1945. The superpowers had argued over Eastern Europe at the Yalta and Potsdam Conferences. From the USA's point of view Stalin was building an empire in Eastern Europe as communists took over Poland, Romania, Hungary and Yugoslavia. Tension was increased further still by clashes over Greece and Czechoslovakia (see pages 63–64). Whilst the West feared Stalin, you should also point out how Stalin saw matters (page 63).
2. The division of Germany really followed on from the events which led to the creation of the Iron Curtain. Again, you need to look at the views of each side, and explain how the views of each side caused concern to the other side (e.g. Stalin's fear of a rebuilt Germany). You should also point out that the West stood firm over Germany because of the events which led up to the Iron Curtain. On the other hand, it was Stalin's fear of Germany which had led him to create the Iron Curtain in the first place.
3. Again, you should briefly describe Marshall Aid, how it worked and what its aims were. You need to explain why Stalin saw Marshall Aid as a threat (see page 65). You should also point out how the question of Marshall Aid caused tensions (e.g. in Czechoslovakia). It is important to explain that the USA genuinely wanted to help rebuild Europe but also wanted to contain communism (see page 64). Again, this brings up the links between Marshall Aid and the events which led to the creation of the Iron Curtain in particular.
4. You should finish with a short conclusion on which of the events was the most important cause of tension. The most effective conclusion would be to point out that each event could claim to be the most serious cause of tension. In addition, the three events are strongly connected and so it would be very difficult to make a firm judgement.

SUMMARY AND REVISION PLAN

Below is a list of headings which you may find helpful. Use this as a check list to make sure that you are familiar with the material featured in this chapter. Record your key words alongside each heading.

A The background to the Cold War

1. Damage caused by the First World War
2. The rise of the superpowers
3. Conflicting ideologies: communism and capitalism
4. Political changes in Europe: occupation, resistance and liberation

B The Allied conferences at Yalta and Potsdam

1. the Yalta Conference, February 1945
2. The Potsdam Conference, July–August 1945 – tensions

C The differences between the superpowers

1. The USA
2. The USSR

D The USSR's policy on Eastern Europe

1. Creating satellites
2. The communists take over in Czechoslovakia, 1947

E US policy on Eastern Europe

1. Greece
2. The Truman doctrine
3. Marshall Aid, 1947

F Crisis points in the Cold War

1. The Berlin blockade and airlift, 1948–49
2. The Korean War, 1950–53

G NATO, the Warsaw Pact and other alliances set up, 1945–55

1. Cominform, 1947
2. Comecon, 1949
3. NATO, 1949
4. The Warsaw Pact, 1955

Changing relations between the superpowers, 1955–90

From 1955 onwards, relations between the superpowers changed dramatically. Sometimes it seemed the Cold War was thawing. At other times it seemed that the superpowers were on the brink of all-out nuclear war. Why were there such extremes?

To answer questions on changing relations between the superpowers you need to be familiar with both the key content and the key themes of this period.

KEY CONTENT

You will need to show that you have a good working knowledge of these areas:

- **A Khrushchev and the 'thaw' in the Cold War in the 1950s**
- **B Relations between China and the USSR**
- **C The crisis points in the Cold War, 1956–80**
- **D Détente and improving relations between the superpowers**
- **E US-Soviet relations in the 1980s: the end of the Cold War**

KEY THEMES

As with any examination questions you will not be asked to simply describe the events of this period. You will need to show your understanding of some important themes connected with the Cold War. These are:

- **The importance of certain key events on Cold War relations and 'détente'**
- **Why there was hostility between China and the USSR**
- **Why relations changed between the USA and China**
- **Why and how superpower relations changed between 1955 and 1990**
- **Why the Cold War ended**

For example, look at this examination question from MEG Paper I, 1993.

(a) (i) Name one country that became a member of NATO in 1949. [*1 mark*]

(ii) Explain what is meant by the 'Cold War'.

Briefly use your knowledge of relations between the USA and the USSR from 1946 to 1955 to support your answer. [*3 marks*]

(b) Why were relationships between the USA and China very poor between 1950 and 1953? [*6 marks*]

(c) In 1956, relationships between the USA and the USSR were poor. By 1988, relationships between the USA and the USSR were much better. Why did the relationships change between 1956 and 1988? Explain your answer fully. [*15 marks*]

For this question you clearly need to show your knowledge of these areas:

- *The Berlin airlift*
- *The Korean War*
- *Crisis in the Cold War and the development of détente*
- *International relations between 1955–88.*

You also need to show your understanding of the following themes:

- *Why there were tensions and conflict between the USA and China in the 1950s*
- *Why relations between the USSR and USA changed.*

We shall look at this question in more detail at the end of the chapter.

CHANGING RELATIONS BETWEEN THE SUPERPOWERS, 1955–90

A Khrushchev and the 'thaw' in the Cold War in the 1950s

1. **Nikita Khrushchev: a new Soviet leader** Stalin died in 1953. There was a power struggle to succeed him as leader of the USSR. The winner was Nikita Khrushchev. Khrushchev seemed to be a less aggressive leader than Stalin and talked of peaceful coexistence (living in peace) with the West. In 1956 at the 20th Congress of the Communist Party, he publicly attacked Stalin for being a dictator.

2. **Peaceful coexistence** The West began to see hopeful signs from the new Soviet leader.
   - Khrushchev seemed to be encouraging greater freedom within the USSR and its allies.
   - On a visit to Warsaw in 1956 he indicated that Polish people should be allowed more freedom.

   Up to 1956 the signs seemed very positive in terms of improving relations between East and West. Khrushchev appeared much less hostile to the West than Stalin had been. He also seemed to be willing to relax the USSR's grip on Eastern Europe.

3. **Eastern Europe** Later in 1956, events in Hungary showed a different side to Khrushchev:
   - In 1956 a reforming government took power in Hungary. It announced its intention of leaving the Warsaw Pact and throwing off the influence of the USSR (see page 76).
   - Khrushchev showed that he was not willing to allow this kind of change inside the Warsaw Pact. He sent Soviet troops and tanks into the Hungarian capital, Budapest. The rebellion was crushed and its leaders were killed.

   ■ ***Many historians doubt whether there was a real 'thaw' in the Cold War. Khrushchev was prepared to show a more friendly attitude to the West and was also prepared to consider reform inside the USSR. However, he was not prepared to let the USSR's iron grip on Eastern Europe be threatened. This inevitably raised the tensions between the USA and the USSR.*** ■

B Relations between China and the USSR

This is also known as Sino-Soviet (China-USSR) relations. The relationship between China and the USSR is an important theme in the Cold War.

1. **Stalin and Mao** The communists took power in China in 1949, and the previous nationalist government fled to the island of Taiwan. The new government was a powerful communist ally for the USSR. In 1950 Stalin and the Chinese leader Mao Zedong signed a 30-year treaty of friendship. Both countries seemed to be champions of communism in a world dominated by capitalist countries. This friendship made the USA suspicious of both China and the USSR. This was evident in the Korean War.

2. **Chinese reaction to Khrushchev** After Stalin's death in 1953, relations between China and the USSR got worse:
   - The Chinese leadership accused Khrushchev of betraying communist ideals and working too closely with Western capitalist governments.
   - The Chinese also accused the Soviets of treating its allies in Eastern Europe like colonies rather than communist equals.

   The dispute between China and the USSR came to a head at a conference in Bucharest in 1960:
   - The Soviets stressed the policy of peaceful coexistence with the USA.
   - The Chinese continued to warn of the Western capitalist threat.

Even after the fall of Khrushchev in 1964, hostility between the Soviets and Chinese continued. Fighting broke out along the border in Manchuria in 1964. By the end of the 1960s relations between Moscow and Peking were at an all-time low.

The relationship between the USSR and China affected East-West relations in two ways:

- Friendship between the two communist powers worried the USA and came to a head in events such as the Korean War (see pages 66–67).
- The dispute between China and the USSR eased the fears of the USA and probably helped to ease relations between the USA and the USSR.

REVISION TASKS

1. Find 4–6 key words to summarise how Khrushchev was:
   a) different from Stalin
   b) similar to Stalin.
2. Describe Khrushchev from the point of view of the USA
   a) early in 1956
   b) towards the end of 1956.
3. Explain why the relationship between the USSR and China was important to the USA.

C Crisis points in the Cold War 1956–80

In Chapter 5 you will have seen how relations in the Cold War varied. They were seldom good, but sometimes there were incidents and crises which raised tension between the superpowers to extremes. You need to be familiar with these crises and what they show about the changing relationships between the superpowers.

1. Hungary, 1956

In July 1956 a reforming government led by Imre Nagy took power in Hungary after repeated rioting by students in Budapest. The new government planned to increase personal freedom and even talked of taking Hungary out of the Warsaw Pact.

The Soviet response was harsh:

- On 4 November Khrushchev sent 6000 Soviet tanks into Hungary to overthrow the rebellion and crush any further protest.
- The Soviets arrested Nagy and installed a loyal communist, Kadar, to set up a new government.
- Nagy was shot for his part in the rebellion.
- Soviet troops remained on Budapest streets until the crisis was over.

An estimated 30,000 Hungarians were killed during the crisis and 180,000 fled to the West. The Western powers protested about the Soviet interference. However, the NATO powers did not assist or send any help to the Hungarian rebels at any point.

■ ***Although they were sympathetic to the Hungarian rebels, Western governments were not willing to risk a possible war with the Soviet Union over reform in Hungary. It is a feature of the Cold War that neither side intervened in the areas of the world that were of most vital interest to their opponents. They preferred to challenge each other in less direct ways.*** ■

2. The U2 incident

On 1 May 1960, another incident occurred which developed into a crisis. The Soviets shot down an American U2 spy plane over the USSR and captured the pilot, Gary Powers. According to the Soviets he admitted he was on a spying mission.

The American government denied that spying flights took place over Soviet territory and claimed that Gary Powers had accidentally strayed into Soviet airspace whilst on a flight to study weather conditions. The Soviets were keen to show the world that the American government was lying so they developed the film taken by Powers on his mission. It showed he had clearly been spying. This severely embarrassed the American government.

The results in terms of Cold War relations were extremely serious. Khrushchev demanded that the Americans must:

- Apologise for the U2 affair
- Stop future spying flights
- Punish those responsible.

Eisenhower refused to apologise. Gary Powers was sentenced to 10 years in prison in the USSR but was in fact exchanged in 1962 for a Soviet agent.

The incident was especially damaging for the American President Eisenhower:

- Not only had a US plane been shot down spying over Soviet territory but the Americans had lied about it for all the world to see.
- The Soviets had scored a propaganda victory.

The U2 affair showed how quickly conflict between the superpowers could develop from a single incident.

3. Berlin, 1961

Berlin had always been a source of conflict between the Soviets and Western allies. Capitalist West Berlin – surrounded by the communist state of East Germany – continued to be a problem for East Germany and the USSR:

- The high standard of living enjoyed by the people of West Berlin contrasted sharply with that of the communist half of the city - East Berlin. It was a continual reminder to the people in East Germany of their poor living conditions.
- It was estimated that 3 million people had crossed from East to West Berlin between 1945 and 1960. Many of these people were skilled workers and it seemed that the survival of East Germany was in doubt if this escape route remained open.

In 1961, Khrushchev and the East German leadership decided to act. Without warning, on 13 August 1961, the East Germans began to build a wall surrounding West Berlin.
- At first the wall was little more than barbed wire but by 17 August this was replaced with a stone wall.
- All movement between East and West was stopped.
- For several days Soviet and American tanks faced each other across divided Berlin streets.

The building of the Berlin Wall had some immediate effects:
- The flow of refugees stopped instantly.
- Western nations were given a propaganda victory since it appeared communist states need to build walls to prevent their citizens from leaving.
- They had to be satisfied with a propaganda victory. It was clear that the USA and NATO were not going to try to stop the building of the wall. In reality, there was little the western powers could do to stop it.

For the West, from the 1960s until the 1980s the Berlin Wall became a symbol of the division between the capitalist West and communist East. US President John F Kennedy made an historic visit to West Berlin and declared that the city was a symbol of the struggle between the forces of freedom and the communist world. For the USSR and East Germany, however, the wall was simply an economic and political necessity. The loss of so many refugees from East Germany was beginning to threaten the existence of the East German state.

REVISION TASKS

1. Create a 5-question quiz on the first three crisis points. You can write your questions (and answers) here.

Question
a.
b.
c.
d.
e.

Answer
a.
b.
c.
d.
e.

4. The Cuban missile crisis, 1962 The Cuban missile crisis was the most serious conflict between the USSR and USA in the history of the Cold War. Cuba was a communist country just 90 miles off the coast of the USA. In October 1962, US spy planes identified nuclear missile sites being built on Cuba. This is what happened.

Position and threat of Cuban missiles

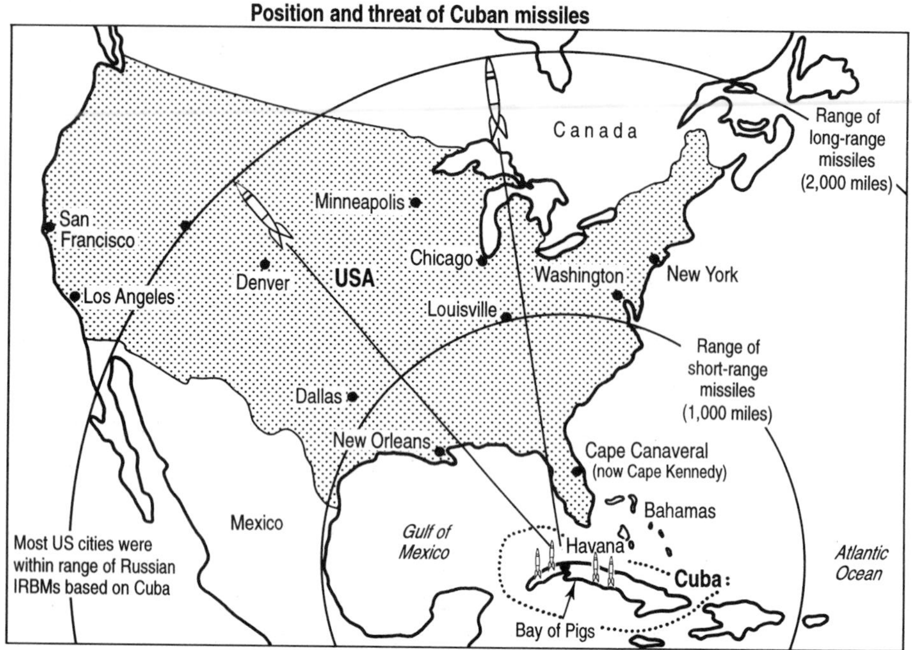

- President Kennedy and his closest advisers discussed what to do about the Soviet missiles in Cuba.
- Kennedy broadcast to the American people informing them of the potential threat and what he intended to do about it.
- The Americans blockaded Cuba and began to stop any ship suspected of carrying arms and equipment.
- The Soviets and Cuban leader Fidel Castro complained about US action to the United Nations and said it was a threat to world peace.
- President Kennedy threatened to invade Cuba and remove the missiles by force. The next 10 days were tense. The world seemed to hold its breath as the USSR and USA headed towards nuclear conflict.

Cuban crisis at its peak, October 1962

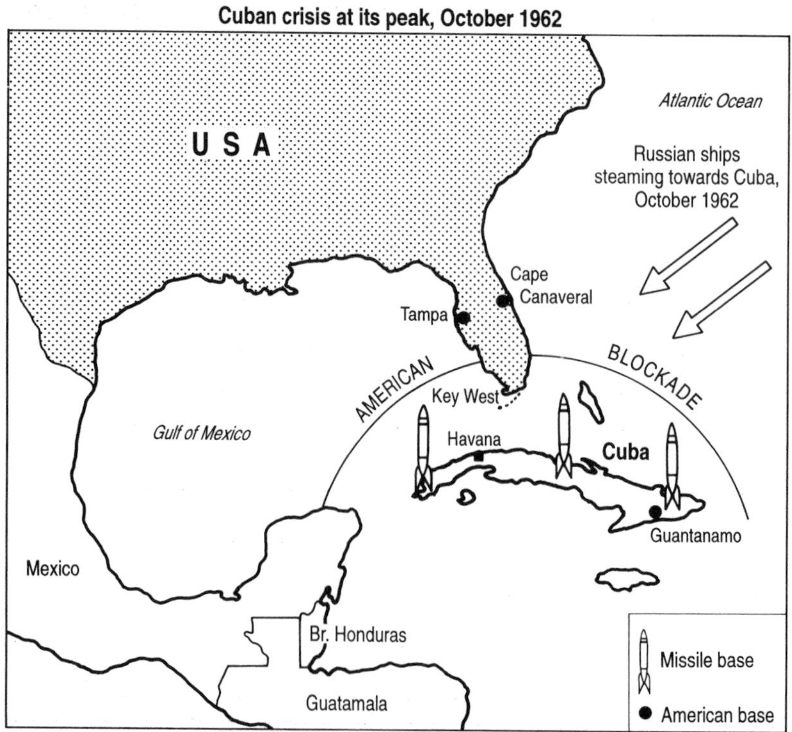

It was Khrushchev who broke the stalemate and on 28 October he agreed to remove the missiles and return them to the Soviet Union. The Cuban missile crisis was over.

The Cuban crisis had a major effect on East-West relations:
- Leaders of both the USSR and the USA realised that nuclear war had been a real possibility and it was vital that a similar crisis should not happen again.
- The Americans and Soviets decided to set up a telephone link (hot line) so that in future direct communications could take place between Moscow and Washington. Nuclear arms talks also began and in 1963 a Test Ban treaty was signed between America, the USSR and Britain.

Debate over the Cuban crisis has continued ever since. President Kennedy became an instant hero in the West for his apparent tough handling of the Soviets. However, questions have been raised as to whether he made a secret deal with the Soviets to remove NATO missiles from Turkey.

■ ***In some ways the Cuban missile crisis was the height of Cold War tension. Never before had the world been so close to nuclear conflict as it was in October 1962. However, the crisis actually resulted in arms reductions and improved communications (if not better relations) between the USA and the USSR.*** ■

5. Czechoslovakia, 1968 In 1967 Alexander Dubcek became Communist Party Secretary in Czechoslovakia. In the spring of 1968 (the 'Prague Spring'), Dubcek began to reform the communist system:
- Censorship of the press was ended.
- Other political parties apart from the communist party were allowed.
- Some political prisoners were released and Czech citizens were given greater freedom to travel abroad.

The reforms in Czechoslovakia became known as 'communism with a human face'. They seemed to represent the general easing of tension between East and West that had taken place after the Cuban crisis.

However, Dubcek's reforms were seen as a major threat by the new leader of the USSR, Brezhnev. As in Hungary 12 years earlier, action was taken to prevent the reforms from sweeping the communists out of power in Czechoslovakia and spreading to the rest of Eastern Europe.
- In August 1968, 400,000 Warsaw Pact troops entered Czechoslovakia and arrested leading reformers and seized key towns and cities.
- Dubcek and the Czeck President Svoboda were flown to Moscow where for four days they talked with the Soviet leader.
- On 27 August the Czech leaders returned and announced that many of their reforms were to be stopped and censorship re-introduced. In 1969 Dubcek resigned and was replaced by a loyal communist, Husak.

As with Hungary in 1956, the Western powers did little to assist those in conflict with the Soviet leadership. Both China and the West condemned Soviet action in Czechoslovakia, but did nothing to support Dubcek and his government.

■ ***The end of the 'Prague Spring' showed once again that the Soviet leadership would not tolerate reform in its satellite states and that the West was unwilling to risk nuclear war over Eastern European countries.*** ■

REVISION TASKS

1. List 2 ways that the Cuban Missile crisis made relations between the USA and the USSR worse.
2. List 2 ways that the crisis made relations better.
3. List similarities and differences between the Czechoslovakian crisis in 1968 and the Hungarian crisis in 1956.

6. Vietnam, 1962–75 Vietnam had been a colony (called Indo-China) of France, but in the 1950s communist rebels had tried to overthrow France's control of Vietnam. After the humiliating defeat of the French army by communist rebels at Dien Bien Phu in 1954, Vietnam was divided into two states:

- communist North Vietnam
- non-communist South Vietnam.

However, communist guerillas (called Vietcong) continued to fight to create one communist state of Vietnam.

The USA had supported the French in Vietnam as a way of preventing communism from spreading throughout South-East Asia. After the French defeat the Americans began sending money and arms directly to the government of South Vietnam to help it against communist guerrillas. In 1961 American assistance was stepped up:

- President Kennedy sent American military advisers to South Vietnam.
- Advisers were soon followed by American troops (50,000 by 1964).
- Kennedy's successor, President Johnson, felt that if South Vietnam fell under communist control, then so would the rest of south-east Asia.

The Vietnam War did not go well for the USA:

- The US commitment increased massively. By 1969 there were half a million American troops fighting in South Vietnam.
- The Vietnam War became hugely unpopular with the American public as thousands of young American men lost their lives. Anti-war demonstrations began to take place in America.

In 1973 a peace agreement was signed in Paris and American troops began to pull out of Vietnam. America had lost the Vietnam War; within two years South Vietnam had also fallen under communist control. American policy had failed, and 55,000 American troops died apparently for nothing.

■ ***The Vietnam War was a case of Cold War tensions causing a local conflict to escalate into a larger conflict. The conflict between North and South Vietnam began as a civil war. However, the involvement of the Americans made it a fight for survival for the North Vietnamese who accepted help from their Soviet allies.*** ■

7. Afghanistan, 1979 The 1970s saw improving relations between the superpowers (see page 83). However, these improving relations were once again damaged by the USSR's invasion of Afghanistan in 1979. The Soviets insisted that they had been invited into Afghanistan to restore order, but Western nations protested that it was a straightforward invasion that could not be justified. Despite world-wide protests, the invasion and occupation of Afghanistan continued.

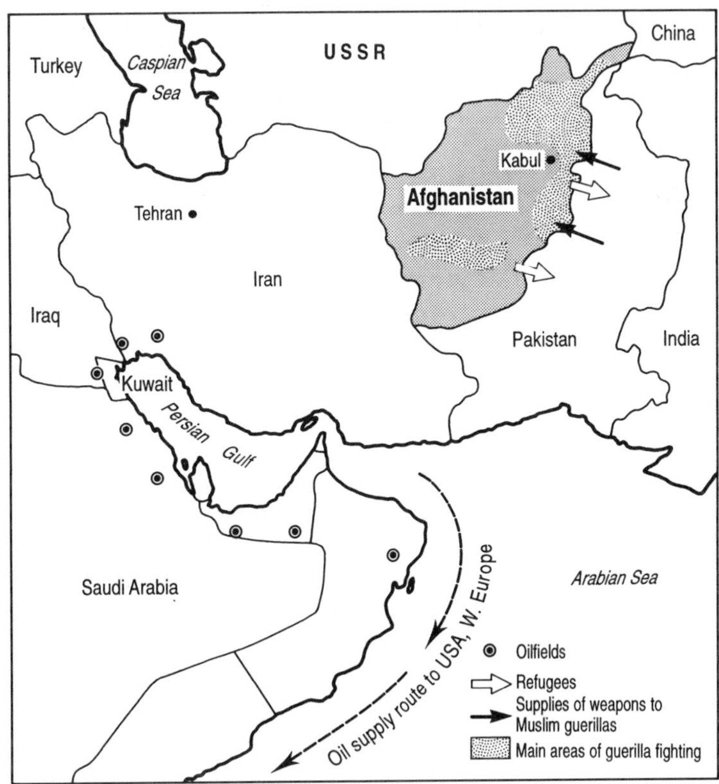

The Soviets invaded Afghanistan for several reasons:

- They were concerned about the Muslim revolution in neighbouring Iran which could have spread to Afghanistan and Muslim areas inside the Soviet Union.
- The political situation in Afghanistan was very unstable at the end of the 1970s and the Soviets wanted to maintain their influence in the area.
- Afghanistan was close to the Middle East oil reserves of the Western powers and the ports of the Indian Ocean. The Soviets were interested in developing their interests in this area.

The invasion of Afghanistan brought a return to Cold War tensions:

- The Americans did not ratify SALT 2.
- They boycotted the Moscow Olympics.
- They stopped grain shipments to the Soviet Union and they increased aid to Afghan rebels.
- Relations did not begin to improve again until Gorbachev became leader of the Soviet Union in 1985.

There were similarities between the USA's experience in Vietnam and the USSR's in Afghanistan.

- Within weeks of the invasion, Soviet troops were being killed by Mujahadin guerrillas using the same tactics developed by the Vietcong against American troops in the Vietnam War.
- There was protest against the war at home in the USSR.
- After a 12-year occupation President Gorbachev announced that Soviet troops would leave Afghanistan – apparently with little to show for their long war.

REVISION TASKS

1. Construct a table like the one below and use the information in this section to complete it. Your aim is to create a summary of the major Cold War crises of the period.
2. When you have completed columns 1–3, give each incident a mark out of 10 which in your view reflects the seriousness of the incident. Put your marks in column 4.

Incident/Date	Countries involved	Cause of tension	How serious?
Hungary 1956	Hungary USSR	New government in Hungary Could leave Warsaw Pact Soviet invasion	

D Détente and improving relations between the superpowers

The Cuban missile crisis in 1962 brought both superpowers to the edge of nuclear war. In the years that followed both the USA and USSR began to look for ways in which future conflict could be avoided. By the end of the 1960s there was a general easing of tension between the superpowers. This easing of tension became known as DETENTE.

1. Reasons for détente Détente came about because a number of favourable factors came together at the same time.

- The Vietnam War had damaged the confidence of the USA. America was keen to find ways to avoid further conflict.
- The cost of the nuclear arms race was escalating.

The arms race was based on the policy of MAD (Mutually Assured Destruction). This meant that in theory neither side would use nuclear weapons because the other side would retaliate – both sides would be destroyed. However, there was a wish to move away from this policy for the following reasons:

- The cost of the arms race was huge.
- Stockpiles of weapons were so large that both superpowers had the capacity to destroy the earth many times over.
- By the end of the 1960s the Soviets were looking to ways to reduce their arms budget to spend more increasing the standard of living of their citizens.
- The Americans also wanted to reduce expenditure on arms in order to increase spending on reducing poverty at home.

The hostility between China and the USSR (see pages 74–75) meant that there was no longer the simple situation of a single communist enemy facing the capitalist countries of the West.

- For America détente was a way of helping to further divide the USSR from China.
- For the Chinese, détente was an opportunity to develop relations with the USA and end her isolation. The Chinese leadership was looking for American investment to help modernise the country.

■ ***Détente came about in the 1970s because several factors coincided. It was in the interests of the superpowers to have better relations.*** ■

2. Key trends in the period of détente The late 1960s saw a series of initiatives which improved relations between the communist and non-communist world.

East and West Germany During the late 1960s, Willy Brandt, Chancellor of West Germany, worked hard to form closer ties with communist East Germany. This policy was called OSTPOLITIK. In 1972, agreements were signed between East and West Germany recognising each other's frontiers and developing trade links.

Strategic Arms Limitation Talks (SALT) In 1969 the USA and USSR began the SALT negotiations in an effort to control the arms race. The talks lasted for three years and in 1972 SALT I was signed. Both sides agreed to keep the numbers of nuclear weapons and warheads within strict limits. They also agreed to begin further talks to discuss weapons systems not included in SALT I.

Cooperation in space Throughout the 1960s the Americans and Soviets had been arch rivals in the 'space race'. Yet in July 1975 three American astronauts and two Soviet cosmonauts docked their Apollo and Soyuz spacecraft together in orbit around the earth. It was one of the most visible signs of détente in action and gave a further impetus to superpower cooperation.

3. The Helsinki Conference, August 1975 In August 1975 at Helsinki in Finland, 35 countries including the USSR and the USA signed the Helsinki Agreement. This was a high point for détente.

- The Western powers recognised the frontiers of Eastern Europe and Soviet influence in that area.
- The Soviets agreed to allow greater freedom in the Soviet Union to Western journalists, give 21 days notice before holding military manoeuvres near to a frontier and allow some inspection of human rights.
- West Germany officially recognised East Germany.
- The Soviets agreed to buy US grain and export oil to the West.
- All countries agreed to improve human rights throughout the world.

It should be remembered that these resolutions were not always entirely put into force. For example, abuses of human rights continued in the USSR and other countries after 1975.

■ ***Although not all aspects of détente in this period were total successes, events such as SALT and Helsinki were important because they showed a commitment by the superpowers to genuinely work to improve relations.*** ■

4. Détente between the USA and China Relations between the USA and China began to improve at the beginning of the 1970s.

- Visits by US and Chinese table tennis teams to each other's countries in 1971/2 led to the term 'ping pong diplomacy'.
- In October 1971 the USA dropped its support for Taiwan as the sole Chinese representative at the United Nations and accepted communist China.
- In 1972 US President Richard Nixon made a historic visit to see the ageing Chairman Mao in Peking.
- Trade talks and improving relations followed. Contact between Western nations and China continued after the death of Mao in 1976.

In the 1980s private firms were given greater freedom in China and communism was relaxed. In 1989, however, student demonstrations aimed at increasing democracy in China were crushed by the army. Relations between China and Western nations deteriorated immediately and have yet to fully recover.

REVISION TASKS

1. Produce your own definition of détente using two examples from this section.
2. Explain why the Helsinki Conference was important (use 6–8 key words).
3. Use 6–8 key words to produce a summary of why arms reduction was so successful in the 1980s.

E US–Soviet relations in the 1980s: the end of the Cold War

1. Gorbachev and Reagan Superpower diplomacy during the 1980s was dominated by US President Ronald Reagan and Mikhail Gorbachev of the USSR. Reagan was elected US President in 1980. He was not worried about standing up to the USSR:

- He began to build up American defence forces and spending.
- He ordered further research into the Strategic Defence Initiative (SDI or Star Wars programme, a satellite anti-missile system which would orbit the earth).

In the USSR, Brezhnev continued to support hard-line communist policies up until his death in 1983. Brezhnev was followed first by Andropov (who only lived a few months longer) and then by Chernenko. Neither lived long enough to make an impact.

In March 1985 Mikhail Gorbachev became leader of the Soviet Union and immediately set about reforming the old Soviet system and improving relations with the USA:

- He realised that the USSR could not afford an arms race with the USA.
- He accepted President Reagan's invitation to meet with him in Geneva in November 1985.
- After several meetings, the USSR and USA signed the Intermediate Nuclear Forces treaty (INF) which removed all medium range nuclear weapons from Europe.
- SALT had developed into START (STrategic Arms Reduction Talks) and on an official visit to Washington in December 1988, Gorbachev also proposed deep cuts in conventional (non-nuclear) US and Soviet forces.

The deciding figure in this period is Gorbachev. He firmly believed that the USSR could not continue to compete with the USA and that the USSR needed to be reformed.

2. The collapse of communism As the period of renewed cooperation developed, the pace of change increased in Eastern Europe. In the USSR Gorbachev had made major reforms to the Soviet system and in neighbouring communist countries old style communist leaders began to face opposition to their rule.

REVISION TASKS

1. Explain how Regan was a new kind of American leader compared to American presidents in the 1970s.
2. In what ways was Gorbachev a new kind of Soviet leader?
3. What progress did disarmament make in the 1980s?

Collapse of communism in Eastern Europe

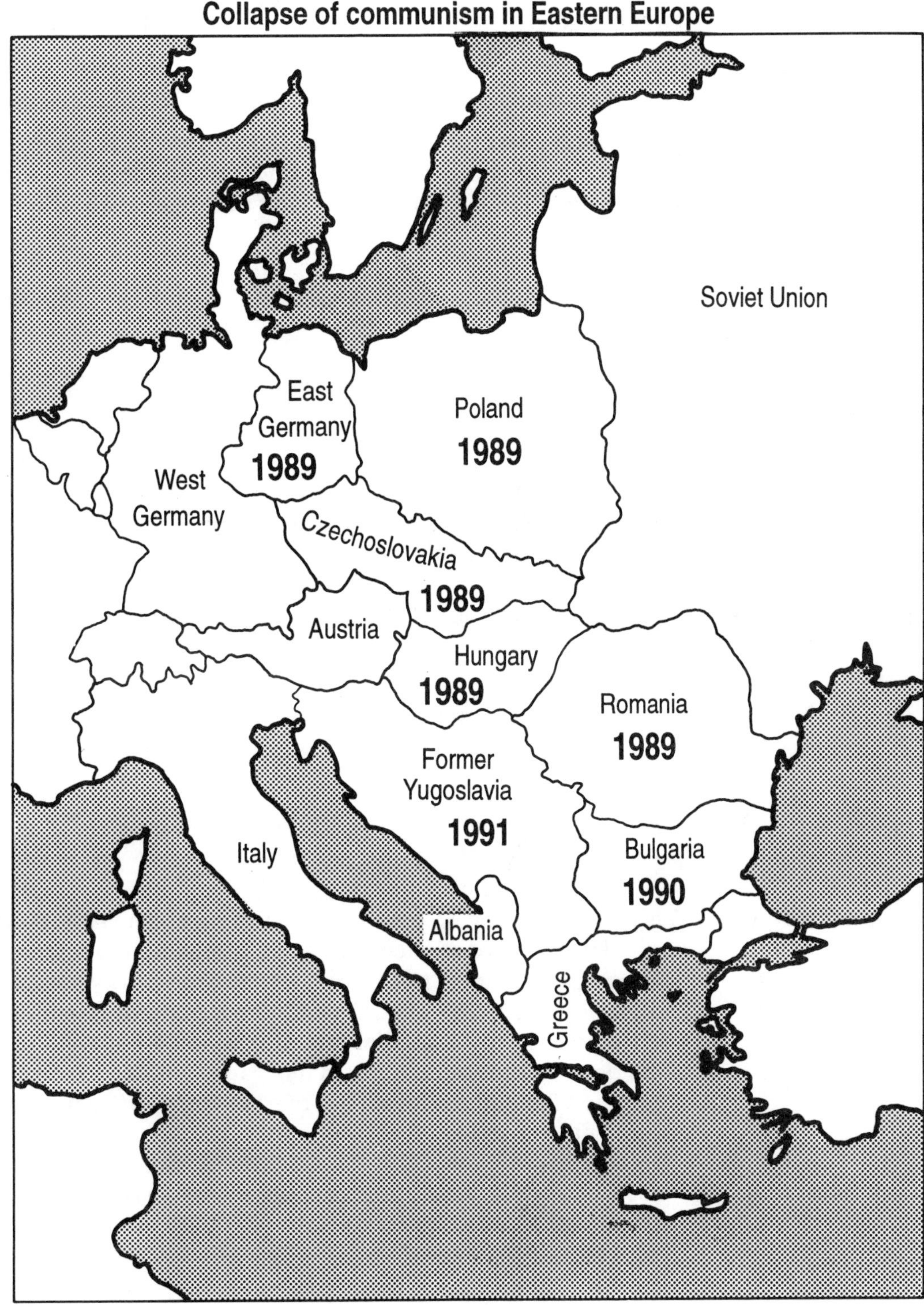

- In 1989 Gorbachev refused to provide assistance to the East German government as it faced protesters demanding increased freedom. In October, crowds in Berlin took the initiative and began taking down the Berlin Wall whilst East German guards stood by.
- Within two years Gorbachev was also swept from power. The Soviet Union began to disintegrate, the Warsaw Pact collapsed and communist governments throughout Eastern Europe fell from power.
- By the beginning of the 1990s the USA remained as the sole world superpower – the Cold War had been won.

REVISION SESSION

The aim of this session is for you to see how you can apply your knowledge of the content in this chapter to the kind of questions you will face in your examination.

Examination questions

The most important theme which examiners ask about in questions on this topic is how and why relations between the superpowers changed at different times after 1955. For example, look at this examination question from MEG Paper I, 1993.

(a) (i) Name one country that became a member of NATO in 1949. [*1 mark*]
(ii) Explain what is meant by the 'Cold War'.

Briefly use your knowledge of relations between the USA and the USSR from 1946 to 1955 to support your answer. [*3 marks*]

What is required?

For Part (i) you need to give a simple factual answer.

To score full marks for Part (ii) you need to show that you understand the term 'Cold War' and give one example.

Ideas for your answer

1. For (i) simply name one of the following countries: Britain, USA, France, Italy, Belgium, Netherlands, Luxembourg, Canada, Portugal, Iceland, Norway, Denmark.
2. Cold War in (ii) refers to relations between the superpowers when there was no actual war but relations between the USA and USSR were poor. An example of a Cold War confrontation is the Cuban missile crisis in 1962.

(b) Why were relationships between the USA and China very poor between 1950 and 1953? [*6 marks*]

What is required?

This question is testing your understanding of causes and consequence. In particular you need to show that you understand *the reasons why* relations between the superpowers were poor. You must also support your answer with examples.

A low level answer (1 mark) would be a general statement, for example: there was a war in Korea. To aim for a higher level (2–3 marks) you must suggest a cause of the poor relations and explain this cause with an example.

To reach the highest level (4–6 marks) you must provide several convincing causes with examples.

Ideas for your answer

1. You should include several reasons for poor relations. You could point to the fact that the USA and China fought against each other in Korea between 1950 and 1953 (see pages 66–67). Also the USA was a capitalist country and China was a communist country. The USA had an open democratic and free market system whilst in China the state owned and operated agriculture and industry.
2. Another valid point is that the USA did not recognise the new communist leadership. Instead the USA supported the nationalist leaders who had been defeated in 1949 by Mao and fled to Taiwan.

(c) In 1956, relationships between the USA and the USSR were poor. By 1988, relationships between the USA and the USSR were much better. Why did the relationships change between 1956 and 1988? Explain your answer fully. [*15 marks*]

What is required?

This question is also testing your understanding of causes and consequence. You will need to explain why relations between the USA and USSR had improved by 1988.

General statements will score at a low level (1–3 marks), for example: relations improved because the superpowers began to talk to each other. To reach the next level (4–6 marks) you will need to describe how the relationship changed, with an example.

For a higher score (7–9 marks) you will need to show you understand how relations between the USA and USSR developed. You could mention some events which helped improve relations, such as the meetings between Reagan and Gorbachev in the 1980s, and events which caused increased rivalry, e.g. the U2 incident in 1960 or the Cuban crisis in 1962.

To improve your score (10–12 marks) you will need to look in detail at the whole period and show how relations have developed and changed. You will need to give examples of events which have caused relations to change.

To score a top mark (13–15) you must use examples to explore USA-USSR relations. In particular you need to show how changing relations have been affected by changes in leadership, development of weaponry, economic, military and political rivalry and key events such as Afghanistan.

Ideas for your answer

There are several ways you may wish to approach this answer. One option is to examine the relationship between the USA and USSR chronologically (over time) and point out how key issues have re-occurred.

1. The period 1956–62: During this period it seemed as if USSR-USA relations might improve. In 1956 Khrushchev denounced Stalin, peaceful coexistence seemed a possibility and for a brief moment both countries came together in the Middle East crisis of 1956 (see page 94 in Chapter 7). Always on the horizon, however, rivalry in Europe unsettled relations (e.g. Hungarian uprising). By 1960 relations had become more strained over the U2 incident and reached crisis point in the conflict over Berlin in 1961 and Cuba in 1962.
2. 1962–68: The lessons of the Cuban missile crisis led to improved communications between the USSR and USA. Both sides had sufficient nuclear weapons to destroy each other many times over. MAD (Mutually Assured Destruction) became a policy that seemed to assure peace.
3. 1968–79: Europe became the centre of another East-West crisis in 1968 with the Soviet invasion of Czechoslovakia. Tensions eased in the 1970s and a period of détente began. Much of this owed its spirit to US President Richard Nixon. The SALT talks began and both countries signed treaties limiting underground testing of nuclear weapons. The Helsinki agreement in 1975 seemed to offer new hope for lasting peace.
4. 1979–85: Cold War rivalry intensified after the Soviets invaded Afghanistan. The USA boycotted the 1980 Moscow Olympics. Changes of leadership in the USSR did not bring continuity.
5. 1985–90: USA-USSR relations improved significantly with the developing relationship between Gorbachev and Reagan. Regular meetings were held and although there were disagreements over Star Wars (SDI) relations improved with the START talks. The collapse of communism in 1989 brought the Cold War to an end.
6. Conclusion: Rivalry and control over areas of interest always caused problems for USA-USSR relations (e.g. Cuba, Vietnam, Afghanistan). New leaders (e.g. Khrushchev, Reagan, Gorbachev) have often helped to improve relations.

SUMMARY AND REVISION PLAN

Below is a list of headings which you may find helpful. Use this as a check list to make sure that you are familiar with the material featured in this chapter. Record your key words alongside each heading.

A Khrushchev and the 'thaw' in the Cold War in the 1950s

1. Nikita Khrushchev
2. Peaceful coexistence
3. Eastern Europe

B Relations between China and the USSR

1. Stalin and Mao
2. Chinese reaction to Khrushchev

C The crisis points in the Cold War, 1956–80

1. Hungary, 1956
2. The U2 incident, 1960
3. Berlin, 1961
4. The Cuban missile crisis, 1962
5. Czechoslovakia, 1968
6. Vietnam, 1962–75
7. Afghanistan, 1980

D Détente and improving relations between the superpowers

1. Reasons for détente
2. Key trends in the period of détente
3. The Helsinki Conference, August 1975
4. Détente between the USA and China

E US-Soviet relations in the 1980s: the end of the Cold War

1. Gorbachev and Reagan
2. The collapse of communism

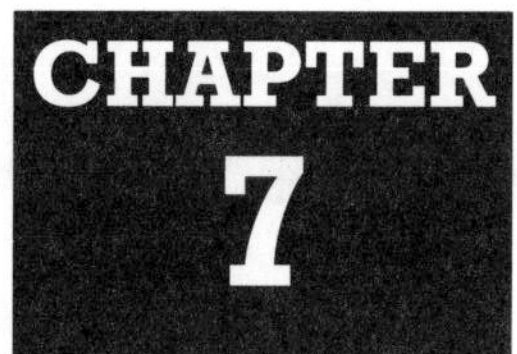

The United Nations Organisation

After the First World War the League of Nations had been set up to keep peace and order in the world. It failed. After the Second World War everyone believed that a similar organisation was needed, but this time it had to be able to do the job.

To answer questions on the United Nations Organisation (UN), you need to be familiar with both the key content and the key themes involved in this topic.

KEY CONTENT

You will need to show that you have a good working knowledge of these areas:

A The establishment of the UNO
B The structure and organisation of the UNO
C The differences between the UNO and the League of Nations
D The UNO and the Cold War
E The peace-keeping role of the UNO
F The humanitarian work of the UNO
G The growth of the UNO

KEY THEMES

As well as being a topic in its own right the United Nations Organisation (UNO) is also an important background topic for the Cold War. As for all topics you will not be asked simply to write down what you know about the UNO. You will need to show your understanding of some of these key themes:

- **The importance of the UNO in the Cold War**
- **Whether the UNO was effective as a peace-keeping organisation**
- **Whether it was effective as a humanitarian organisation**
- **The strengths and weaknesses of the UNO**
- **The successes and failures of the UNO**
- **Why the membership of the UNO grew and the issues that raises**
- **The importance of the UNO to the developing world**

For example, the question below is from MEG Paper I, 1992.

(a) (i) Name two countries which were permanent members of the United National Security Council between 1945 and 1987. *[2 marks]*

(ii) State two differences between the Security Council and the General Assembly of the United Nations Organisation. *[2 marks]*

This question is asking you to show your knowledge and understanding of this topic. To answer the question you will see that you need to know about these important areas:

- The structure of the UNO (how it is organised)
- How the UNO operates in practice and the role of each of the bodies which make up the UNO
- The membership of the UNO
- The role of the UNO as a peace-keeping force.

You will also need to show your understanding of important themes:

- Why and how the membership of the UNO has grown since 1945
- The effectiveness of the UNO in dealing with major world problems
- The attitudes of the members of the UNO towards its peace-keeping role

We will look at this question in detail at the end of the chapter.

THE UNITED NATIONS ORGANISATION

A The establishment of the UNO

1. Background The Second World War had been even more destructive than the First World War. Millions had been killed or injured as the table on page 58 shows.

Many cities had been bombed into rubble. Refugees were to be found throughout the world and hardship and suffering was everywhere.

As well as all of this, there was now a new weapon more destructive than had ever been thought possible.

- In August 1945 two Japanese cities were completely destroyed by atomic bombs. The world had entered the atomic age and it was now more important than ever to try to avoid future wars.

2. The origins of the UNO The first important step was the Atlantic Charter agreed by Churchill (Britain) and Roosevelt (USA) in 1941. The other important stages were the Bretton Woods Conference and the Dumbarton Oaks Conference, both in 1944.

The Charter of the United Nations was not officially signed until 1945 in San Francisco. The aim was to set up an organisation which:

- Could keep the peace
- Could remove the factors (e.g. poverty) which helped to cause war in the first place.

B The structure and organisation of the UNO

The UNO was (and still is today) a huge organisation. Its membership is very large and its agencies and personnel deal with an enormous number of different questions and issues. Because of its size the UNO is organised into a number of different bodies.

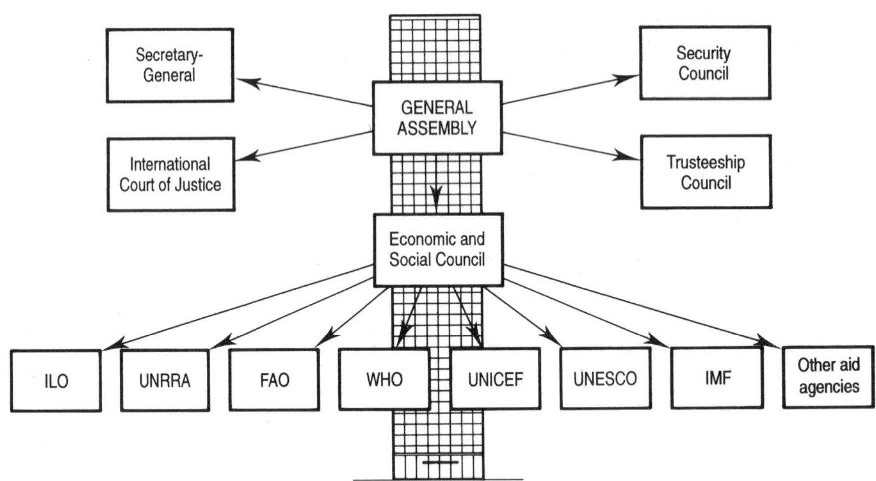

1. The General Assembly The General Assembly is the parliament of the UNO. Every member of the UNO is represented and has one vote. The original assembly in 1945 contained 51 members but by 1985 the number had risen to over 150.

- It discusses major issues and can make recommendations about what to do.
- It elects the non-permanent members of the Security Council and also controls the budget of the UNO.
- It can pass resolutions if a majority of members vote for them, although particularly important resolutions may require a two-thirds majority.
- It is a strong influence on public opinion throughout the world.

The General Assembly has limited powers but it is very important as members are free to act individually. From the 1950s countries with shared interests (e.g. some of the newly independent colonial states) often acted and voted together in blocs. This made the views of these countries more likely to be listened to by the major powers and in some cases influenced the actions of the Security Council.

2. **The Security Council** In some ways this is the most powerful part of the UNO. There are five permanent members (UK, France, China, USSR, USA) and 10 others elected for two years at a time by the General Assembly. The job of the Security Council is to concentrate on keeping order and opposing aggressive nations.

- It has the power to enforce ECONOMIC SANCTIONS (e.g. cutting off oil supplies).
- It can also take military action (e.g. in the 1991 Gulf War against Iraq).

Security Council actions need nine out of the 15 votes. However, each permanent power has a VETO, which means it can block any action even if all other members are in favour.

The Security Council has a mixed record:

- It has great powers but has not always been able to use them.
- It was caught up in the Cold War in the 1950s and 1960s as the USSR and USA both used the veto to put their own interests ahead of the interests of the UNO.

The relationship between the General Assembly and the Security Council is not completely clear. The USSR believed that resolutions of the Security Council should come first. However, this has not always happened. For example, in 1950 a resolution was passed which allowed the General Assembly to take military action in certain circumstances.

3. **The Trusteeship Council** This body took over the work of the League of Nations Mandates Commission. Its job was to prepare former colonies or MANDATED territories for independence. This task was almost complete by 1970 although Southern Africa remained a troubled region into the 1980s, with Namibia finally achieving independence in 1990.

This was a good example of the UNO in action and being largely successful. Under the old mandates the question of independence was often delayed or held back. This has not been the case under the UNO.

4. **International Court of Justice** This is based in the Netherlands and has 15 judges from different nations. Its purpose is to try to reach judgements in disputes between nations, usually about borders, territories or similar issues. It also has authority to make judgements about international treaties.

The Court has had limited success because relatively few nations have actually used it, and even then countries can ignore the judgement, as when South Africa refused to give independence to Namibia in 1983. However, it has had some successes as well, such as sorting out British and Norwegian fishing rights.

5. **The Secretariat and Secretary-General** The secretariat keeps the UNO running. It supplies information, translates speeches – in short it runs the administration of this huge organisation. The head of the secretariat is the Secretary-General. This is a very important position. The Secretary-General can bring matters before the Security Council and has greater influence on world politics.

REVISION TASKS

1. Use 4–6 key words to describe the main aims of the UNO.

2. Construct a summary table like the one below and insert details of the organisations which make up the UNO.

Name	Members	Responsibilities	Powers
General Assembly	All UNO members	Discussion Advise Security Council	Make resolutions
Security Council			

3. Name the responsibilities of the following:
a) the Trusteeship Council b) the UN secretariat.

C The differences between the UNO and the League of Nations

1. Membership

The UNO was (and is) much larger than the League in terms of its membership.
- The League never had more than 50 members.
- The UNO by 1980 had 150 member states.

Both superpowers (USA and the USSR) were members of the UNO. The absence of the USA had been a major weakness of the League (see page 18).

As well as the superpowers, many developing nations joined, particularly in the 1960s. These were mainly the new Asian and African states. By working together and acting as a bloc they were able to make their views heard, and as a result the UNO was much more representative than the League had been. The League had been dominated by Britain and France.

2. Effectiveness

The UNO has been stronger and more effective than the League for the following reasons:
- It has a larger and more powerful membership.
- It is able to act more quickly and decisively because the General Assembly can pass resolutions on a simple majority, which the League assembly could not do.
- The Security Council sits all of the time (unlike the Council of the League) and so issues can be dealt with promptly.
- The Security Council has economic and military power which the League never had.

The UNO was and is a true world organisation. It is listened to by most states in the world and it has the power to make its resolutions stick, if it wishes to. Many states have been in dispute with the UNO, including the USA. The USSR (in 1950) and France (in 1958) even left for periods of time. However, the importance of the UNO is shown by the fact that both countries returned. This contrasts sharply with the actions of Japan, Italy and Germany who left the League in the 1930s.

REVISION TASK

1. Create your own summary of the differences between the League of Nations and the UNO. Concentrate on the following points:
   – membership (number of members, size of new members)
   – effectiveness (past record of League, record of UNO).

D The UNO and the Cold War

One overwhelming problem which faced the UNO in the 1950s and 1960s was the Cold War – the war of ideas between the superpowers and their allies. The Cold War is dealt with in Chapters 5 and 6 of this book. However, the examples in this section demonstrate the problems which faced the UNO in dealing with the conflict.

1. The Korean War

In 1950 communist North Korea invaded non-communist South Korea. The Security Council acted immediately and decisively. Troops were sent to help the South Koreans push back the invaders.

At first sight the UN action looked impressive. However, several factors must be taken into account:
- The Security Council vote was only possible because the USSR were boycotting (refusing to attend) the UNO at the time.
- This in turn was because the USA was blocking communist China's entry into the UNO. The Korean War was therefore more of a US than a UN operation. If China

and the USSR had been in the UNO at the time it is unlikely that the UNO would have played a decisive role in a Cold War confrontation such as Korea.

2. **The Cuban crisis and Vietnam** These two crises showed how difficult it was for the UNO to take action in Cold War problems.
   - In the Cuban crisis in 1962 the UN building was the scene of furious debates and arguments between the US and USSR representatives. However, it was the powers themselves – not the UNO – who eventually resolved this dispute.
   - The UNO also failed to stop or make peace in the Vietnam War. It was a Cold War conflict – the USSR and China aiding one side and the USA the other. The UNO did not and could not intervene. Again, the war ended with little or no help from the UNO.

When the superpowers were in agreement it was clear that the UNO could achieve much. However, when it came to Cold War confrontations it was equally clear that cooperation between the superpowers in the UNO was virtually impossible. This in turn meant that the UNO would be powerless to resolve conflicts.

REVISION TASKS

Note down the key points from this section:

1. Explain why the Security Council veto made the UNO virtually powerless in the event of Cold War confrontations.
2. Did the UNO seem to play any real part in settling the Korean War, the Cuban crisis and the Vietnam war?

E The peace-keeping role of the UNO

One of the key roles of the UNO since 1945 has been to try to bring about and keep peace in areas where fighting has broken out. Since 1945 the UNO has been involved in many peace-keeping operations. Some of these are described in the map below:

Peace-keeping by the UN

Hungary
Date: 1956
Dispute: Hungarians tried to get away from the control of the USSR. Soviet tanks and troops moved in and crushed the revolt.
UN action: This time the Security Council was paralysed by the USSR's veto. The Assembly condemned the invasion but the USSR simply ignored it.
Conclusion: The USSR was able to ignore the UNO and the UNO could do nothing – a failure, although negotiations behind the scenes continued for many years.

Cyprus
Date: 1964
Dispute: Civil war between Greek and Turkish Cypriots broke out in 1963.
UN action: Peace-keeping forces stopped fighting in 1964. However, fighting broke out again in 1974, again stopped by UN troops keeping the two sides apart. UN troops are still there.
Conclusion: UNO acted successfully as a peace-keeper but once again failed to solve the problem permanently.

Suez (Egypt)
Date: 1956
Dispute: Britain and France sent troops to seize control of the Suez Canal which had been nationalised by President Nasser.
UN action: Security Council action was stopped by French and British veto but General Assembly condemed the invasion. Pressure on Britain and France forced them to pull out.
Conclusion: Great success for the UNO.

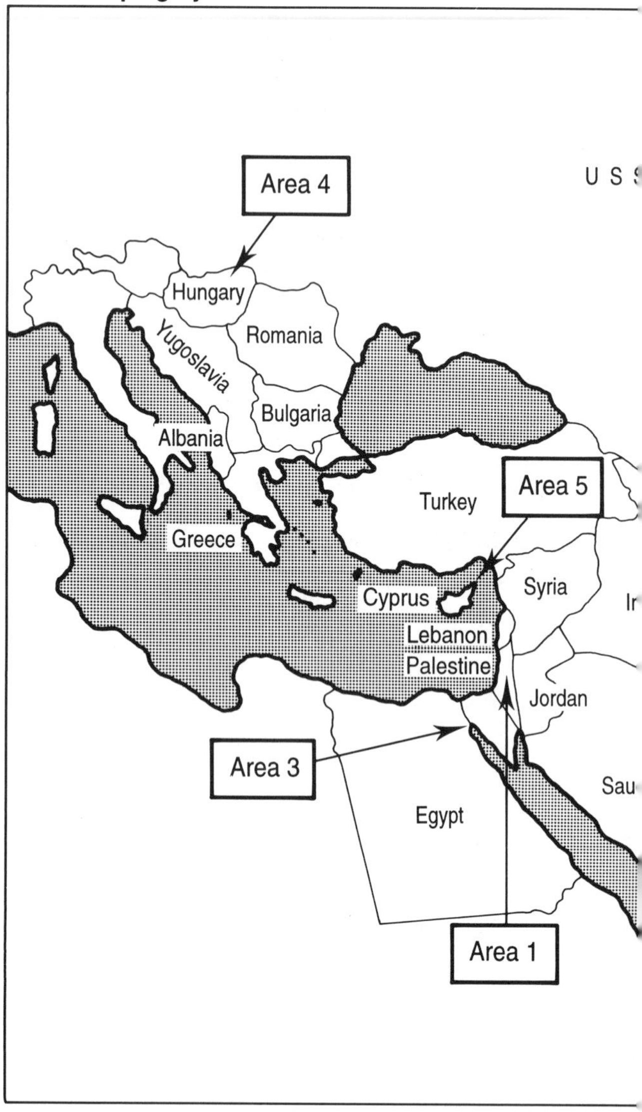

Palestine
Date: 1967–present day
Dispute: The new state of Israel set up in 1948 was clai
by the Arabs as their land.
UN action: UNO was unable to prevent wars in 1967
1973.
Conclusion: Limited success – UNO not able to solve
problem but did some good work (e.g. arranging ceasefi

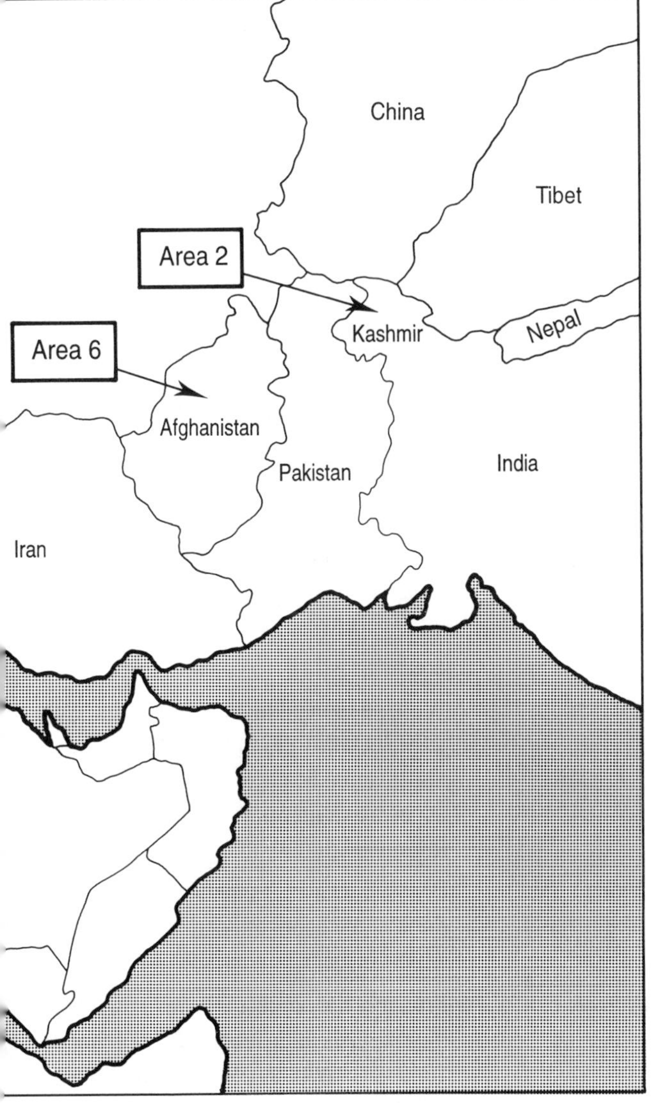

Kashmir
Date: 1947, 1965
Dispute: Both India and Pakistan claimed the border province of Kashmir.
UN action: UN troops kept peace by keeping the two sides apart, although a short war broke out in 1965, again stopped by UNO.
Conclusion: UNO successful as peace-keepers but unable to end the problem.

Afghanistan
Date: 1979
Dispute: USSR's troops invaded to put the man they wanted in power in Afghanistan.
UN action: Security Council again faced Soviet veto. Assembly condemned the USSR but the troops did not withdraw.
Conclusion: This was another demonstration of how powerless the UNO could be against one of the superpowers.

REVISION TASK

1. Look at the events described in this section. Choose one example which fits into each of these categories and explain your choice.
   Category 1 Failure for the UNO
   Category 2 Success for the UNO
   Category 3 Partial success/failure

F The humanitarian work of the UNO

1. Aims One of the key aims of the UNO when it was set up was to remove the factors which cause future wars. The UNO has tried to do this by providing health care, education and economic help to all parts of the world.

The UNO's work in health and education and with problems such as refugees is probably its greatest success. UN workers have saved many lives and improved the lives of many more.

2. The Economic and Social Council (ECSC) The ECSC is the part of the UNO responsible for humanitarian and development work. The ECSC controls the special UN agencies which bring help to people around the world. These are shown in the table below:

The UN agencies

Agency	Type of work	Examples
ILO (International Labour Organisation)	Protects and improves working conditions.	International treaties on inspection, minimum wages, holidays.
FAO (Food and Agricultural Organisation)	Studies world food supplies and improves agricultural methods in developing countries.	Irrigation projects in SE Asia, World Food Programme in 1970 helped 40 million people in 75 countries.
The World Bank	Provides loans, mainly to developing countries.	Work of the IDA (International Development Agency).
UNESCO (UN Educational, Scientific and Cultural Organisation)	Supports and organises research, conferences and education throughout the world.	Pays for exchange students to learn about and bring skills back to their own countries.
WHO (World Health Organisation)	Provides health care and health education where it is most needed.	Working alongside other agencies (FAO, UNRWA, UNICEF) to fight disease and improve medical care and knowledge. An especially high priority has been projects to provide pure drinking water.
UNICEF (UN International Children's Emergency Fund)	Primarily helps children, although this of course often means helping parents.	Drugs, vaccines, essential equipment donated by sponsors and transported to wherever help is required.
UNRWA (UN Relief and Work Agency)	Mainly concerned with refugees and people made homeless by war.	Probably the biggest job was rehabilitating the refugees after World War II ended in 1945. UNRWA has also been busy in Palestine, Hungary and many other regions.

The work of the agencies does not often make the news headlines, but it is important to the people who receive help from them. Millions of people's lives have been saved or improved by these agencies and their work is a major success of the UNO.

REVISION TASK

1. Choose 4 examples from the list above and create key word summaries for each. For each one you should be able to provide:
   a) The name of the agency
   b) The work of the agency
   c) Examples of the agency in action
   d) How the agency has contributed to the importance of the UNO.

G Growth of the UNO

1. Increased membership The UNO has grown dramatically since 1945 as the table below shows. This has had some important consequences for the UNO and its members.

Number of new nations joining UNO	
1945–54	59
1955–64	55
1975–84	21
1985–93	28

The growth of the UNO began in the 1950s. The majority of the new members were states which had been colonies (mainly of France and Britain). The growth in the size of the membership has had some important effects on the UNO. In at least one way it is a source of great strength. Because of its membership the UNO truly represents world opinion.

This has been an important development in the workings of the UNO. These new countries tended to work together, and on the whole they shared common interests. For example, the General Assembly voted a resolution in 1960 to end colonial rule by any country, clearly showing that the ex-colonies were making their views heard.

2. The effects of increasing membership Growing membership meant that the UNO became truly representative. This had other effects, too.

- As the UNO grew it cost more to run. This has often been a problem for the UNO and by the 1980s was almost a crisis.
- The priorities of the UNO became broader, reflecting the large number of smaller states. One consequence of this was that disputes arose between the members of the UNO about what its aims were. This was demonstrated by the complaints of the USA in 1983 about the cost of the agency UNESCO.
- At the same time, states tended (from the 1960s) to vote in blocs rather than on what they thought about particular issues. For example, the communist states supported the USSR against criticism by the USA whatever the issue.

REVISION TASKS

Note down the key points from this section:

1. How has the growing membership of the UNO made it stronger?

2. In what ways has its growing membership caused problems for the UNO.

REVISION SESSION

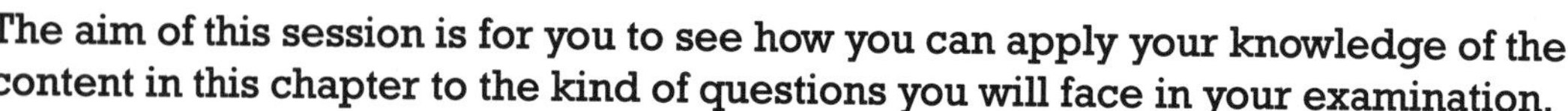

The aim of this session is for you to see how you can apply your knowledge of the content in this chapter to the kind of questions you will face in your examination.

Examination questions

Like the Great Depression and its effects in Chapter 3, the UNO is an important topic on its own as well as being a key background topic for areas such as the Cold War. Because of the contrasts within the UNO, examination questions often target the concepts of cause and consequence and particularly similarity and difference. For example, look at the question below from MEG Paper I, 1992.

(a) (i) Name two countries which were permanent members of the United National Security Council between 1945 and 1987. *[2 marks]*

(ii) State two differences between the Security Council and the General Assembly of the United Nations Organisation. *[2 marks]*

What is required?

Part (i) needs only a simple factual answer. Part (ii) is also testing your factual knowledge but you must take care. Simply describing the two bodies will not gain you the two marks, you must point out two differences between the Security Council and the General Assembly.

Ideas for your answer

(i) You can name any two from the five permanent members of the Security Council – USA, Britain, France, China, USSR

(ii) The examiner is looking for you to point straight to differences and then explain them clearly. Perhaps the most obvious difference is the membership of the two bodies. The Security Council contains 15 members, five permanent and 10 elected on a rolling term, whereas the Assembly is a forum for all members of the UNO and all members can be represented there at all times. The two bodies also operate differently. To pass a motion, the Security Council must have nine of its 15 members in favour of the motion, and even then one of the permanent members has the power to veto any decision made (see page 91). In contrast, the Assembly can pass some motions on any majority, however small, and there are no powers of veto in the Assembly.

(b) Explain why the membership of the United Nations Organisation increased between 1945 and 1987. *[6 marks]*

What is required?

In this section the examiner wants you to focus on reasons and causes of the growth of the UNO rather than describing the growth. General comments will only gain 1–2 marks. To reach the next level (3–4 marks) you need to identify at least one reason for the growth in the membership and use your knowledge of the topic to explain your reason, to demonstrate that you are not simply guessing. To reach the highest level marks (5–6 marks) you must give several reasons, all supported by your factual knowledge.

Ideas for your answer

1. It is worth beginning your answer by pointing out that there are a number of reasons for the growth in membership of the UNO. Perhaps the main reason for the growth of the UNO has been the large number of new countries which have been created since 1945. The break up of the British Empire has seen the emergence of an independent India and many former African colonies (such as Kenya and Nigeria). The French (mainly in North Africa) and Dutch (mainly in the Pacific) overseas possessions have also become independent.
2. Another important reason is the fact that the UNO has actively encouraged new nations to join it. The aim of the UNO is to be a truly representative world organisation and the larger the membership, the more truth there is in this claim.

3. You should also mention that nations, particularly in the developing world, had much to gain from joining the UNO. They could get access to UNO aid programmes and to important development projects run by the UNO's agencies such as FAO or WHO (see page 96). Also, the UNO General Assembly was a place where small nations could complain about the actions of larger nations and by working together in the Assembly, smaller nations have been able to have a voice on the world stage (see page 97).

(c) Why was the United Nations Organisation unable to prevent wars and international tension between 1945 and 1987? Explain your answer carefully. *[15 marks]*

What is required?

This question is asking you to show your understanding of cause and consequence (effects). It is important that you let the examiner know:

- Whether the UNO's failure was due to weaknesses in the UNO
- How far the failure was due to causes outside the UNO's control (the attitudes of the superpowers).
- How these two factors combined.

General statements will receive 1–3 marks, depending on how well they are explained. A description of conflict and tension in the period 1945–87 will get you 4–6 marks. To reach the next level (7–9 marks) you must choose one of the issues listed above and provide examples to show how this was a reason for the UNO's failure. To get top marks (10–15 marks) you must use examples to show how each of the points above was important in explaining why the UNO failed to prevent conflict. Overall, the examiner is looking for a balanced and well-explained view, supported by examples.

Ideas for your answer

1. It would be useful to set out your line of argument at the beginning of your answer. In this question you are arguing that the UNO failed to prevent wars and international tension in the years after the Second World War because of a combination of factors. These factors were the way in which the UNO was set up and organised, and the way in which international relations worked in this period, particularly the behaviour of the superpowers.

2. To tackle the first point we must look at the structure of the UNO. The most important cause of tension in the years 1945–87 was the growing rivalry between the USA and the USSR. However, they were both members of the UN Security Council and therefore both had a veto. As a result, if one of these two superpowers took any action which was felt to be unjust by the members of the Security Council, then either the USA or USSR could veto that action.

3. This problem is shown up by the example of the Korean War. When Communist North Korea invaded South Korea the Security Council voted to send UN troops to remove the Communists. This was not vetoed because the USSR was boycotting the UNO at the time. This in turn was because the USA was vetoing the entry of Communist China into the UNO. You can make the point from this that the UNO had all the necessary powers to enforce peace, but it could do little if one of the superpowers was determined to stop it from acting.

4. To make matters more complicated, France and Britain also had powers of veto and could in theory defy the UNO. However, when Britain and France invaded Suez in 1956 the UNO (including the USA and USSR) put enough pressure on them to make them pull out. From this you could make the point that the UNO was able to prevent conflict as long as it had the support of the superpowers.

5. In later examples of international tension, the superpowers ignored the UNO altogether, except as a place to criticise each other. During the Cuban missile crisis American and Soviet delegates argued in the Assembly but the issue was settled by personal negotiations between President Kennedy and the Soviet leader, Khrushchev. In the case of Vietnam, the UNO did not support US troops going into action in Vietnam, but the Americans sent troops anyway. Similarly, the Soviet invasion of Afghanistan in 1980 was condemned by the UNO but because of the Soviet veto it was unable to do anything practical about it.

6. In conclusion, therefore, you could point out that while the UNO could keep peace in theory, it could do little if one of the superpowers refused to accept the views of the UN Assembly or Security Council.

SUMMARY AND REVISION PLAN

Below is a list of headings which you may find helpful. Use this as a check list to make sure that you are familiar with the material featured in this chapter. Record your key words alongside each heading.

A The establishment of the UNO

1. Background
2. The origins of the UNO
   - aims

B The structure and organisation of the UNO

1. The General Assembly
2. The Security Council
3. The Trusteeship Council
4. The International Court of Justice
5. The Secretariat and the Secretary-General

C The differences between the UNO and the League of Nations

1. Membership
2. Effectiveness

D The UNO and the Cold War

1. The Korean War
2. The Cuban crisis and Vietnam

E The peace-keeping role of the UNO

- Palestine
- Kashmir
- Suez
- Hungary
- Cyprus
- Afghanistan

F The humanitarian work of the UNO

1. Aims
2. The Economic and Social Council
   - ILO
   - FAO
   - The World Bank
   - UNESCO
   - WHO
   - UNICEF
   - UNWRA

G The growth of the UNO

1. Increased membership
2. The effects of increasing membership

CHAPTER 8 ■ Answering source-based questions

Historical sources

In every GCSE History course, it is important to make use of *historical sources*. In examination questions, you will be asked to evaluate these sources.

An historical source can be virtually anything that survives from the past, such as:

- A poster or photograph
- An extract from a diary
- An extract from a textbook
- A recorded interview written down at a later date.

You have probably seen many other types of historical sources in your GCSE course. Make your own list of sources.

Answering source-based questions

In this short section we look at the particular skills of answering source-based questions. One important point to remember is that you cannot demonstrate your skills in analysing sources without a good background knowledge of the period you are studying. So it is extremely important to revise for these questions.

In examinations you will come across questions such as:

- Does Source A prove that Hitler wanted to ...?
- How could Source D be useful to an historian studying ...?
- Which of Sources A and B is more reliable?

To answer such questions you must be able to:

- Understand what a source is saying
- Find in a source the relevant pieces of information to answer questions
- See the difference in a source between facts, opinions, or judgements
- Recognise how and why a source is or is not biased.

Two key words crop up again and again in source-based questions: 'useful' and 'reliable'. Let's see why these words are important.

Utility

'How could Source A be useful for ...' is obviously asking you about the usefulness or relevance. To tackle this type of question, you need to ask yourself:

1. Is the source *relevant* to the topic or question?
   It is not useful if it does not provide information on the topic you are studying – an account of life in the trenches is not much use if you are studying the Wall Street Crash, although it might be very useful if you are studying the First World War.
   However, examiners won't try to trick you this way. If they ask 'is something useful' then it almost certainly will be. The question is therefore 'How useful ...' so ask
2. What information does it give you which could be useful in your study?
3. Does the information it gives you provide a complete picture or does it still leave you with unanswered questions?

Reliability

A reliable person is someone you can trust to do something. A reliable source is one you can trust to tell you something. An unreliable source is one that you think might be biased, untrue, exaggerated or otherwise not to be trusted.

Usefulness and reliability are closely linked but they are not exactly the same thing. A source could be unreliable but still be useful. For example, an anti-Jewish cartoon from Nazi Germany will not give you reliable information about the Jews but it is very useful for understanding what the Nazis thought of Jews.

ANSWERING SOURCE-BASED QUESTIONS

A source is never useless or unreliable in itself. A source which is useless or unreliable for one purpose may well be useful or reliable for another. For this reason you will often be asked to compare the reliability of two sources.

This is how you can test a source for reliability:

- Who wrote it or made it? (Might he/she be biased?)
- When did he/she make it? (Be careful here – a source produced at the time is not necessarily more reliable than a source produced years later. The later writer has usually *researched* what he/she says using a range of sources, but the author of a source produced at the time is often expressing his/her views or might be influenced by things going on at the time.)
- Why did he/she make it? (To express an opinion, to make someone laugh, or to record facts?)
- Does the source fit your own knowledge of events at that time?
  This is a most important question. Be confident. If your background knowledge helps you understand the source, then use it. Your own knowledge of the topic is one of the best factors upon which to base a *judgement* of the reliability of the source.

If you use these questions on a source, you are evaluating it rather than simply accepting it at face value. Source-based questions are designed to test your skills in evaluation.

Making judgements Remember there are no black and white answers to source questions. Examiners usually choose a range of sources in questions which present different viewpoints. Your task is to show that you:

- Understand each source
- Know the context or background of each source
- Can express views on its usefulness
- Can express views on its reliability
- Can look at several sources, evaluate them against each other, decide whether they fit in with your own knowledge and reach a conclusion.

You are being asked to think about the sources and to make judgements about them. In practice this means producing answers along the lines of:

- Source A is useful for ... but it has these drawbacks ...
- Source B seems reliable as evidence for ... but ...
- At the time the source was written ... was happening. This might affect the author's views about ...

If you need help in evaluating sources then this memory aid summarises the questions you have to ask yourself:

Source: where it comes from (date/author etc.)
Objective: why it was written (for a diary/a newspaper)
Usefulness: how useful to the enquiry or question you are doing
Reliability: how reliable it is for your purposes
Context: How does your background knowledge help you understand or explain the source
Example: always use examples from the source to back up what you say.

The aim of the next four chapters is to help you apply these principles to the most popular option topics in your GCSE examination.

The First World War, 1914–18

Between 1914 and 1918 the great European powers fought each other to dominate Europe. In 1914 everyone predicted a short war. But after four years of horrific slaughter Europe was in ruins and many former European rulers gone forever. The First World War was a turning point which changed both the nature of war and the face of Europe.

To answer source-based questions on the First World War, you need to be familiar with both the key content and the key themes of the topic. This will help you to show your understanding of documents and other sources from this period.

KEY CONTENT

You will need to have a good working knowledge of these areas:

A How the major powers planned for war
B How the war started (particularly the events of July 1914)
C Events on the Western Front, 1914–18
D Events on the Eastern Front, 1914–18
E The war in Africa, the Pacific and the Middle East
F The war at sea
G The 'Home Front' – how the war affected civilians
H The changing technology of war

KEY THEMES

You will also need to show your understanding of some key themes for the period. These are:

- **Why the war became a stalemate on the Western and Eastern Fronts**
- **Why there was little change in tactics despite the stalemate**
- **The importance of the war at sea and the Allied blockade of Germany**
- **The effects of the First World War on the role of women in society**
- **The importance of changing military technology**
- **Why conscription was introduced in Britain in 1916**
- **How far people in Britain supported the war effort**

Source-based questions test both your knowledge of the topic and your understanding of documents and other sources from the period being studied. For example, look at this question from the MEG Paper 2, 1994.

SOURCE E *An extract from King George V's 'Message to his people', 25 May 1916*:

To enable our country to organise more effectively its military resources, I have, acting on the advice of my ministers, agreed to the Military Service Bill.

I wish to express my thanks for the splendid patriotism and self-sacrifice which my people have shown by voluntary enlistment since the start of the war. I am confident that they will endure this additional sacrifice.

Study Source E. What changes to the system of recruitment were made by the Military Services Bill of May 1916? [*2 marks*]

This question is asking you to show that

- *You understand the source and can select information from it*
- *You understand the context of the source. In other words, you must also show that you know that conscription was introduced in Britain in 1916 and be able to place that in the context of the unfolding events of the First World War.*

We will look at this question in detail at the end of this chapter.

THE FIRST WORLD WAR, 1914–18

A How the major powers planned for war

In 1914 Europe was divided into two armed camps:
- The Triple Alliance: Germany, Austria and Italy
- The Triple Entente: France, Russia and Britain.

Each member of these alliances promised to support the others if they were attacked. Britain had also guaranteed to protect Belgium in the Treaty of London, 1839. Each country had a plan of action if war broke out.

1. Germany

Because of the Alliance system, Germany knew it might have to fight France and Russia at the same time. It therefore developed the Schlieffen Plan to overcome the problem of fighting on two fronts:
- The German army was to sweep quickly through Belgium and defeat France in the first few weeks of war.
- This would allow the German army to move to the Eastern Front to defeat the Russians.

Germany in 1914 had approximately 2.3 million well-trained troops. Her navy had 17 Dreadnoughts (warships).

2. France

The French plan of attack was called Plan 17. In a war, French troops would invade Germany through the territories of Alsace and Lorraine. These territories had been lost to Germany in 1871. The French had approximately 2 million well-trained troops.

The Schlieffen Plan and Plan 17

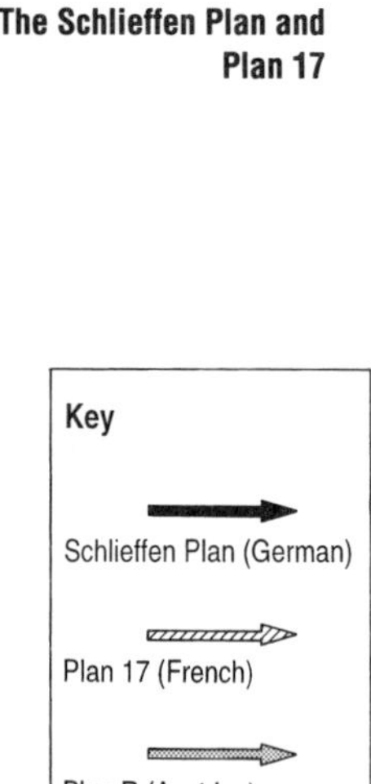

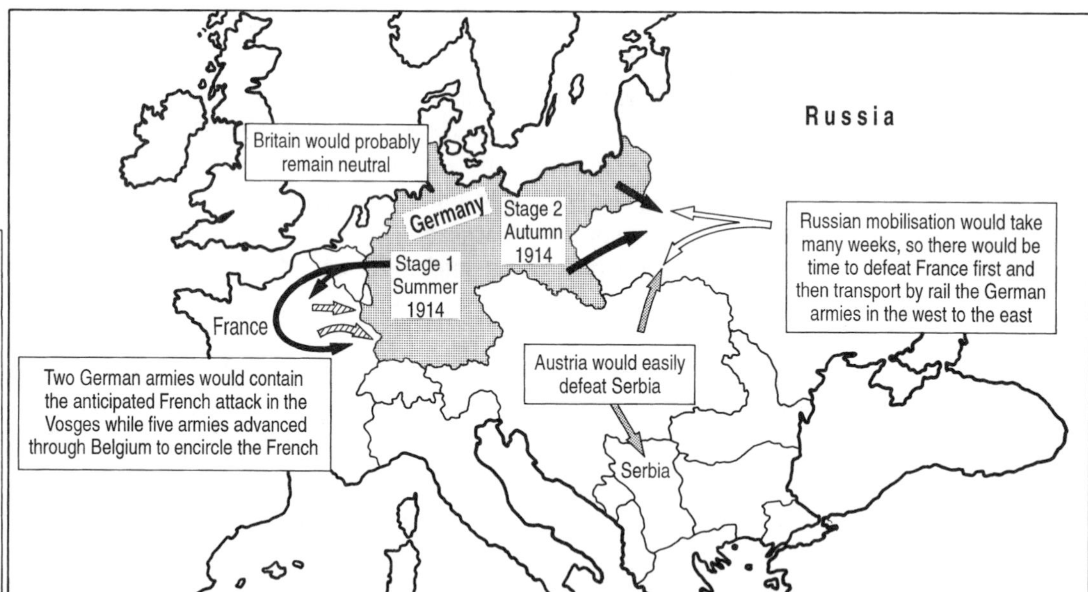

3. Britain

British plans for war were based on supporting the French army with a small but highly trained expeditionary force. Britain would rely on its powerful navy to blockade German ports and use her forces overseas to harass the Germans.

The British had approximately 600,000 well-trained troops. The navy included 29 Dreadnoughts.

4. Austria

The Austrian plan of attack was called Plan R. In a war Austria would invade Russia with thousands of troops and at the same time attack Serbia in the south. The Austrians had approximately 1.25 million troops.

5. Russia

The Russian plan of attack relied upon using its huge army to defeat the Germans and Austrians. It had approximately 3 million poorly trained and poorly equipped troops.

B How the war started

Each country had to mobilise (get its army ready for battle) quickly to gain an advantage. This is what happened:

- Huge numbers of troops were moved into position mainly by rail transport.
- Once one country began to move its troops to the front line, then the enemy had to do the same or risk immediate defeat.
- Once mobilisation began therefore, it was very difficult to stop.

This diagram summarises the steps that began the First World War. Note how quickly war began once Austria mobilised its forces (on 25 July).

28 June Austrian Archduke Franz Ferdinand and his wife are shot dead in Sarajevo.

23 July Austria blames Serbia for the death of the Archduke and his wife. (Later it became clear that Austria was looking for an excuse to crush Serbia.)

24 July Serbia accepts most of the Austrian demands and suggests that the Court of Arbitration in the Netherlands should decide upon the rest.

25 July Austria rejects the Serbian proposals and begins to mobilise troops.

28 July Austria declares war on Serbia.

30 July Russia starts moving its armed forces to help Serbia defend itself against Austria. Germany warns that it will enter the war if Russia continues to mobilise. Russia ignores this and continues to move troops.

1 August Germany declares war on Russia. But following the Schlieffen Plan it also begins to move its army towards France and Belgium.
Italy declares that it will remain neutral despite its membership of the Triple Alliance with Germany and Austria.

3 August Germany declares war on France.

4 August Germany invades Belgium as part of Schlieffen Plan.
Britain declares war on Germany.

REVISION TASKS

1. Construct a table like the one below and use the information in this section to make a summary of the war plans of the Great Powers.

Country	Plan	How was it meant to work?
Germany		
France		
Britain		
Austria		
Russia		

2. The outbreak of the First World War has been compared to a team of climbers being roped together; one of them falls and pulls down the rest. What evidence is there to support this view?

C Events on the Western Front, 1914–18

1. The failure of the Schlieffen Plan The Schlieffen Plan was designed to give Germany a quick and decisive victory against France.

However, the plan failed for several reasons:

- The Belgian army fought very bravely and delayed the German advance at Liège.
- The British expeditionary force slowed the German advance at the Battle of Mons.
- Some German troops were transferred from the Western Front to the Eastern Front because the Russians had mobilised their forces more quickly than expected.
- The German commander Kluck decided to turn his forces south rather than encircle Paris. This allowed the British to continue sending troops ashore since the channel ports were not attacked.

2. The battles of the Marne and Ypres, 1914 At the Battle of the Marne, 5–11 September, the commander of the French army, Joffre, was able to halt the German advance and push them back. The French even transported fresh troops to the front in taxis in order to face the exhausted Germans.

Both the British and German forces now abandoned their original plans and tried to cut each other off from fresh supplies and equipment. This led to a race to the English Channel between the British expeditionary force and the German army. At the First Battle of Ypres, the British managed to stop the German advance but at a terrible cost. It is estimated that one British division lost nearly 11,000 of its 12,000 men.

3. Stalemate, December 1914 At the beginning of the war, the French forces also carried out their plans. They launched Plan 17 against the Germans but their advance was also halted. It has been estimated that French casualties were 300,000 in just three months.

By December 1914, the war of movement had come to a halt. From the English Channel in the north to the Swiss border in the south, troops on both sides dug trenches in order to prevent the enemy from advancing further. The soldiers expected to be home by Christmas. But instead the war reached stalemate. No side could make the vital breakthrough.

4. The Western Front, 1915 Some generals on the side of the Allies (Britain and France) were convinced that the Germans could be beaten back if large numbers of troops charged at enemy trenches. Through 1915, wave after wave of soldiers were sent 'over the top' – only to be mown down by enemy machine guns:

- At Neuve Chapelle, the British suffered 11,000 casualties in only three days.
- At the battle of Loos in September 1915, 60,000 British soldiers were killed in less than two weeks.

There are many first-hand accounts of the horrors of trench warfare. They are often used in examination questions. The following are two such examples. Both are from novels written by men who had fought in the war.

SOURCE 1 Robert Graves, *Goodbye to All That* (written in 1929 by a former British soldier):

Going along whistling, I saw a group of men bending over a man lying in the bottom of a trench. He was making a snoring noise mixed with animal groans. At my feet lay his cap slashed with his brains. One can joke with a wounded man, one can disregard a dead man, but no one can joke over a man who takes three hours to die after the top of his head has been taken off by a bullet fired at twenty yards range.

SOURCE 2 E. M. Remarque, *All Quiet on the Western Front* (written shortly after the war by a German soldier):

We were able to bring in the wounded who did not lie too far off. But many had to wait and we listen to them dying. For one we search for two days in vain. Kat thinks he is hurt in the spine or pelvis... his chest cannot be injured otherwise he would not cry out. We crawl out at night but cannot find him. The first day he cries for help, the next day he is delirious and cries for his family. In the morning we suppose he has gone to his rest. The dead lie unburied. We cannot bring them all in. If we did we should not know what to do with them.

5. The Western Front, 1916 The most significant events on the Western Front in 1916 were two battles, Verdun and the Somme.

Verdun

Verdun was a heavily fortified French city in north-east France. The Germans believed they could defeat the French army by concentrating their troops in one small area. They believed that since Verdun was seen as such an important fortress by the French people, its loss would destroy French morale and lead to France's defeat.

- On 21 February 1916 the Germans launched a bombardment of Verdun and within three days it looked as if the city was about to be captured.
- The problem of saving Verdun was given to General Pétain. He moved food, ammunition and equipment into the city and after five months the Germans stopped their attack.
- Pétain became a national hero. The cost to the French and Germans had been high. The Germans lost 281,000 men and the French 315,000.

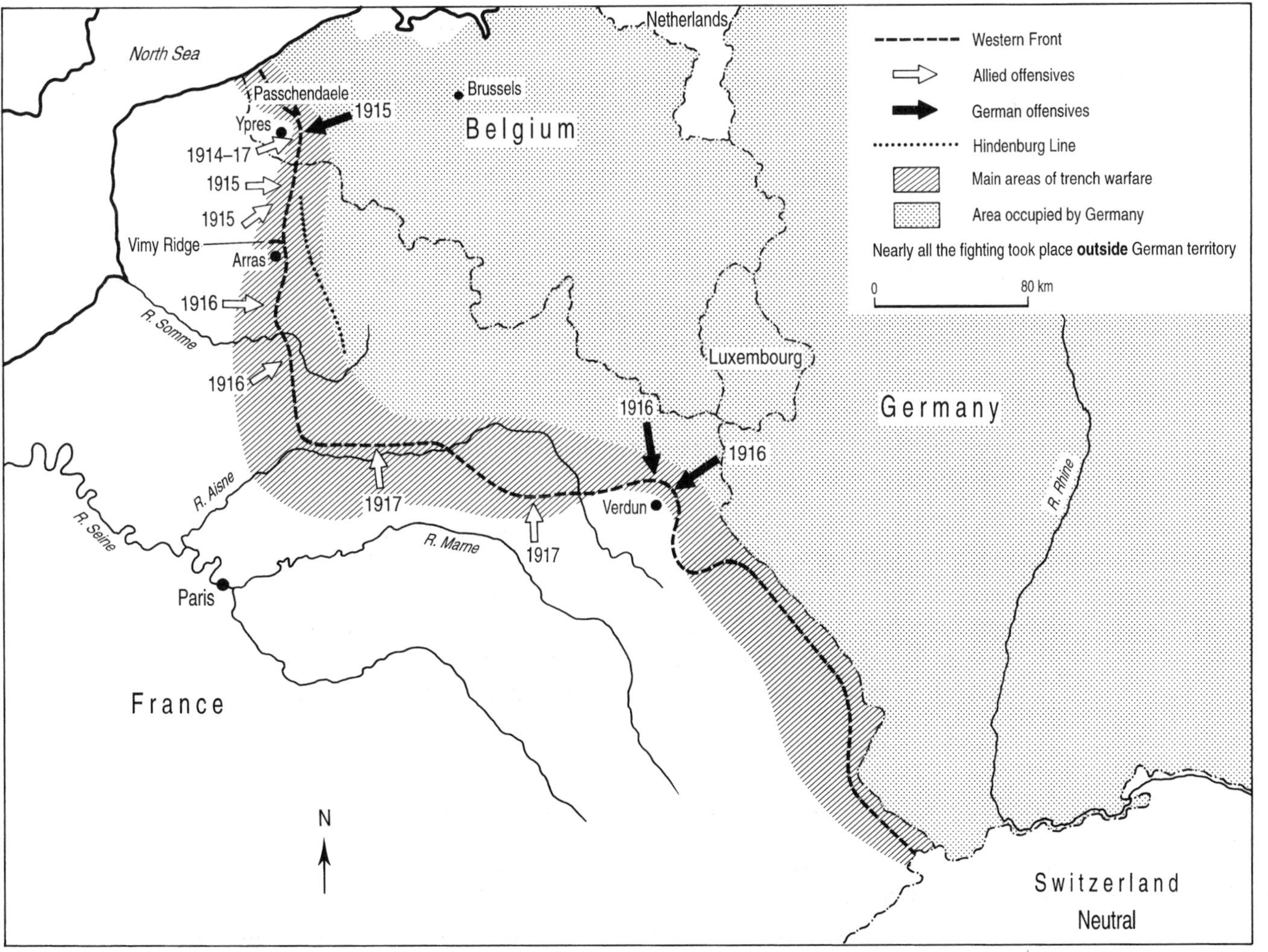

The Somme

General Haig, the British commander, decided to launch a major attack against the Germans along the Somme river. He hoped that by using heavy artillery he would be able to weaken the German front line and so allow the British troops to advance. He also hoped to relieve the pressure on Verdun. This is what happened:

- The battle began with a five-day bombardment of the German positions along an 18-mile front.
- The German troops had prepared dugouts deep underground in order to survive the bombardment.
- On 1 July, 200,000 Allied soldiers attacked the German trenches along the Somme. British troops were ordered to walk not run since each man was carrying up to 66 pounds of equipment.
- In the ten minutes between the end of the bombardment and British attack, the Germans were able to return to their trenches and machine guns.
- On the first day of the battle, the British lost 20,000 men killed and 40,000 wounded.

The battle of the Somme ended in the middle of November 1916. Only nine miles of land had been gained by the Allies at a cost of 600,000 casualties. At the end of 1916, there was still no breakthrough on the Western Front.

▲ *Viewpoints and evidence*

There have been conflicting views on several of these key questions on the first years of the war:

- Why did the plans of the Great Powers not work?
- Why did the war become a stalemate and could anything have been done?
- What were conditions like in the trenches and how did the soldiers feel about them?
- How effective were the tactics used at the Somme in 1916?

For example, these two sources present two differing views about the effectiveness of artillery on enemy defences at the Somme.

SOURCE 3 Sir Douglas Haig,the British general in charge of the offensive, writing about the battle of the Somme:

The work of our artillery was wholly admirable, though the strain on the personnel was enormous. The excellence of the results attained was the more remarkable, in view of the shortness of the training of most of the junior officers and the NCOs.

SOURCE 4 From an interview with George Coppard, a British machine-gunner at the Somme:

How did the planners imagine that Tommies [British soldiers], having survived all other hazards – and there were plenty in crossing No Man's Land – would get through the German wire? Had they studied the black density of it through their powerful binoculars? Who told them that artillery fire would pound each wire to pieces, making it possible to get through? Any Tommy could have told them that shell fire lifts wire up and drops it down again, often in a worse tangle than before.

REVISION TASK

1. Read Sources 1–4 carefully. Note three factors that might affect the reliability of each source.

6. The Western Front, 1917 1917 was another mixed year for the Allies, particularly for the French.

A new French commander, General Nivelle, launched his troops against what he thought was the weakest section of the German front line. Unfortunately, the Germans had discovered the French plans and prepared for their advance. The French suffered nearly 125,000 casualties and made no breakthrough. French morale suffered as a result.

- In early 1917, thousands of French troops mutinied and refused to obey orders.
- General Pétain restored discipline by having hundreds of mutineers shot, improving food rations and extending leave for his soldiers.

The British also had a mixed year.

- They had a major victory in June 1917 at Messines when they blew up a hillside occupied by German troops by placing TNT explosive in tunnels dug out by engineers.
- In the summer, however, at the Third Battle of Ypres (Passchendaele), 400,000 British troops were killed or wounded in a sea of mud created by heavy rain.
- At Cambrai in November the British successfully used tanks against the Germans. But the British advance had been so swift that the soldiers were unable to keep up and in a counter-attack the Germans regained the lost ground.

▲ *Viewpoints and evidence*

People disagreed about the military tactics used on the Western Front during the war. Here are two examples of differing views expressed at the time.

SOURCE 5 Extract from the diary of a New Zealand officer whose men fought at Passchendaele in 1917:

My opinion is that the generals who direct these battles do not know of the conditions, mud, cold, rain, and lack of shelter for the men. The Germans are not so played out as our High Command think. Exhausted men struggling through mud cannot compete against dry men with machine guns.

SOURCE 6 Telegram sent by British Prime Minister, Lloyd George, to Field Marshal Haig, October 1917. The telegram would be read out to the officers:

The war cabinet desires to congratulate you upon the achievements of the British armies in the great battle which has been raging since 31st July. Starting from positions from which the enemy had every advantage and despite being hampered by most unfavourable weather, you and your men have nevertheless driven the enemy back with skill and courage and filled the enemy with alarm. I am personally glad to pass this message to you and to your gallant troops and to state again my confidence in your leadership.

In Source 5 we are told about the weariness of the troops and determination of the enemy. In Source 6, however, the Prime Minister, Lloyd George, is congratulating his commander-in-chief for success on the battlefield. Historians could therefore argue that:

- Source 6 takes a much wider view of events.
- Source 5 only sees events in a specific area.
- A Prime Minister would not want to be critical or negative in a 'public' telegram (Source 6).
- A diary writer might feel more free to express doubts and criticisms (Source 5).

In order to resolve these points and reach a balanced judgement about whether people actually supported the military tactics at the time, we need to examine the contexts (drawn from our background knowledge) of these statements and look at further evidence.

7. The Western Front, 1918: victory for the Allies

For some time German U-boats (submarines) had been sinking American merchant ships and in 1915 the liner *Lusitania* was sunk. Amongst the passengers were 100 American citizens. Despite American protests, German submarines continued to sink American merchant ships. In April 1917 the USA joined the Allies in the war against the enemy.

The Germans knew it would take time for the USA to recruit and train an army, so they drew up plans to win a swift victory before the full impact of the American army was felt on the Western Front.

By March 1918, the Russian army had been defeated. The Germans could now move a million of their own men to the Western Front. This is what happened:

- Ludendorf, the German commander, decided that since he now had many more men than the Allies, he must make an all-out attack on the Western Front before large numbers of American troops arrived in Europe.
- On 21 March 1918 the Ludendorf offensive began and the Germans advanced rapidly; they had soon moved forward 40 miles along an 80-mile front.
- They reached the river Marne in July and once again the French capital looked as if it might fall to the Germans.

The Allied commander, General Foch, began his counter-attack on 18 July and with the help of newly arrived American troops was able to reverse the German advance.

- In August with the help of tanks the British defeated the Germans at Amiens.
- More victories followed in Flanders (e.g. at Ypres).

On 4 October, with the the German army in full retreat, Ludendorf asked the Allies for a truce. On 11 November an ARMISTICE was signed and the First World War was over.

REVISION TASKS

1. Use the information about the Western Front to create a timeline of key events 1914–18. Try to keep it as brief as possible.

1914	Schlieffen Plan	Mons	Marne	Stalemate
1915				
1916				
1917				
1918				

2. First World War generals on the Western Front are usually seen as uncaring and incompetent. What evidence can you find for and against this view, either from these notes or from other sources which you know?

D Events on the Eastern Front, 1914–18

1. The Eastern Front, 1914 At the beginning of the war the Russians invaded East Prussia and won a number of small victories against the Germans. However, the Germans soon recovered.

- They heavily defeated the Second Russian army at Tannenberg. The Russians lost 125,000 men.
- At the beginning of September, the First Russian army was defeated at the battle of the Masurian Lakes in which the Russians lost a further 100,000 men. The Russians were much more successful against the Austrian army. After initially advancing into Russian territory, the Austrians were driven back over 100 miles into Galicia.

2. The Eastern Front, 1915–16 The Russian campaign against the Germans continued to go badly in 1915. In August the retreating Russian army was forced to abandon Warsaw and by the end of the year, the Russians had been driven out of Poland.

1916 saw mixed fortunes for the Russians:

- In June General Brusilov launched an offensive against the Austrian army and won some early successes.
- The Romanians also joined the war on the Russian side.
- However, Hindenburg moved German forces to help the Austrians and soon Russia was in retreat.
- The Russians lost 500,000 men – killed, wounded or taken prisoner. The Germans also moved into Romania and captured the capital city, Bucharest.

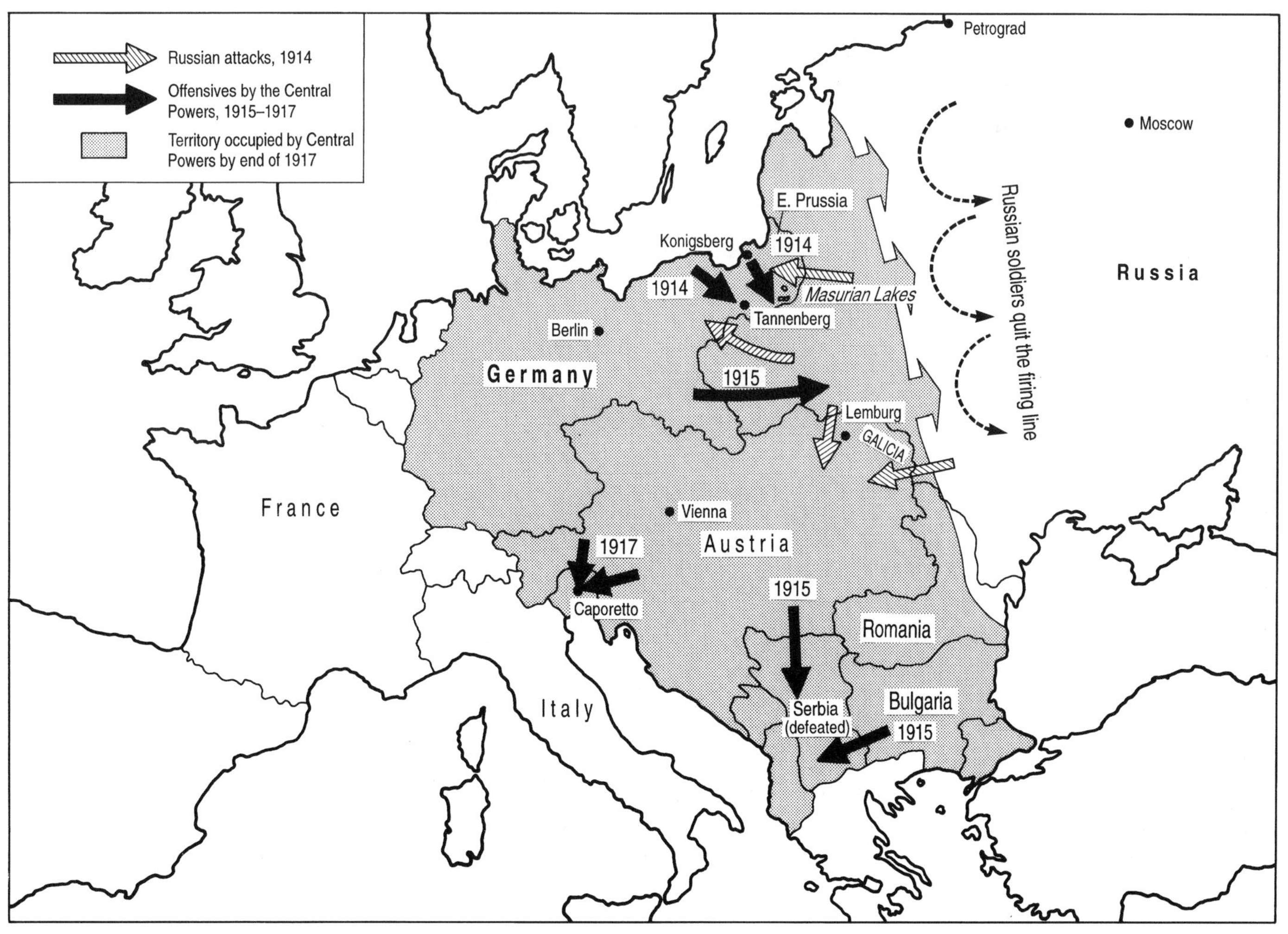

3. The Eastern Front, 1917–18 Russia's heavy losses in the First World War added to the discontent and unrest at home. This is what happened:

- Russian defeats on the Eastern Front forced the Tsar to abdicate in February 1917.
- The new Russian government led by Kerensky continued the war and hoped for a victory to help its cause.
- In the summer of 1917, however, the Russian army began to fall apart and in October Kerensky's government was overthrown by the BOLSHEVIKS. The Bolsheviks wanted to take Russia out of the war and signed an armistice with Germany in December.

The Russians and Germans signed the Treaty of Brest-Litovsk. Russia had been defeated and had to pay a heavy price. In the peace treaty with Germany and Austria, Russia lost Poland, Latvia, Lithuania, Finland, Estonia and the Ukraine. She also gave up one-third of Russian land, along with most of her coal and iron industries.

E The war in Africa, the Pacific and the Middle East

1. Africa

German colonies were attacked in the early stages of the war. In Africa, there was little resistance. In 1915, the German colonies of Togoland, Cameroon and South-West Africa fell to the Allies.

However, for four years Colonel von Lettow-Vorbeck hindered allied forces in southern Africa. His small group of German and native soldiers were still in action when the war ended in November 1918.

2. The Pacific

In the Pacific, Australian and New Zealand forces took possession of Samoa and New Guinea. Japan had made an alliance with Britain in 1902 and joined the war against Germany in August 1914. The Japanese successfully captured the German colony of Kiachow in China and took control of the Caroline and Marshall Islands in the Pacific.

3. Turkey

Before the war, both the British and German governments had been trying to win the support of the Turks. Just before the outbreak of war, however, the British refused to deliver two Dreadnought battleships they had been building for the Turkish navy, but the Kaiser sent two German ships to help the Turkish navy.

In October 1914 Turkey joined the war on Germany's side.

4. Gallipoli

By the end of 1914, with stalemate on the Western Front and the Russians under pressure on the Eastern front, Winston Churchill, First Lord of the Admiralty, came up with an imaginative and daring plan to shorten the war.

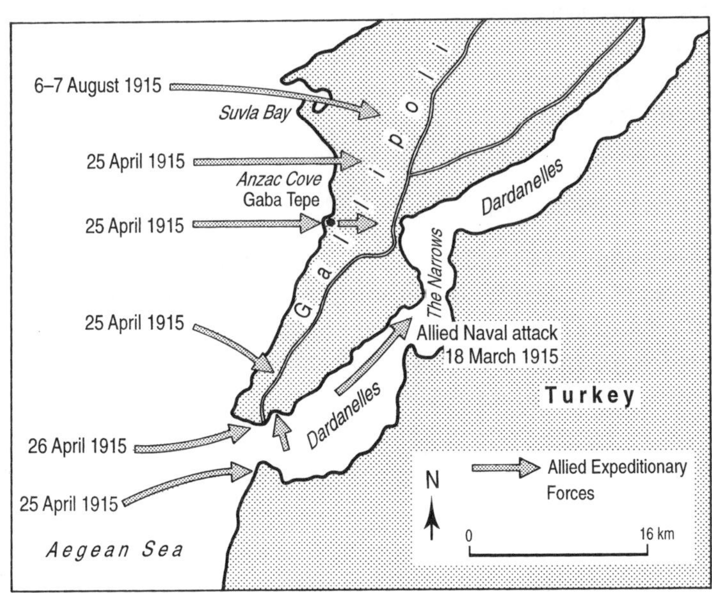

Gallipoli campaign

Churchill's plan was to :

- Capture the Turkish capital Constantinople and force Turkey to surrender
- Re-open a supply route to Russia
- Encourage the neutral countries of Bulgaria, Greece and Romania to join the war on the side of the Allies
- Surround Germany and Austria-Hungary.

But what actually happened?

- In February 1915 the British navy failed to open the stretch of water known as the Dardanelles. The fleet retreated.
- In April a force of British and ANZAC (Australian, New Zealand and Canadian) troops landed on the Gallipoli peninsula. They were soon pinned down by Turkish machine guns.
- In August, the Allies attacked again, this time landing a force at Suvla Bay. By delaying their advance the Allies gave the Turks the chance to regroup and no further advance was made. Many Allied soldiers died of disease.

At home in Britain, the commanders of the Gallipoli campaign were heavily criticised. After several weeks, the decision was taken to evacuate the Gallipoli peninsular. At the end of 1915 the Allies withdrew, having suffered 200,000 casualties.

5. Mesopotamia

The Turks defeated a combined British and Indian army at Kut el Amara in 1916. The Allies recovered, however, and in March 1917 went on to capture Baghdad.

6. Palestine

At the beginning of the war, Turkey controlled Palestine. This was seen as a threat to British-controlled Egypt. In Arabia, local tribes rose against the Turks and were

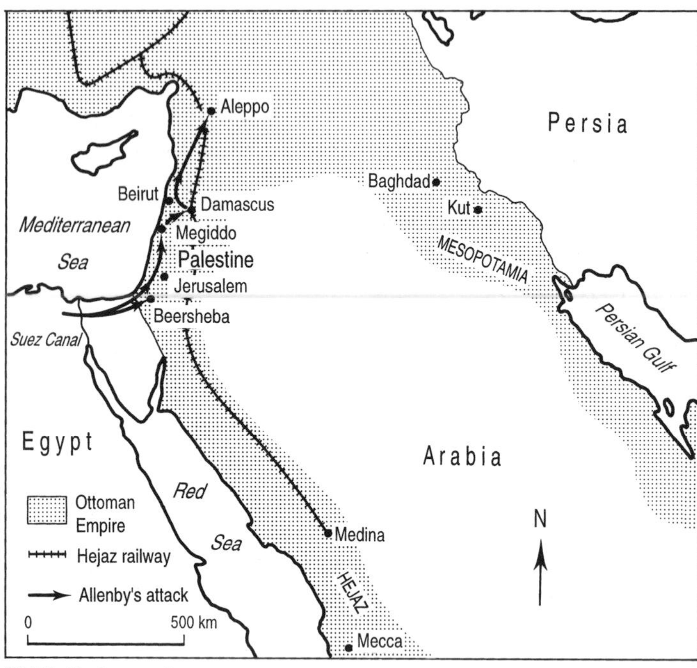

Middle East camapign

assisted by army officers sent by the British. One of these officers, Colonel T. E. Lawrence, organised guerrilla attacks on the important Hejaz railway. By December 1917 the British (under the leadership of General Allenby) had captured Jerusalem from the Turks and in September 1918 Damascus was also taken.

▲ *Viewpoints and evidence*

There are several important issues concerning the campaigns outside the Western Front:

- Why and how were tactics different in the other campaigns?
- Were they any more effective?
- How important were the campaigns when compared with the Western Front?

But perhaps the most important of these questions is:

- Why was the Gallipoli campaign a failure?

Sources 7 and 8 give the views of two historians about Gallipoli.

SOURCE 7 A. Wood, *Europe 1815–1960*, 1984:

There was only one serious strategic attempt made by the British to open up a new flank – the Gallipoli expedition of 1915 inspired primarily by Winston Churchill – and this failed largely through the constant demand for troops on the Western Front... It [Gallipoli] had been a daring and imaginative campaign and, but for certain errors in command, might have succeeded.

SOURCE 8 W. Robson, *20th-Century Britain*, 1983:

The Gallipoli campaign was disastrously mismanaged. From the start, the commander, Sir Ian Hamilton, was short of men because Sir John French and General Joffre [the leading British and French commanders in France and Belgium] resisted every attempt to divert troops from the Western Front. But Hamilton's own incompetence was the main cause of the failure.

REVISION TASKS

1. Create your own timeline for these fronts, like the one shown below.

	Africa	The Pacific	The Middle East
1914			
1915			
1916			
1917			
1918			

2. Compare Sources 7 and 8. What do they agree about? What do they disagree about?
3. Were the commanders to blame for the failures of the Gallipoli campaign? What evidence can you find, either here or in your own reading?

F The war at sea

1. Background The British and German navies were the most powerful in the world and control of the seas was an important factor in the final outcome of the war. The aim of the Royal Navy was:

- to keep shipping lanes free from German attack
- blockade German ports
- re-supply British troops in the colonies.

The German navy aimed to disrupt Britain's food and munitions supplies and protect German colonies from British attack.

2. Minor clashes Before 1916 there were only a few clashes between the Allies and the other powers at sea.

- In 1914 German raiders bombarded Scarborough and in 1915 another group of German vessels clashed with the British near the Dogger Bank in the North Sea.
- In the Pacific region German ships were sunk at the battles of Coronel in November 1914 and the Falkland Islands in December 1916.

3. The battle of Jutland, May/June 1916 At the end of May 1916 Admirals Hipper and von Scheer led the German Fleet into the North Sea. In a carefully worked-out plan, they aimed to destroy the British Grand Fleet by tempting the British ships into a trap. However, the British had discovered the German radio codes and were able to decode all German messages.

On the evening of 31 May 1916, the two fleets had a running battle off the coast of Jutland in Denmark. The outcome of the battle was indecisive although both sides claimed victory. The losses were as follows:

	Germany	**Britain**
Ships	11	14
Men (killed)	2,500	6,000

German casualties were much lighter than the British but the German fleet never set sail into the North Sea again. The British Grand Fleet had not proved its superiority but Admiral Jellicoe claimed it had been the Germans who had fled and headed for home.

4. War against the submarine Most of the food and raw materials which Britain needed to keep up its war efffort came into Britain by ship.

In 1915 the German government announced it would attack any ships it suspected of carrying supplies to Britain.

- The most famous victim of the German U-boat (submarine) war was the large British passenger line, *Lusitania*, sunk in 1915.
- By 1917 the Germans had over 300 submarines and began unrestricted submarine warfare.
- This tactic was so effective that at one stage Britain was reduced to six weeks supply of grain.

The German submarine campaign had severe consequences. On 6 April 1917 the USA entered the war on the side of the Allies. American President Woodrow Wilson said the German policy of unrestricted submarine warfare was a major factor in America's decision to declare war on Germany.

Towards the end of the war, various tactics were used by Britain against the German submarines:

- The British developed the convoy system to protect merchant ships.
- Nets and mines were used, particularly in the English Channel, to trap and destroy U-boats.
- Some Allied ships were equipped with depth charges.
- Q-boats (disguised merchant ships) were developed to trick U-boats to attack.

5. The British blockade of Germany Despite the attacks on shipping, Germany was unable to isolate Britain by using her navy or submarines. In fact, Germany was successfully blockaded by the Allies. This led to severe food shortages in Germany in 1918 and speeded up the German surrender in November of that year.

▲ *Viewpoints and evidence*

The key questions on the war at sea are:

- How effective was the British blockade of Germany?
- How effective was the German attempt to cut off Britain's supplies?
- How successful were the British and German navies at Jutland in 1916?

SOURCE 9 The Kaiser speaking to the sailors of the German fleet, June 1916:

A brave leader led our fleet. The superior English armada appeared. What happened? The English were beaten. The spell of Trafalgar has been broken.*

(* Trafalgar was a great British naval victory in 1805)

SOURCE 10 An extract from a British history of the Great War published in 1988:

After Jutland, despite losing more ships and more men, the British navy kept control over the North Sea. The blockade of Germany continued. The Germans had to turn to submarine warfare and the morale of the surface fleet was damaged.

Sources 9 and 10 give a different view of the outcome of the battle of Jutland. Source 9 is a PRIMARY SOURCE whilst Source 10 is SECONDARY EVIDENCE written by a British historian over 60 years after the battle. However, this shows how important it is to test all sources for reliability – Source 9 is actually a piece of propaganda (see page 117). It is understandable that the Kaiser in Source 9 speaks of a British defeat. Whatever the outcome of Jutland we would not expect a wartime leader to admit a defeat. In wartime, official reports on events were often propaganda.

Source 10, on the other hand, is likely to be more balanced. We would hope that 60 years after the event, an historian, whether British or German, would be able to provide an unprejudiced view of this major episode of the war.

REVISION TASKS

1. In your view, which side won the Battle of Jutland? Give reasons for your answer.
2. Was the U-boat campaign a major threat to Britain in the First World War? What evidence is there for this?

G The 'Home Front': how the war affected civilians

1. Recruitment Between August 1914 and March 1916, 2.5 million men volunteered for the British Army. The recruitment campaign launched by the government in 1914 worked far better than was predicted. Around 750,000 men joined up during the first few weeks of the campaign alone. Sometimes, whole groups of friends from one area joined up together as a 'pals battalion'.

However, despite the steady flow of volunteers, there was a high casualty rate at the front, so more troops were needed. By late 1915, the British government was considering CONSCRIPTION (compulsory military service).

This was highly controversial and a debate raged through the winter of 1915–16. The original proposal was for only unmarried men to be conscripted. However, by May 1916 the needs of war and unrest in Ireland meant that the government was given the power to conscript all men aged 18–41 under the Military Services Act. According to the Act:

- Only men involved in 'reserved occupations' such as munitions work or mining were exempt from military service.
- Conscientious objectors (often known as 'conshies') had to appear before local tribunals to explain why they refused to fight.(Most conshies joined up to do war work in the medical or support services. About 1500 conshies went to prison until the end of the war.)

2. Emergency measures In 1914 the British government passed the Defence of the Realm Act or DORA as it became known. The Act gave the government wide powers during wartime to censor the press, imprison troublemakers and ration food.

- By 1916 food prices were nearly 60 per cent higher than the 1914 level. Rationing was introduced locally in a number of areas, although there was no nationwide rationing before 1918.
- It was widely believed by government ministers that absenteeism from work (and therefore the war effort) was partly caused by excessive drunkenness. Using DORA, therefore, the government passed a very unpopular measure: from 1915 pubs were only allowed to open from noon to 2.30 p.m. and 6.30 to 9.30 in the evening. The price of beer also rose despite the fact that it was made weaker.
- Under DORA, the government was able to control the reporting of conditions on the Western Front. Newspapers ran stories about heroic soldiers, and portrayed the war as a great British success. It was very difficult for ordinary people to find out the truth about the trenches.

3. The employment of women As more men joined the armed forces, their civilian jobs were increasingly taken by women. The contribution of women to the war effort brought about some important and lasting changes in women's economic and political lives.

- SUFFRAGETTES who had been aggressively campaigning for voting rights for women stopped their violent activities and supported the war effort.
- By 1916, in addition to working in the munitions factories making explosives for use in the war, many women were working on trams and buses, in iron foundries and farming. These were all traditionally men's jobs.
- With women doing so much for the war effort, parliament finally agreed to give women the vote. The Representation of the People Act of 1918 gave women over the age of 30 the vote for the first time.

4. The cost of war The First World War changed the face of Europe and directly affected the lives of hundreds of millions of people. In loss of life alone, the First World War was the most costly conflict there had ever been. As well as the troops, many civilians were killed, injured, made homeless or died from disease. It is estimated that 8.5 million people died in war during the period 1914–18:

- 750,000 British men were killed.
- Another 200,000 Empire troops also died in the war, including 60,000 from India.
- France lost twice as many troops as Britain.

Despite the few Zeppelin raids (see page 120), civilian casualties in Britain were light. Fewer than 1,500 civilians were killed – considerably less than the losses in France, Germany or Russia.

▲ *Viewpoints and evidence*

The following sources show some reactions to the role played by women in the First World War.

SOURCE 11 Prime Minister Asquith speaking in 1918 about women's work in the war:

I think that some years ago I used the expression 'let the women work out their own salvation'.

Well sir, they have worked it out during the war. How could we have carried on the war without them?

SOURCE 12 Extract from the radical periodical, *New Statesman*, 1917:

They [women] appear more alert, more critical of the conditions under which they work, more ready to make a stand against injustice...

SOURCE 13 A British historian, writing in 1988:

During the war, women took over a great many new jobs. Some took over the work their husbands had been doing. Others did the work which had always been done by men. Women were also needed to work in the munitions factories.

These sources do not disagree in content. They all comment favourably on women's war work. However, they show how important it is to consider not just the content of the sources, but also their tone and emphasis. The tone of the above sources differs – surprised (in Source 11), enthusiastic (Source 12) and with a more objective, factual emphasis in Source 13.

REVISION TASKS

1. How did the First World War change the life of civilians?
   Use 6–8 key words to summarise your main points.
2. In your opinion, what were the two most important effects of the war for women? What have you based your decision on?

H The changing technology of war

1. Machine guns

Most soldiers killed in the First World War were gunned down by machine gunfire. In 1914, many military commanders had thought the machine gun an unreliable and untested invention. However, Lloyd George was so impressed with these new weapons that by the end of the war nearly 250,000 had been manufactured for the British army.

On the battlefield the machine gun had a devastating effect. The water-cooled machine guns used by both sides could fire up to 600 rounds a minute and frequently cut down hundreds of troops before they were able to advance more than a few yards.

SOURCE 14 Recollections from a German machine-gunner at the Somme, 1916:

The officers were in front. I noticed one of them walking calmly carrying a walking stick. When we started firing we just had to load and reload. They went down in their hundreds. You didn't have to aim, we just fired into them.

2. Gas

Poison gas was used for the first time by the Germans at the second battle of Ypres in April 1915. It was later used by both sides in the war. There were different kinds of gas:

- Chlorine and phosgene gas destroyed the victim's lungs.
- Mustard gas was particularly horrible and destroyed flesh.

Gas attacks were widely feared. But they did not have a major impact on the outcome of the First World War. Gas was unpredictable in battle – a change in wind direction could blow the gas back to the sender – and by 1917 effective gas masks had been produced to protect soldiers on the battlefield.

Most people have regarded gas as a particularly horrific weapon. In fact, the use of poison gas in war had been banned by international agreements signed at the Hague in 1899 and 1907.

There are first-hand accounts of gas attacks. Sometimes, these accounts are full of personal detail and emotion. But they are a vital tool for the historian who is trying to find out what life at the front was really like.

SOURCE 15 G. Chapman, *Vain Glory*:

We have heaps of gassed cases. I wish those who call this a holy war could see the poor things burnt and blistered all over with great mustard coloured, suppurating blisters, with blind eyes all sticky and glued together, always fighting for breath with voices a mere whisper saying their throats are closing and they will choke.

SOURCE 16 Anthony Hossack, Queen Victoria Rifles:

Suddenly down the road from the Yser Canal came a galloping team of horses, the riders goading on their mounts in a frenzied way; then another and another... Plainly something terrible was happening... In the northerly breeze there came a pungent nauseating smell that tickled the throat and made our eyes smart. The horses and men were still pouring down the road... while over the fields streamed mobs of infantry, the dusky warriors of French Africa; away went their rifles, equipment, even their tunics that they might run faster...

Historians must balance accounts like these against what they also know about the significance of gas in the outcome of the war. The descriptions in Sources 15 and 16 show how awful the results of a gas attack could be, but they do not prove that gas was a significant weapon in deciding the outcome of the war.

3. Tanks

The British used tanks for the first time at the battle of the Somme in July 1916. They were successful in battle but there were not enough of them to break the stalemate on the Western Front.

The first tanks were armour-plated with cannon and machine guns and moved at three miles per hour. These models were unreliable and often broke down. Those that were successful often advanced too quickly for supporting troops and were captured or destroyed. At the battle of Cambrai in 1917, the British used 381 tanks with great success to begin with. But the infantry soldiers could not keep up with the tanks and in the later stages of the battle much of the land captured by the tank crews was recaptured by the Germans.

4. Aeroplanes

One of the most important new weapons to be introduced in the First World War was the aeroplane. At first aeroplanes were slow and unarmed and used only for reconnaissance, such as taking photographs from the air behind enemy lines. The British had 63 aircraft at the beginning of the war and commanders used them to report on enemy troop movements.

In 1915 the Germans produced an aircraft (Fokker EI) which was capable of firing a machine gun safely through a rotating propeller. The British and French soon copied the idea and 'dogfights' between rival aircraft became more common over the battlefield. These fights captured the public interest, and the newspapers gave them more publicity than the fighting in the trenches.

By 1917 the Germans had developed a twin-engine bomber and when war ended both sides had developed four-engine bombers. However, their range and power were very limited, and they had little impact on the outcome of the war.

5. Balloons and Zeppelins

Small balloons were frequently used on the battlefield for observation purposes before the widespread use of aircraft. Hydrogen-filled Zeppelins were also used by the Germans for reconnaissance and bombing purposes. A small number of Zeppelins bombed London and the east coast of England during April 1915. Although the actual damage was slight, it was the first time civilians far from the front line had been attacked in this way. The effect upon civilian morale in Britain was alarming.

REVISION TASKS

1. Construct a chart like the one below and use the information in this section to complete it.

Type of weapon	When was it first used?	How was it used?	Why was it important?

2. In your opinion which of the weapons described in this section had most impact in the war? What evidence have you found here or from your own reading to support your view?

The aim of this session is for you to see how you can apply your knowledge of the First World War to answering some source-based questions.

Examination questions

This example is from MEG Paper 2, 1994 on the First World War.

SOURCE D *Men of the St. Helens (Lancashire) Pals Battalion in February 1915. The photograph was printed in a local newspaper.*

Study Source D. What was a 'Pals Battalion'?

[*2 marks*]

What is required? The aim of this question is to test your background knowledge of the period and your understanding of the source. A suitable answer would be a simple definition supported by an example.

Ideas for your answer A straightforward definition would be useful, for example: groups of friends from one area who joined up together. You should then follow up with examples such as the St Helens Pals (Source D) or the Accrington Pals. It might also be worth pointing out that calling the Battalions 'Pals' was a way to encourage young men to join up.

SOURCE E *An extract from King George V's 'Message to his people', 25 May 1916.*

To enable our country to organise more effectively its military resources, I have, acting on the advice of my ministers, agreed to the Military Service Bill.

I wish to express my thanks for the splendid patriotism and self-sacrifice which my people have shown by voluntary enlistment since the start of the war. I am confident that they will endure this additional sacrifice.

Study Source E. What changes to the system of recruitment were made by the Military Services Bill of May 1916?

[*2 marks*]

What is required? This question has the same aims as the first one – clear information backed up by examples.

Ideas for your answer Begin with the changes brought by the new Bill. This basically means the extension of conscription to married men. It would be worth providing more details e.g. when conscription had first been introduced, reserved occupations, the effects of conscription.

SOURCE C *Army recruiting figures August 1914 to December 1915. The figures were published in 1923.*

1914:		**1915:**	
August	300,000	January	156,000
September	450,000	February	88,000
October	137,000	March	114,000
November	170,000	April	119,000
December	117,000	May	135,000
		June	114,000
		July	95,000
		August	96,000
		September	71,000
		October	113,000
		November	122,000
		December	55,000

Study Source C. In what ways might these figures be useful to an historian studying British recruitment in the First World War? Explain your answer. [*6 marks*]

What is required? **This question is testing the concept of the usefulness or utility of historical sources. To score the lowest level (1 mark) you must make a simple statement (e.g. it gives useful figures). To hit the next level (2–3 marks) you must explain your statement further (e.g. why the figures are useful). To reach higher levels (4–6 marks) you must evaluate Source C. This means you need to explain how historians could use the statistics, but also point out the weaknesses of the source.**

Ideas for your answer

1. A useful point to start with is the information contained in the source. It is certainly relevant information to an historian studying recruitment as it contains recruitment figures. The figures themselves are useful in that they show patterns and trends in the period shown.
2. You should point out that an historian could probably use the figures to look at how effective particular recruiting campaigns were. For example, Source B mentions the recruiting campaigns in May 1915 and Source C shows a rise in recruitment in May 1915.
3. Of course, other factors might explain this. Your background knowledge will tell you that the key period of debate about conscription was in the winter of 1915–16, and so the figures for the winter months of 1915 are particularly relevant.

SOURCE B *Extracts from the diary of an Essex clergyman, the Reverend Andrew Clark.*

1 May 1915:
William Milton, foreman of Lyons Hall farm, does not approve of all the recruiting posters on tree trunks and walls. 'If the government want more men let them take idlers not workmen. Unless the war is over before August there will not be enough men for the harvest.'

The men say 'We will go when we like, or when we are ordered.' Conscription, being just, would be welcome.

9 May 1915:
The annoyance of farm-labourers with the recruitment campaign is shown by the fact that every recruiting poster has been torn down.

SOURCE A

Study Sources A and B. Which of these two sources gives the more reliable view of British attitudes to recruitment? Explain your answer. [*8 marks*]

What is required? Your aim here is to show that you understand the idea of the reliability of a source. For the lower levels (1–3 marks) you must produce either a general statement (e.g. one is primary) or evaluate one source in outline (e.g. Source A is a kind of propaganda).

For the next level (4–5 marks) you must evaluate at least one source, explaining why it is or is not a reliable view.

To reach the top levels (6–8 marks) you must 'test' both sources and reach a conclusion – you must also explain that conclusion.

Ideas for your answer You will find it helpful to take each source in turn.

1. Source A is a government poster. It has a clear aim which is to get men to join up. We therefore have to be careful as to whether this reflects ordinary British people's attitudes to recruitment, as its message seems to be that all British people expect men aged 19–38 to join up. Source A clearly reflects the government's view.

   You can now test the source. By using examples from your background knowledge you can show that there was enthusiasm for joining up in 1914. You could also use Source C to support this. However, we also know that there was less enthusiasm later on in 1914, which is also backed up by Source C. In addition, the poster is very insistent and persuasive and this may imply that the government issued the poster because it was becoming concerned about the levels of recruitment.

   Overall, then, the source is clearly a biased source. The poster suggests that all British people expect all men to volunteer. However, its origin and its insistence suggest that this may not be an entirely reliable view of British attitudes.

2. Source B presents a different picture about attitudes to recruitment. At face value it appears that by May 1915 enthusiasm for joining up has gone. There is no hidden aim of getting men to join up in this source as there clearly is in Source A, so you could conclude this means it is a reliable view of the feelings in that part of Essex. The mention of idlers also fits in with our background knowledge of the issue of recruitment. In addition, you could point out that these men are not against joining up as long as there is a fair system for doing so.

   However, you should also point out that it may not be a reliable view of British attitudes as a whole. The feelings against recruitment are expressed in a farming community with harvest on the way – they cannot spare men. Again, you could use your background knowledge and Sources C and D to show that recruitment in other areas seemed to be fairly strong.

Study all the Sources. 'Conscription was introduced because voluntary recruitment was not working'. Do these sources provide reliable evidence to show this view to be true? Explain your answer. [*12 marks*]

What is required? This question is the most important of the set. You must reach a conclusion on the question and support your answer by referring to these sources. For each of the sources you should comment on its value, reliability, usefulness.

At the lowest level (2–3 marks) examiners will look for general comments about conscription, not really using the sources.

The next level of answer (4–5 marks) should have a conclusion, but not really well backed up by evidence or examples.

To reach the next level (6–7 marks) you must reach a conclusion and explain which sources support your conclusion. To score the highest marks (8–12 marks) you must do all of this, but you must also show that you understand that all of the sources have their strengths and weaknesses. Overall, your aim is to produce a balanced response.

Ideas for your answer The best approach is to work systematically through the sources.

1. As we saw in the fourth question Source A sends conflicting signals to us about recruitment. However, careful analysis suggests that on balance Source A supports the view that voluntary recruitment was

not working and that the government was worried about recruitment even in 1914. However, you should point out that while it has its value it is dated 1914. As a result it cannot really provide entirely reliable evidence on how recruitment was working by 1916.

2. You can take a similar line with Source B. This source clearly indicates that there is a problem with the voluntary recruiting system (e.g. posters being pulled down). It suggests that men are not opposed to joining up but they feel that it could be organised better and more fairly. However, in order to produce a balanced answer, you should again point out its narrow representation (Essex farm workers) and that like Source A, it is dated more than a year before conscription was finally introduced.

3. Source C again seems to support the idea that voluntary recruitment was not working. There are increases and decreases in recruitment figures in 1914 and 1915 but the overall trend is definitely downwards. You could back this up with your background knowledge. Again, you should question the reliability of this evidence. Government figures for this period were not always accurate but of all the countries in the war British figures are generally the most reliable. On balance, this source could be seen as fairly reliable evidence to support the idea that voluntary recruitment was not working.

4. Source D seems to give a clear indication that voluntary recruitment was working as the Pals battalion marches off to war. However, we must look at the context of this evidence. Source C suggests that February 1915 was a bad month for recruitment, although we do not know exactly when these men joined up. Your background knowledge tells you that the real debate about conscription took place in the winter of 1915. On balance, therefore, this source does not provide particularly reliable evidence either way.

5. Source E seems to support the statement. After all, why introduce conscription if voluntary recruitment was working? In addition it is an official statement as the King specifically mentions the advice of his ministers. This would appear to be clear and reliable evidence that the system is not working as these are the people in charge of the system.

6. In your conclusion you could therefore point out that the sources generally seem to support the view that voluntary recruitment was not working. Source E is the most reliable evidence to support the view while Sources A, B, and C provide less reliable supporting evidence.

Below is a list of headings which you might find helpful. Use this as a check list to make sure you are familiar with the material featured in this chapter. Record your key words alongside each heading.

A How the major powers planned for war

1. Germany
2. France
3. Britain
4. Austria
5. Russia

B How the war started

1. Key factors
2. Key dates, 1914:
   - June
   - July
   - August

C Events on the Western Front, 1914–18

1. Failure of the Schlieffen Plan
2. The battles of the Marne and Ypres, 1914
3. Stalemate, December 1914
4. The Western Front, 1915
5. The Western Front, 1916
   - Verdun
   - The Somme
6. The Western Front, 1917
   - for the British
   - for the French
7. The Western Front, 1918

D Events on the Eastern Front, 1914–18

1. The Eastern Front, 1914
2. The Eastern Front, 1915–16
3. The Eastern Front, 1917–18

E The war in Africa, the Pacific and the Middle East

1. Africa
2. The Pacific
3. Turkey
4. Gallipoli
5. Mesopotamia
6. Palestine

F The war at sea

1. Background
   - British aims
   - German aims
2. Minor clashes
3. Jutland, May/June, 1916
4. War against the submarine
5. The British blockade of Germany

G The 'Home Front' – how the war affected civilians

1. Recruitment
   - conscription
2. Emergency measures
   - DORA
3. Employment of women
4. The cost of war

H The changing technology of war

1. Machine guns
2. Gas
3. Tanks
4. Aeroplanes
5. Balloons and Zeppelins

CHAPTER 10

The USA between the wars, 1919–41

After the First World War, people in Europe looked to the United States for leadership – both to help prevent future wars and for money to help rebuild Europe's shattered economies. But Americans had problems of their own...

To answer source-based questions on the USA between the wars, you need to be familiar with both the key content and the key themes of the period. This will help you to show your understanding of documents and other sources relating to this topic.

KEY CONTENT

You will need to have a good working knowledge of these areas:

A The US system of government
B The economic boom of the 1920s
C American society in the 1920s
D The Wall Street Crash and the Depression
E Roosevelt and the New Deal
F Successes and failures of the New Deal

KEY THEMES

You will also be asked to show your understanding of some key themes:

- **The differences between the myth and reality of life in the USA in the 1920s**
- **The policies of the main political parties**
- **Why there were divisions within American society**
- **What Americans thought of their Presidents**
- **The relationship between Presidents and important groups in society**
- **How films and newspapers reported events**
- **Theories about the causes of the Great Depression and ideas about how to solve it**
- **The arguments over the New Deal**
- **The successes and failures of the New Deal**

Source-based questions test both your knowledge of the topic and your understanding of documents and other sources from the period being studied. For example, look at this question from the MEG Paper 2, 1993.

SOURCE C *A notice displayed on the walls of 'Thomas Edison Inc.', New Jersey, in April 1933, by the owner.*

President Roosevelt has done his part: now you do something. Buy something – buy anything, anywhere: paint your kitchen, give a party, get a car, pay a bill, rent a flat, get a haircut, see a show, build a house, take a trip, sing a song, get married. It does not matter what you do – but get going and keep going. The old world is starting to move.

Study Source C. How would the instruction: 'Buy something' help President Roosevelt's policies succeed? [*2 marks*]

This question is asking you to show that

- You understand the source and can select information from it
- You understand the context of the source. In other words, you must show that you know what was happening in the USA when this source was produced, and how this might affect what people were saying.

We will look at this question in more detail at the end of this chapter.

A The US system of government

To understand this topic and the evidence from this period in America's history you need to have some knowledge of how America's system of government worked (and still does).

- Federal system: the USA's federal system meant that all the individual states looked after their own internal affairs (e.g. education). Questions which concerned all of the states (e.g. war) were dealt with by Congress.
- Congress: Congress was made up of the Senate and the House of Representatives. Congress and the President (elected every four years) ran the country.
- The Supreme Court: this was made up of judges, who were usually very experienced lawyers. Their main task was to make sure that American governments did not misuse their power or pass unfair laws.
- Political parties: there were two main political parties. The Republicans were strong in the industrial north of the USA while the Democrats had more support in the south. The important difference between the two was that Republicans believed that government should let people and businesses be free to do what they wanted, while the Democrats were more prepared to try to control business life.
- The President: he was the single most important politician in the USA. However, the American Constitution was designed to stop him from becoming too powerful. Congress and the Supreme Court both acted as 'watchdogs' on how the President behaved.

	US Presidents 1921–45	Party	In Office
	Warren Harding	Republican	1921–3
	Calvin Coolidge	Republican	1923–8
	Herbert Hoover	Republican	1928–32
	Franklin D. Roosevelt	Democrat	1932–45

REVISION TASK

1. Complete this diagram with details about the key people and institutions in the US system of government.

STATE GOVERNMENT

Albany

New York City

US system of Government

FEDERAL GOVERNMENT
President
Congress
Supreme Court

Washington D.C.

Congress	President	Supreme Court
Powers ______	Powers ______	Powers ______

B The economic boom of the 1920s

1. Background: the USA up to 1920 America's industry and farming had grown steadily since the 1860s.

- The country had huge resources (coal, iron, timber, oil).
- It had a growing population, many of them immigrants willing to work hard.
- Railways, mining and manufacturing were all strong.

In the early years of the First World War, US businesses profited from the war in Europe.

- American industries supplied arms and equipment.
- American firms were able to take over much of the export business of the European powers while they were caught up in the fighting.

The First World War made the USA wealthy and confident. Americans felt they were doing well. It also made them ISOLATIONIST. They did not want to be dragged into Europe's wars.

2. Republican policies Through the 1920s Republican presidents were in power, and they implemented Republican policies. President Harding believed in what he called 'normalcy'; letting America get back to normal life as it had been before the war.

President Coolidge followed Harding. His key policies were:

- Isolation – the USA was not to get involved in foreign disputes.
- Tariffs – (e.g. the Fordney-McCumber tariff) were placed on foreign goods to make them expensive in the USA so that people would buy American goods instead.
- Low taxes – these helped businesses to grow, and workers had money to spend.

3. The boom period In the 1920s the profits of many American companies rose enormously. More goods were produced more quickly and more cheaply because of new mass-production techniques.

The biggest boom came in the industries making consumer goods – goods for ordinary families to buy. Sales of household goods such as vacuum cleaners and washing machines boosted the electrical industry.

The single most important industry was the motor industry – Henry Ford's cars were becoming increasingly common and by 1930 there were 30 million of them on the roads. A healthy car industry helped to create further jobs in related areas, such as car parts, and roadbuilding.

The figures in Source 1 below seem to support this image of a boom in the USA during the 1920s.

SOURCE 1 US government statistics (1929) on economic performance in the 1920s:

Production of cars	*1926*	*4.3 million*
	1929	*5.3 million*
Number of cars registered	*1920*	*8.1 million*
	1929	*23.0 million*
Value of radios sold (in US dollars)	*1922*	*60.0 million*
	1929	*824.5 million*

Advertising, credit and hire purchase all made it easy to spend. Wages for many Americans did rise, and there was a feeling of confidence, as the next source (from a 1991 examination paper) shows.

SOURCE 2 President Hoover in a speech in 1928:

We in America are nearer to the final victory over poverty than ever before in the history of any land.

As well as buying goods, Americans wanted a share of some of the profits which companies were making. To do this they bought and sold shares in companies.

4. Weaknesses in the US economy There were worrying weaknesses in the US economy during this period.

- Some major industries did not grow in the 1920s (e.g. coal, textiles).
- Farmers had produced too much food and prices were very low.
- Many ordinary Americans did not share in the boom. Black Americans in particular suffered from discrimination, getting the worst jobs.
- Some industries were struggling against foreign competition.
- Other industries could not export goods because of tariffs in other countries. Often these tariffs were simply a reaction to American tariffs.

The following source (from a 1991 examination paper) shows some of the differences in earnings.

SOURCE 3 US social survey of wages in 1929:

Average wages per month of American workers (in US dollars)

Farmers in South Carolina	*129*
Town workers in South Carolina	*412*
Town workers in New York	*881*
Fruit farmers in California	*1246*

Trusts were another problem. These huge companies dominated the business world. They worked together to keep wages down and to keep prices high, to ensure the largest profits possible. Republican policy (laissez-faire) gave them the freedom to operate in this way. However, the combination of low wages and high prices actually stopped many people from buying goods, and this stored up problems for the future.

REVISION TASKS

1. Use 4–6 key words to explain US industrial growth in the 1920s.
2. Construct and complete a table like the one below to show the main features of the US economy in the 1920s.

Signs of 'boom' or prosperity	Signs of weakness

C American society in the 1920s

Like its economy, American society was full of contrasts in the 1920s. There were very real advances for some Americans – they owned cars and electrical goods, and enjoyed themselves as never before.

1. Entertainment

During the 1920s films became a national obsession. Millions of Americans went to the cinema each week to watch new stars like Buster Keaton and Charlie Chaplin. Hollywood became the centre of a multi-million industry. At the same time, jazz music became a craze and the USA became the centre of a world entertainment industry.

2. Women

After the First World War women were given the vote in the USA. At the same time they gained greater freedom by working and earning their own money. One light-hearted symbol of this new independence was the flappers – independent young women named after their short skirts.

However, although about 8 million women were working, mainly as teachers or secretaries, most women were housewives doing the work they had always done.

3. Intolerance and isolationism

The 'Red Scare'

The communist revolution in Russia (see page 169) alarmed some Americans, particularly leading industrialists. They saw America's trade unions as a threat which could lead to a revolution.

The RADICALS in America's immigrant communities were immediate targets. They were suspected of planning revolution. Police, soldiers and ex-servicemen disrupted meetings, raided offices and thousands of people were arrested. The government was involved in and supported this campaign.

It was nothing like the scale of what was to come in Nazi Germany, but it was an unpleasant aspect of the USA in the 1920s.

In one extreme case, two Italian radicals, Vanzetti and Sacco, were executed for murder. Most historians are now convinced that they were innocent of this crime.

Immigration

Most Americans were immigrants or the children of immigrants. However, after the First World War the USA tried to slow down the flow of immigrants with the 1921 Immigration Act.

- By 1929 immigration had fallen from 850,000 a year (before the First World War) to 150,000.
- The 1924 Amendment to the Immigration Act meant that the majority of new immigrants came from Britain, Ireland and Germany rather than from Eastern Europe or Italy.

The Ku Klux Klan

The Klan was another example of the darker side of the 1920s in the USA. It was originally formed to terrorise black slaves after they had been given freedom in the nineteenth century. As well as blacks, the Klan also attacked Catholics and Jews. It was a movement of mainly poor whites concerned about their livelihoods in 1920s America – one sign that the 'Roaring Twenties' were not great times for all. The following gives some idea about the Klan.

SOURCE 4 R. A. Patton, writing about the actions of the Klan in Alabama in *Current History*, 1929:

A lad whipped with branches until his back was ribboned flesh: ...a white girl, divorcee, beaten into unconsciousness in her home; a naturalised foreigner flogged until his back was pulp because he married an American woman; a negro lashed until he sold his land to a white man for a fraction of its value.

4. Prohibition and crime By the end of the First World War, there was a strong temperance (anti-alcohol) movement in the USA. Temperance groups pressured the government to pass the 18th Amendment to the US Constitution – PROHIBITION. Brewing or selling alcohol was now illegal in the USA.

Prohibition was essentially a failure. It didn't stop the alcohol trade – it simply drove it underground. Bootleggers (criminal dealers in alcohol) made large amounts of money smuggling alcohol into the USA, or through illegal brewing. Secret bars called speakeasies were easy to find if you wanted to drink. Even the US President was known to drink.

Gangs of criminals began to run bootlegging and other forms of crime (gambling, drugs, prostitution) almost like a business. These gangs would sometimes fight with each other for control of the trade.

The most notorious gang leader was Al Capone, who virtually controlled the city of Chicago by bribing the mayor and other politicians. Capone was almost certainly responsible for the St Valentine's Day Massacre in 1929 when six members of a rival gang were killed.

▲ *Viewpoints and evidence*

When looking at this period, it is important to consider whether the 1920s were good times for all Americans. For example, were they good times for:

- women
- immigrants
- political radicals
- black Americans?

It is possible to make a selection of sources that will support either argument. Source 4, for example, would suggest that the USA was a terrible place in the 1920s, but Source 2 shows a very different picture. As historians we must look at a wide range of sources to make a balanced judgement. From the information in this section, it is clear that the USA in the 1920s was good for some, but much less so for others.

REVISION TASK

1. Construct a table like the one below and use the evidence and information in this section to complete it.

The USA in the 1920s	
High points	**Low points**

D The Wall Street Crash and the Depression

1. The causes of the Crash Historians can identify long-term and short-term causes of the Crash. The longer-term causes were the weaknesses in the US economy (see page 131):

- Overproduction in agriculture – driving prices down
- Overproduction of consumer goods – driving prices down
- Inequality – the rich were very rich while the poor were very poor
- Foreign competition – reducing demand for American goods.

Short-term causes related to shares. Many ordinary Americans bought shares in companies. Normally this is good for business.

However, in the USA in the 1920s the rush to buy shares caused problems:

- People bought and sold shares to make quick profits instead of keeping their money in one business.
- Companies were forced by shareholders to pay out profits to shareholders rather than re-investing them.
- Americans borrowed money on credit to buy their shares.

These kinds of share dealings depended on confidence that share prices would continue to rise. Once people started worrying about the long-term weaknesses in the American economy, disaster struck. In September 1929, the prices of shares began to edge down – slowly to start with – but people soon began to realise that the shares they owned were worth less than the loans they had used to buy them in the first place. All of a sudden, everyone tried to get rid of their shares, selling them for less and less. The worst day was 'Black Tuesday', 29 October 1929. As a result, share prices collapsed, as you can see in Source 5.

SOURCE 5 Share prices, 1928–9 (from the *Wall Street Journal*):

Company	*Share Values in cents*		
	3 Sept 1928	*3 Sept 1929*	*13 Nov 1929*
New York Central	*256*	*256*	*160*
Union Carbide and Carbon	*413*	*137*	*59*
Electric Bond and Share	*203*	*186*	*50*

2. The effects of the Crash The effects of the Crash were disastrous:

- Many individuals were bankrupt – they could not pay back the loans they used to buy their (now worthless) shares.
- Some home owners lost their homes as they could not pay their mortgages.
- Even some who had savings lost their money when banks collapsed.
- Many farmers suffered a similar fate as banks tried to get back their loans.

The confidence of individuals was shattered. Many faced unemployment, and those in work faced reduced hours and wages. They tightened their belts and stopped spending.

Big institutions also suffered:

- About 10,000 banks stopped trading between 1929 and 1933.
- At the same time demand for goods of all types fell.
- As a result, production fell and so did wages and jobs.

Unemployment rose dramatically as shown in the diagram:

3. President Hoover's response to the Crash

Most Americans blamed President Hoover for the Crash.

> **SOURCE 6** Slogan of protesting farmers in Iowa:
>
> *'In Hoover we trusted, now we are busted!'*

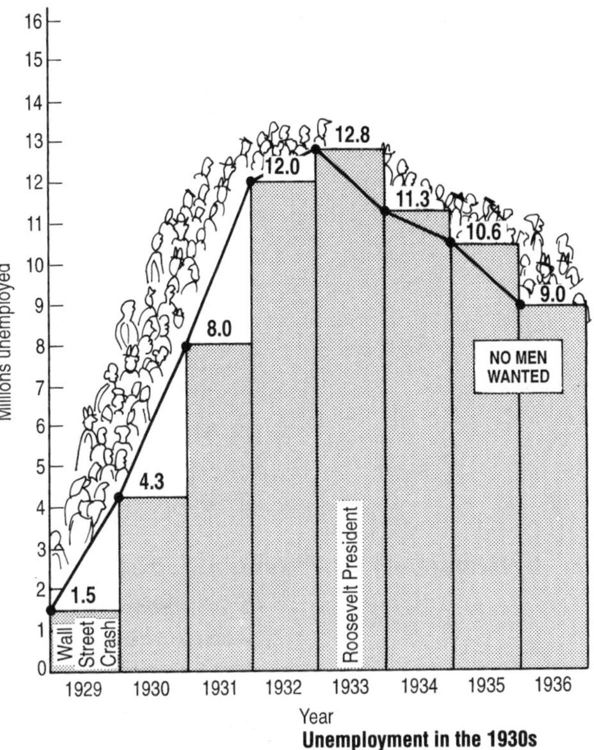

Unemployment in the 1930s

This was not really fair as there were larger forces at work than Hoover's policies. However, people blamed Hoover partly because of what he *did not do* as much as what he did. Hoover insisted that the situation was not too serious, and that 'prosperity is just around the corner'. This upset many Americans.

In some ways Hoover was unfairly criticised. He did take action between 1929 and 1933:

- He set up the Reconstruction Finance Corporation (RFC) which lent money to banks, industries and agriculture.
- He tried to encourage American exports (without much success).

Overall, however, he still believed in 'rugged individualism' and showed little sympathy for poor, starving Americans living in shanty towns called 'Hoovervilles'.

Among the most serious events of this troubled time was the 'Bonus Army' march of 1932. The 'Bonus Army' was made up of ex-servicemen who had fought in the First World War. They were due to be paid a bonus by 1945, but because of massive unemployment they were asking for it early. The marchers moved on Washington but were dispersed by troops. Hoover's reaction was to condemn the marchers.

REVISION TASKS

1. In your view what were the main causes of the Crash. Construct and complete a summary table like the one below.

Short-term causes	Long-term causes

2. How did the Crash affect Americans? Find 4–6 key words for your answer.

3. 'Hoover deserved all of the criticism and blame he got.' How far do you agree with this statement? Make a list of key words to summarise 'for' and 'against' arguments.

E Roosevelt and the New Deal

1. The presidential election, 1932 The main candidates in the presidential election of 1932 were opposites in many ways.

Franklin D. Roosevelt was well educated and a talented, passionate politician. He had complete faith in his ideas for bringing the USA out of the Depression and he communicated these ideas in his 'fireside chats' on the radio. His key phrase was his offer of a 'New Deal' for the American people in which the government would support them.

THE BUSINESS CYCLE

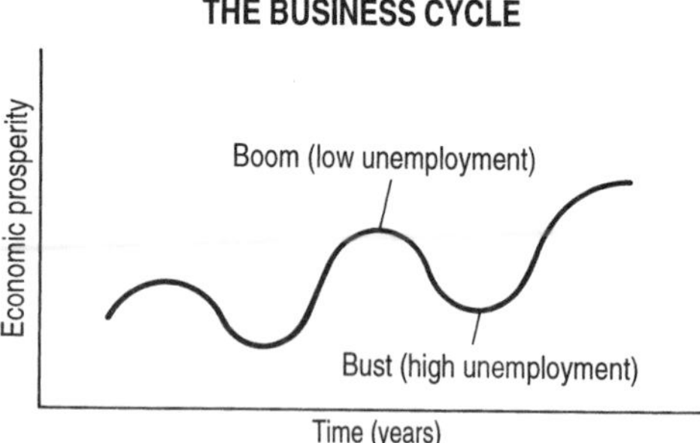

Comment: This graph shows the view of Classical Economists on how business works. Notice how economies go through periods of prosperity and then slump. Classical economists said that governments could do nothing to prevent the boom/bust cycle.

2. Roosevelt as President Roosevelt won the election by a large majority, although not all Americans supported him.

During the campaign it was clear that some powerful people and interests in America were lined up against him.

US Presidential Election result, November 1932

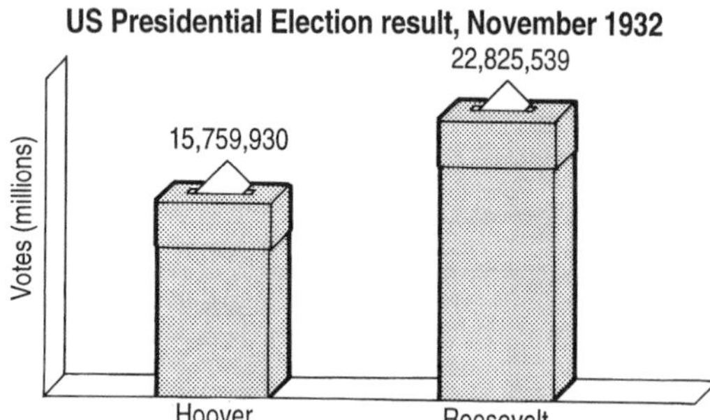

3. Roosevelt's first 'Hundred Days' Roosevelt was determined to act quickly. From March to June 1932 (the 'Hundred Days') he managed to get the US Congress to pass a huge amount of legislation. This is summarised in the table opposite.

4. Other 'New Deal' legislation As well as passing new legislation in his first hundred days of office, in later years Roosevelt updated some laws and created further legislation where it was needed.

- The Works Progress Administration (1935) replaced the CWA. It extended the range of work provided, from building work to the Federal Theatre Project which gave work to unemployed artists and writers.
- Wagner Act (1935) forced employers to recognise trade unions after the National Recovery Administration (NRA) was declared illegal by American courts. This law meant that workers kept the protection which the NRA had given them.
- Social Security Act (1935) allowed each of the USA's states to take part in an unemployment and old-age welfare scheme. However, the provisions were still far less comprehensive than in Germany or Britain.

▲ *Viewpoints and evidence*

To people at the time the New Deal was extraordinary. No US government had ever played such a large role in the lives of ordinary Americans. The key question on this topic is therefore:

- Was the New Deal an American social and economic revolution?

Historians disagree as Sources 7 and 8 show:

SOURCE 7 Historian Carel Degler, 1959:

The conclusion seems inescapable that the New Deal was a revolutionary response to a revolutionary situation.

Hundred Days Legislation March–June 1932		
Legislation	**Problem**	**Action**
Emergency Banking Act and Securities Exchange Commission	Americans had little confidence in the banks and might withdraw all their savings – this would lead to collapse.	Government closed all banks, and then officially backed 5,000 banks and reassured American people their money was safe. Securities Exchange Commission made sure that the speculation which caused 1929 Crash could not happen again.
Federal Emergency Relief Administration (FERA)	Poverty and unemployment	500 million dollars allocated to help relieve suffering of poor (food, clothing etc.). Seed and equipment for farmers, schemes to create jobs.
Civilian Conservation Corps (CCC)	Unemployment among young men	Men aged 18–25 given six months work. Had to send most of their pay home to parents/wives. About 300,000 joined in 1933; by 1940 there were 2 million.
Civil Works Administration (CWA) (became Works Progress Administration in 1935)	Unemployment	Paid for public works projects (e.g. schools, roads, hospitals) and used unemployed workers.
Agricultural Adjustment Administration (AAA)	Poverty, unemployment and low prices	Advised farmers on marketing and farming techniques and helped solve problem of overproduction by US government buying up produce. Farmers became more organised but wealthy farmers gained most.
National Industrial Recovery Act	General economic condition of USA	Set up NRA (National Recovery Administration) which set standards on working practices (hours, child labour). This helped create more jobs. Employers in the scheme displayed the Eagle symbol of government approval and the government encouraged people to use these firms. Over two million employers joined the scheme.
Tennessee Valley Authority (TVA)	Agricultural overproduction and regular flooding had ruined livelihoods of farm workers in Tennessee Valley. No alternative jobs in industry. Area covered parts of six states and was too big for any one state to deal with.	Huge public works projects: dams, irrigation, canals and water transport. Hydro-electric power created thousands of jobs. Farmers given loans and training in soil conservation. New housing built.

SOURCE 8 Historian Barton J. Bernstein, 1969:

The New Deal was neither a third American Revolution as Carl Degler suggests, nor even a half-way revolution ...

Sources 7 and 8 show how two historians can interpret the evidence differently. Later in this chapter we will look at different viewpoints expressed at the time.

5. Opposition to Roosevelt There were a number of groups in the USA who were critical of the New Deal.

1 Business leaders

They were unhappy about various aspects of the New Deal:

- Regulations on working conditions
- Trade unions
- Farmers had little freedom
- Its huge cost (which came from taxes paid by Americans).

2 The states

They were concerned about the New Deal because:

- Measures like the TVA cut right across the rights of individual states.
- Some states feared that the Federal government was becoming too powerful.

3 Politicians

Some politicians opposed the New Deal:

- Republicans (not surprisingly) bitterly opposed the Democrat Roosevelt.
- Even some conservative Democrats opposed him.
- Some radicals in the USA like Huey Long believed the New Deal did not go far enough.

4 The Supreme Court

The Supreme Court clashed with Roosevelt.

- Its judges (mainly old, Republican judges) ruled that several of the New Deal measures were illegal.
- Matters came to a head in 1937 when Roosevelt wanted to make some of his own supporters into Supreme Court judges. This plan failed but afterwards Supreme Court opposition was lessened.

REVISION TASKS

1. Produce your own profile of Hoover and Roosevelt.
2. Produce a key words list to summarise Roosevelt's plans.
3. Find three examples from this section which you could use to argue that the New Deal was a revolution.

▲ *Viewpoints and evidence*

The New Deal and its measures caused huge divisions in opinion in America. This is reflected in evidence from that time, such as Sources 9 and 10 which were published in American newspapers in election year, 1936. Are they supporting or opposing the New Deal? We can use our background knowledge of 1936, the election, Roosevelt's policies and his opponents to work out the purpose of both these cartoons.

The cartoon in Source 9 pokes fun at the industrialists. The 'poor' (but well-fed and well-dressed) industrialists are complaining about Roosevelt's New Deal. However, all around are newspaper headlines which show prosperity. This is a pro-New Deal cartoon.

SOURCE 9

The cartoon in Source 10 is anti-Roosevelt. We see him pumping away billions of dollars on a leaky pump and the water is supplied by the poor taxpayer. The clear message is that Roosevelt is wasting money on stupid schemes. This source comes from opponents of Roosevelt.

SOURCE 10

F Successes and failures of the New Deal

1. Roosevelt and the voters The most obvious success of Roosevelt in this period was that he won re-election in 1936, 1940 and 1944 – the only President ever to serve four terms of office. However, most historians agree that the New Deal had mixed results.

2. Assessing the New Deal

Weaknesses:

- When Roosevelt cut back his programmes in 1937 unemployment rose dramatically.
- He never really conquered unemployment in the 1930s; unemployment was only really solved by America's entry into the Second World War in 1941.
- America's trade (and the world's trade) did not recover.
- He failed to win over a large number of his own people (e.g. the Supreme Court).
- Black Americans gained relatively little from the New Deal.

Successes:

- In the USA the Depression did not lead to extreme movements like Communism or Nazism taking hold.
- Many millions of jobs were created and vital relief (food, shelter, clothing) was supplied to the poor.
- Agriculture and industry benefited from efficient infrastructure (roads, services).

▲ *Viewpoints and evidence*

Historians and others at the time argued about the success or failure of the New Deal. Here are two contrasting views expressed in the 1930s.

SOURCE 11 Letter sent to President Roosevelt in the 1930s:

Dear Mr President,
This is just to tell you everything is alright now. The man you sent found our house alright and we went down to the bank with him and the mortgage can go on for a while longer. You remember I wrote to you about losing the furniture too. Well, your man got it back for us. I never heard of a President like you, Mr Roosevelt. Mrs — and I are old folks and don't amount to much, but we are joined with millions of others in praying for you every night. God bless you Mr Roosevelt.

SOURCE 12 R. Shaw, *The New Deal – Its Unsound Theories and Irreconcilable Policies* (1935):

The New Deal is nothing more or less than an effort to take away from the thrifty what the thrifty and their ancestors have accumulated, and give it to others who have not earned it, or whose ancestors haven't earned it for them, and never would have earned it and never will earn it.

As historians, we have to take care in using these sources, for several reasons:

- Neither source is attempting to balance the successes and failures of the New Deal – each represents a single view.
- Each source could be a 'one-off'. We do not know how many letters like this Roosevelt received, and we are not sure how many agreed with Source 11. However, our knowledge of the period does help, because we know millions did vote for Roosevelt.
- As for Source 12, the title of the book from which this source has been taken is in itself an attack on the New Deal. It indicates the biased nature of the writer's argument.

The aim of this revision session is for you to see how you can apply your knowledge of the USA 1919–41 to answering some source-based questions.

Examination questions

This example is taken from MEG Paper 2, 1993. The set of questions is based on a series of extracts which deal with the attempts of President Roosevelt to restore prosperity to the USA during the Depression in the 1930s.

SOURCE A *From an interview published in 1970, with Blackie Gold who had been unemployed during the Depression.*

I was in the CCC for six monthes, I came home for fifteen months, looked around for work and couldn't make $30 a month, so I enlisted back into the CCC and went to Michigan. I spent another six months there planting trees and building forests. And came out. But still no money to be made. So back into the CCC again and spent four and a half months fighting fires.

Study Source A. What is meant by the CCC? *[2 marks]*

What is required? This question is essentially testing your knowledge (or recall). It requires a short definition and explanation of the CCC.

Ideas for your answer Explain that the CCC stands for Civilian Conservation Corps and that this organisation provided work for unemployed young men.

SOURCE C *A notice displayed on the walls of 'Thomas Edison Inc.', New Jersey, in April 1933, by the owner.*

President Roosevelt has done his part: now you do something. Buy something – buy anything, anywhere: paint your kitchen, give a party, get a car, pay a bill, rent a flat, get a haircut, see a show, build a house, take a trip, sing a song, get married. It does not matter what you do – but get going and keep going. The old world is starting to move.

Study Source C. How would the instruction: 'Buy something' help President Roosevelt's policies succeed? *[2 marks]*

What is required? This is similar to the question above, although you should show a little more background knowledge.

Ideas for your answer Roosevelt was trying to get people back to work and buying some item would give someone else a job producing or selling that item.

SOURCE D *A graph showing the numbers of unemployed people (in millions) in the USA, 1929 to 1942*

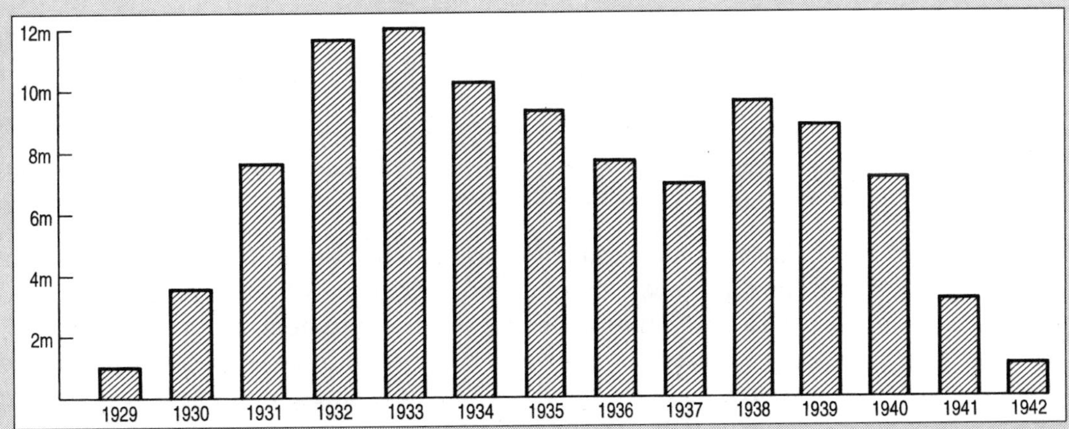

Study Source D. In what ways would this graph be useful to a historian studying the New Deal? Explain your answer. *[6 marks]*

What is required? This question carries 6 marks and examiners are looking for different levels of answers to award marks. A simple statement, for example: 'it gives useful information on unemployment' will only gain 1 or 2 marks. You need to give examples of how historians would use the source; point out that although it has some value it also has some limitations. If you do this then you will score higher marks.

Ideas for your answer

1. You could start by pointing out that Source D does give useful information on unemployment. Another point worth making is that graphs are not usually biased sources (unlike the cartoon Source B).
2. To reach the higher levels you need to explain how historians could use the figures. For example, historians could use the numbers of unemployed as a way to measure how well (or badly) Roosevelt's policies were working in the 1930s.
3. For a top level answer you should also explain that Source D itself is limited on its own. For example, it does not show whether unemployment is higher or lower in different parts of the USA, or among different groups of people.

SOURCE B *A US newspaper cartoon entitled: 'The spirit of the New Deal', published during Roosevelt's presidency. All three figures are wearing the badge of the National Industrial Recovery Administration.*

SOURCE E *Louis Banks recalls his life under the New Deal. He was interviewed in 1970.*

I was so glad when war came and I got in the army. I knew I was safe. I put a uniform on, and I said, 'Now I am safe'. I had money coming, I had food coming, and I had a lot of friends round me. I knew that on the streets or Hoboing*, I might be killed any time.
*(NB hoboing means being homeless and travelling round the country as a tramp)

Study Source B and Source E. Which of these two views of the results of the New Deal is the more reliable? Explain your answer. [*8 marks*]

What is required? This question requires you to show a range of skills. You must show that:

- you understand each source
- you can make use of different types of sources
- you can use your background knowledge of the topic to evaluate each source.

Simple statements of what the sources contain will score about 1–3 marks. To reach the next level you must explain how and why the sources are different.

To reach the top levels you need to 'test' each source for its reliability and explain your conclusion to the examiner. You do not really need to 'choose' one source as more reliable; it is more important to explain the strengths and weaknesses of each source.

Ideas for your answer

1. It is a good idea to take each source in turn. When you look at Source B you could first point out that it gives a rosy picture of the New Deal. We see 'Uncle Sam' (the USA), workers and bosses all pulling together in the NRA. Source E, however, gives a different view. Louis Banks obviously suffered as a 'hobo' in the New Deal years. You can now 'test' each source.

2. Source B is a newspaper cartoon. These are nearly always biased for or against whatever they show – in this case for. However, your background knowledge tells you that although many Americans supported the NRA, many also opposed it (see page 138–9 for examples). Overall, then, Source B is rather one-sided.

3. Source E is a different type of source – one man's memory of the 1930s. As historians we might question the accuracy of his memory. However, your background knowledge (and Source D) tells you that there were millions of unemployed 'hobos' in the 1930s. Overall, then, you might conclude that this source is a reliable view of one man's experiences, but is only evidence about one man.

Study all the sources. 'The New Deal was not successful in restoring prosperity'.
Do these sources show this view is true? Explain your answer fully. [*12 marks*]

What is required? This question is the most important in the set. The examiner wants you to reach a conclusion on the question and support your answer by referring to these sources and commenting on their value, reliability and usefulness.

At the lowest level (2–3 marks) examiners will look for general comments about the New Deal, not really using the sources.

The next level of answer (4–5 marks) should have a conclusion, but not really well backed up by evidence or examples.

To reach the next level (6–7 marks) you must reach a conclusion and explain which sources support your conclusion. To get higher still (8–12 marks) you must do all of this but you must also show that you understand that all of the sources have their strengths and weaknesses. Overall, your aim is to produce a balanced response.

Ideas for your answer

1. A good way to start is to point out what your conclusion will be. In this case, the sources present a mixed view on whether or not the New Deal was successful.

2. Source A presents a mixed view. First, it is the view of just one man. On the one hand he cannot get a normal job in the 1930s but on the other he can get a job with the CCC.

3. Source B suggests that the New Deal was successful in bringing prosperity but we have already looked at how reliable this source is in the fourth question – it is a cartoon and almost certainly biased, and background knowledge of events of the period suggests that the NRA had its failures as well as successes.

4. Source C also presents a mixed view. The writer seems to support Roosevelt and is confident about recovery saying 'the old world is about to move'. However, the date of the source (April 1933) suggests that maybe people had to be pushed to spend money – in other words they did not feel prosperous in 1933.

5. Source D again presents a mixed view. From 1933–7 it shows some success for the New Deal as unemployment falls. Even so unemployment is still high, even in 1937. In 1938 it rises and only war actually solves the problem. Overall, then, Source D suggests partial success for the New Deal but again it does not present a complete picture, as we saw in the third question.

6. Source E presents a negative view of the New Deal. Again we saw in the fourth question that this is the view of only one man. However, our background knowledge tells us that there were many thousands like him. This source does support the view that the New Deal was not successful.

Conclusion: The general impression is that most of the sources support the view that the New Deal was not successful. However, at least one source does not support the view and some of the others suggest that while the New Deal was not entirely successful it was not entirely unsuccessful.

SUMMARY AND REVISION PLAN

Below is a list of headings which you might find helpful. Use this as a check list to make sure you are familiar with the material featured in this chapter. Record your key words alongside each heading.

A The US system of government
- Federal system
- Congress
- Supreme Court
- political parties
- the President

B The economic boom of the 1920s
1. The USA up to 1920
2. Republican policies
3. The boom period
4. Weaknesses in the US economy

C American society in the 1920s
1. Entertainment
2. Women
3. Intolerance and isolationism
   - the 'Red Scare'
   - immigration
   - the Ku Klux Klan
4. Prohibition and crime

D The Wall Street Crash and the Depression
1. The causes of the Crash
2. The effects of the Crash
3. President Hoover's response

E Roosevelt and the New Deal
1. The presidential election, 1932
2. Roosevelt as President
3. Roosevelt's first 'Hundred Days'
4. Other 'New Deal' legislation
5. Opposition to Roosevelt

F Successes and failures of the New Deal
1. Roosevelt and the voters
2. Assessing the New Deal
   - weaknesses
   - successes

CHAPTER 11 Germany, 1918–45

In 1918 Germany was defeated in the First World War. The country was in chaos. There were attempts at revolution. In the 1920s Germany recovered but the Depression caused enormous problems which allowed Hitler and the Nazi party to gain power. From 1933 to 1945 Hitler ruled Germany which had disastrous consequences for both Germany and the wider world.

To answer source-based questions on Germany between 1918 and 1945, you need to be familiar with both the key content and the key themes of the period. This will help you to show your understanding of documents and other sources relating to this topic.

KEY CONTENT

You will need to have a good working knowledge of these areas:

A The origins of the Weimar Republic
B Economic and political problems in Germany during the 1920s
C German recovery in the 1920s under Stresemann
D The effects of the Depression on Germany
E How the Nazis took power
F Life in Nazi Germany
G Nazi treatment of the Jews
H Opposition to the Nazis
I Nazi economic policy and foreign policy
J Germany and the Second World War

KEY THEMES

You will also be asked to show your understanding of some key themes:

- **The effects of the Treaty of Versailles on Germany**
- **The effects of German defeat in the First World War on the German people**
- **The problems caused by hyper-inflation and economic collapse in 1923**
- **The successes and failures of the Weimar Republic**
- **The impact of the Depression on Germany**
- **The reasons for the rise of the Nazi party**
- **The extent of opposition to the Nazis after 1933**

Source-based questions test both your knowledge of the topic and your understanding of documents and other sources from the period being studied. For example, look at this extract from MEG Paper 2, 1994.

SOURCE B *Table showing food prices (in Reichsmarks) 1918–23:*

Commodity	1918	1922	August 1923	Nov 1923
1 egg	0.25	180	5,000	80,000,000
500g butter	3.00	2,400	150,000	6,000,000,000
1kg bread	0.53	163	69,000	201,000,000

Study Source B. In what ways might this source be useful to an historian studying Weimar Germany? Explain your answer. [*6 marks*]

This question is asking you to show that

- *You understand the information in the source and the idea of utility (how useful a source is)*
- *You know the context of the source. In other words you understand the links between inflation and social problems in Germany 1918–23.*

We will look at this question in more detail at the end of this chapter.

A The origins of the Weimar Republic

When Germany was clearly losing the First World War, the German Kaiser William II abdicated. In November 1918, the government of Germany was left in the hands of the Chancellor, Fredrich Ebert. Ebert and his colleagues drew up a new democratic constitution for Germany. In the summer of 1919, Ebert was elected the first President of the new Weimar Republic.

1. A democratic Germany In theory, the new Weimar constitution gave Germany a nearly perfect democratic system.

- The 'lower house', or Reichstag, was elected by PROPORTIONAL REPRESENTATION (the number of representatives from a given party was determined by how many votes that party gained nationally). The vote was by secret ballot and universal suffrage (everyone could vote). Elections were to be held at least every four years.
- The 'upper house', or Reichsrat, was made up of representatives from each of the German states. It could delay new laws.
- The President was also the head of state and was elected every seven years. The President appointed a Chancellor (usually the head of the largest party in the Reichstag) to form a government. The Chancellor's role was therefore similar to the Prime Minister's role in Britain.

In practice, it proved very difficult to get one party into power. Governments were usually COALITIONS of different parties and they tended not to last very long.

2. Problems in the new Republic In the years immediately after the First World War, the new Weimar Republic was constantly under threat from extreme political groups.

Opposition from the left

Communists in Germany, known as Spartacists, wanted a revolution similar to that in Russia in 1917 (see page169).

- In January 1919 communist activists led by Karl Liebnecht and Rosa Luxembourg seized power in Berlin and the Baltic ports.
- In Bavaria, an independent socialist state was created under the leadership of Kurt Eisner.
- Within weeks, however, all the revolts had been crushed by regular troops and ex-soldiers (Freikorps). The communist leaders were assassinated.

The Kapp putsch

German nationalists saw democracy as weak. For many nationalists the new Weimar Republic was a symbol of Germany's defeat in the war. They were furious with the government for signing the hated Treaty of Versailles. Source 1 below expresses what many people in Germany felt about the treaty at the time.

SOURCE 1 *Deutsche Zeitung*, 28 June 1919:

VENGEANCE, GERMAN NATION!
Today in the Hall of Mirrors, the disgraceful treaty is being signed. Do not forget it. The German people will reconquer the place among the nations to which they are entitled. Then will come vengeance for the shame of 1919.

They associated the Weimar government with Germany's defeat in the war. They wanted to see a strong government that would make Germany great once again.

- In March 1920, Wolfgang Kapp, an extreme nationalist, and a group of Freikorps units seized power in Berlin.
- Kapp was not supported by the workers in the factories. The workers organised a strike in Berlin in support of the government. Within hours, the German capital came to a halt and supplies of gas, water and coal stopped.

- After four days Kapp and his supporters gave up and fled Berlin. Ebert and the Weimar government returned to power.

Source 2 below gives us Kapp's view of the new Weimar Republic:

SOURCE 2 Wolfgang Kapp, March 1920:

The nation is in grave danger. We are approaching the collapse of law and order. Hardship is growing. Starvation threatens. The government has no authority and is corrupt. We are threatened with Bolshevism. We shall get rid of this weak republic and replace it with a strong government.

Kapp was obviously biased against the Weimar government. Even so, the source shows how some people viewed the government in 1920: weak, corrupt and having no authority.

Other political murders

There was much political violence during the early years of the Weimar government. Riots and lawlessness were common, and two leading Weimar politicians were murdered.

- On 26 August 1921 the German Finance Minister Matthias Erzberger was murdered by extreme nationalists. He had been the leading German representative at the signing of the peace treaty in 1918.
- On 24 June 1922 four extreme nationalists shot the popular German Jewish Foreign Minister Walther Rathenau. He had recently negotiated the Treaty of Rapallo to improve relations with communist Russia. Many nationalists were fanatically anti-communist and anti-semitic.

REVISION TASKS

1. Make a list of key words to show that the new Republic was not popular in Germany.
2. Give two examples of threats to the new Republic.

B Economic and political problems in Germany during the 1920s

1. Reparations and the invasion of the Ruhr According to the terms of the Treaty of Versailles, Germany would have to pay for the damage caused during the First World War. These payments were known as reparations and were a major burden to the new state:

- The Reparations Commission announced that Germany would be required to pay £6,600 million in gold in annual instalments.
- In 1922 the German government announced it would not be able to pay and asked for more time.

The British government agreed to this but the French government insisted that Germany must pay. In January 1923 the French and Belgian governments sent troops into the Ruhr, the centre of German industry. The results were disastrous for Germany:

- German workers used 'passive resistance' against the invaders (they did not fight but they refused to co-operate).
- The German economy ground to a halt.

2. Hyper-inflation The problem of making the reparation payments encouraged the Weimar government to print more and more money. However, printing money simply caused prices to rise out of control and hyper-inflation set in. The German mark became virtually worthless:

Value of the German mark against US dollar, 1914–23	
1914	\$1 = 4 marks
1922	\$1 = 7,000 marks
July 1923	\$1 = 160,000 marks
Nov 1923	\$1 = 4,200,000,000 marks

- As prices rose people's savings became worthless (this hit the middle classes particularly hard). In 1923, prices in shops were increased almost every hour.
- At times workers were paid twice a day so that they might be able to buy food before prices rose again.
- People (such as pensioners) on fixed incomes suffered badly.
- Prices rose much faster than incomes and many people starved as they were unable to afford food or fuel.

SOURCE 3 A middle-class woman recalls her experience of hyper-inflation in 1923:

My husband set up his practice as an eye surgeon. My own income was fixed at 30,000 marks. However, 80 per cent of my husband's patients paid their fees three months after the treatment. We were virtually without any income. My brother-in-law owned a factory and, like all businessmen, was well off. His wife and I had our babies within a few days of each other and I remember how I was lying in a borrowed iron bedstead with my baby in a borrowed cradle, while she had everything for herself and her baby in pure silk. And yet we both came from the same sort of family background.

3. Crisis under control In September 1923, at the height of the economic crisis, a new government was formed by Gustav Stresemann.

- He stopped the printing of worthless paper money in November 1923.
- He created a new currency called the Rentenmark.

- He also called off the resistance against the French occupation by German workers in the Ruhr. The German economy began to recover slowly, although French troops did not withdraw from the Ruhr until 1925.

4. The Munich putsch Weimar Germany faced political as well as economic troubles in this period. In 1923 a new nationalist leader called Adolf Hitler first came to prominence.

In November 1923 Hitler and the Nazis tried to seize control of the Bavarian government. The plan was to capture Munich and from there march on Berlin. Hitler was convinced people would join him in overthrowing the failed Weimar regime.
- On 9 November, Hitler forced members of the Bavarian government to join him.
- The Nazi plan soon began to go wrong. Bavarian police opened fire on Nazi stormtroopers in Munich and 16 Nazis were killed.
- Ludendorff (the former First World War general who was now a Nazi supporter) and Hitler were arrested and charged with high treason.

However, it was clear that Hitler's views had some support in Germany.
- Hitler received the minimum sentence. Many Nazi supporters also received light sentences.
- Hitler served his sentence in the comfortable Landsberg Fortress and spent his time writing his memoirs.
- The memoirs were later published as *Mein Kampf* (My Struggle). In this book, Hitler outlined his view of German history and his views on Germany's rightful place in the world.

▲ *Viewpoints and evidence*

The Munich Putsch became an important piece of Nazi propaganda once they gained power. The sources below show two differing accounts of Hitler's role in the events.

SOURCE 4 From the official biography of Hitler published by the Nazi party in 1934:

The body of the man with whom Hitler was linked shot up into the air like a ball, tearing Hitler's arm with him, so that it sprang from the joint and fell back limp and dead ... Hitler approached the man and stooped over him ... a boy severely wounded. Blood was pouring from his mouth. Hitler picked him up and carried him on his shoulders.

SOURCE 5 Rudolf Olden, *Hitler the Pawn* (written in 1936):

At first shot Hitler had flung himself to the ground. He sprained his arm, but this did not prevent him from running. He found his car and drove into the mountains.

Which of these two sources gives us the most reliable version of this event? To answer this, it is important to think about why they were written. Source 4 was written as a piece of Nazi propaganda and its purpose was to portray Hitler as a hero. The actions described are improbable – especially for someone who has sustained a severe injury. It is therefore unreliable as a piece of evidence.

Source 5, however, also has its problems. We do not know if Rudolf Olden was a Nazi, communist, liberal or none of these. His evidence is so uncomplimentary about Hitler that we must be a little suspicious about this in the same way that we are about Source 4.

REVISION TASKS

1. Is Source 3 a reliable source about hyper-inflation in 1923? Use 4–6 key words to outline your view.
2. Use the information and evidence in this section to complete the table below. Your aim is to produce a key words summary of each and to give each one a rating on a scale of 1–10 in terms of its seriousness for the Weimar Republic.

Threat	Date	Outline of events	Rating
1. Spartacist revolt			
2. Kapp Putsch			
3. French invasion of the Ruhr			
4. Hyper-inflation			
5. Munich Putsch			

C German recovery in the 1920s under Stresemann

1. Economic recovery From the end of 1923 the German economy began to recover.

- There was a new currency, the Rentenmark, and industries in the Ruhr had begun production again.
- In 1924 Stresemann, now the Foreign Minister, signed the Dawes Plan (see page 25). Germany received huge loans from the USA and reparation payments were made easier.
- German industry began to benefit from new investment and unemployment fell sharply.

2. The Locarno treaties During the mid 1920s, Stresemann's aim was to get Germany accepted again as a member of the international community. He had great success in this field:

- Germany signed the Locarno treaties in 1925 (see page 26).
- In 1926 Germany was admitted into the League of Nations.

3. Extremist groups Despite the gradual recovery of the German economy, extreme political groups in Germany continued to grow.

- In the elections of 1924 and 1928 the Nazis won only 14 and 12 seats in the Reichstag. Throughout the country, however, Hitler was building a small but firm base of support.
- The communists were also organising themselves throughout the country. They created the Red Fighting League and regularly fought street battles with Nazi thugs. In 1924 the Communists held 45 seats in the Reichstag and this grew to 54 in the 1928 election.

REVISION TASK

1. How had Germany changed by the end of the 1920s? Use a key words list to summarise the changes under the following headings.

	1921	1928
Economy		
Employment		
International affairs		
Politics at home		

D The effects of the Depression on Germany

1. Effects of the Wall Street Crash, 1929

The recovery of the German economy was fragile. It depended heavily on American money. In 1929 disaster struck with the Wall Street Crash:

- Many American banks were forced to recall their loans. German companies were unable to pay.
- German businesses began to close. Millions lost their jobs.

2. Unemployment and the rise of extremism

Between 1928 and 1930 German unemployment rose from 2.5 to 4 million. This provided an opportunity for extremist groups such as the communists and Nazis.

- As unemployment rose, more and more people felt let down by the Weimar government and began to support extremist parties.
- In the 1930 election the Communists increased their number of seats in the Reichstag from 54 to 77.
- Nazi support increased from 12 seats in 1928 to 107 in 1930. The Nazis were now the second largest political party in the Reichstag.

REVISION TASK

1. What factors changed the prospects for the Nazis between the beginning and end of the 1920s? Use 4–6 key words for your answer.

E How the Nazis took power: the German elections, 1932–3

1. How the Depression helped Hitler The Depression helped Hitler in several ways:

- It caused a period of chaos in Germany.
- No government could take control of the situation and solve Germany's terrible economic problems.
- Unemployment was the big issue. By July 1932 it stood at 6 million. Hitler promised to get these people back to work. Through clever campaigning and his brilliant speaking skills Hitler gained support in many parts of German society, including the support of wealthy and powerful industrialists.

In two years he led the Nazi party from being the second largest party in the Reichstag to being the only legal party in Germany. By July 1933 the Weimar Republic and the democracy it represented had been destroyed.

2. The presidential election, 1932 In the 1932 election Hitler stood against the ageing President Hindenburg for the position of President.

- In his speeches, Hitler blamed the 'November criminals' (those who had signed the Treaty of Versailles) and Jews for the problems Germany was facing.
- He promised to build a better Germany, and many people believed him.

Hitler did not win, but he only lost to Hindenburg on a second vote. The Nazis felt they were close to success.

3. Elections for the Reichstag, July 1932 The 1932 general election campaign was very violent. Nazis and Communists fought each other in street battles and nearly 100 people were killed.

The Nazis became the largest party in the Reichstag and Hitler demanded to be made Chancellor. However, Hindenburg was suspicious of Hitler and refused. Instead, he appointed a moderate, Franz von Papen (leader of the Social Democrats), as Chancellor.

4. **Fresh Reichstag elections, November 1932** To achieve his aims von Papen needed to increase his support in the Reichstag and so he called another election in November 1932.

The Nazis lost seats in this election, but they still remained the largest party. Von Papen did not get the increased support he needed.

5. **Hitler becomes Chancellor** It was becoming increasingly clear that President Hindenburg could not continue to work with a Chancellor who did not have support in the Reichstag. He simply could not pass any of the measures he wanted.

- Hindenburg and von Papen decided to make Hitler Chancellor.
- They believed they would be able to control him once he was in power.
- On 30 January 1933 Hitler became German Chancellor and von Papen Vice-Chancellor.

As soon as he was appointed, Hitler tried to find a way of increasing the number of Nazis in his government. He persuaded his colleagues there should be another general election.

6. **The Reichstag fire, February 1933** During the election campaign, the Reichstag was burnt to the ground. A communist, Marianus van der Lubbe, was arrested for the crime. It presented Hitler with an excellent opportunity:

- The Nazis were quick to blame the communists.
- Hitler persuaded President Hindenburg to pass an emergency law restricting personal liberty.
- Using the law, thousands of communist supporters were thrown in prison and the Nazis increased their control of the Reichstag in the election.

Despite increasing their share of the vote, the Nazis still did not have an overall majority in the Reichstag. They were forced to join together with the 52 nationalist members to create a government.

Election results, 1932–3

Presidential election result, 1932

Candidate	No of votes
Hindenburg	19 million
Hitler (Nazi)	13 million
Thalman (Communist)	4 million

General election results, July 1932

Moderate parties	No of seats
Social Democrats	133
Centre Party	75
Extremists	
Communists (left wing)	89
Nazis (right wing)	230
Nationalists	40

General election results, November 1932

Moderate parties	No of seats
Social Democrats	121
Centre Party	70
Extremists	
Communists (left wing)	100
Nazis (right wing)	196
Nationalists	51

General election results, March 1933

Moderate parties	No of seats
Social Democrats	120
Centre Party	73
Extremists	
Communists (left wing)	81
Nazis (right wing)	288
Nationalists	52

▲ *Viewpoints and evidence*

The Nazis' rise to power presents a number of important questions for historians. These often form a focus for examination questions:

- Could the Nazis have gained the support they did without the impact of the Depression?
- How was Hitler helped by the failings of the Weimar constitution?
- How much support did the Nazis really have?
- Did Hindenburg and other leading German figures underestimate Hitler?

The Reichstag fire was a particularly important moment in the Nazis' rise to power. A key question here is whether the fire was in fact staged by the Nazis. The following sources address this possibility.

SOURCE 6 Rudolph Diels, head of the Prussian (German) military police explaining what he found at the police office in the Reichstag:

Marianus van der Lubbe was being questioned. He was smeared in dirt and sweating. He panted as if he had completed a tremendous task. There was a wild triumphant gleam in his eyes. He had communist pamphlets in his pockets.

SOURCE 7 William Shirer, an American writing about the Reichstag fire in 1959:

From Goering's palace an underground passage ran to the Reichstag building. Through this tunnel Karl Ernst, a former hotel porter who had become the leader of the Berlin SA, led his stormtroopers. They scattered petrol and quickly returned to the palace. At the same time, van der Lubbe climbed in and set some fires of his own.

SOURCE 8 Adolf Hitler, 28 February 1933:

This act of arson is the most outrageous act yet committed by communists in Germany. The burning of the Reichstag was to have been the signal for a bloody uprising and civil war....

These sources illustrate the problem of dealing with conflicting evidence. They suggest three possible explanations of the fire:

- van der Lubbe acted alone.
- van der Lubbe acted on behalf of the communists.
- Nazi stormtroopers (the SA) caused the fire hoping to blame the communists and win more support for Hitler in the general election.

The historian needs to consider each source carefully. Source 7 sounds balanced and confident, but where did Shirer get his evidence? Source 6 may be a primary source but it is evidence from a Nazi police officer. Source 8 shows Hitler quickly taking the opportunity to spread anti-communist propaganda.

7. Hitler takes control: the Enabling Act, March 1933 Hitler still did not have enough support to have complete control of Germany. An Enabling Act would give him the right to pass laws for the next four years without having to obtain the support of members in the Reichstag. However, to pass an Enabling Act Hitler needed to obtain the votes of two-thirds of Reichstag members, but he only had the support of just over a half. This is what happened:

- Hitler ordered his SA (stormtroopers) to continue intimidating the opposition.
- The 81 communist members of the Reichstag were expelled and the Enabling Act was passed by 441 to 91.

- Hitler was given the power to rule for four years without consulting the Reichstag.

In July 1933 Hitler increased his grip on power even further. Using the powers of the Enabling Act he outlawed all other parties and Germany became a one-party state. The democratic Weimar Republic had been destroyed and Germany had become a dictatorship.

8. Hitler turns on the SA Once he had gained power, Hitler's priority was to rid himself of possible rivals. Ernst Röhm, leader of the SA (stormtroopers) had played a major role in helping Hitler achieve power. However:

- The SA was seen by the German army as a rival. It would not support Hitler unless the SA was disbanded.
- Some members of the SA looked to Hitler to follow a socialist programme of reform. Hitler was opposed to this since he knew he would lose the support of wealthy industrialists.
- Röhm was a threat to Hitler's dominance of the Nazi party.

Hitler made a deal with the generals of the German army. They promised to support him as commander-in-chief of the armed forces if the SA was disbanded, and if he started a programme of rearmament. On 30 June 1934 SS assassination squads murdered Hitler's potential SA rivals (including Röhm). It has been estimated that up to 400 people were killed in the 'Night of the Long Knives'.

Just over one month later, President Hindenburg died. Hitler combined the posts of Chancellor and President and also became commander-in-chief of the armed forces. From this point onwards soldiers swore personal allegiance to Hitler who officially became known as *der Führer* (the leader).

REVISION TASKS

1. Use the information and evidence in this section to create a timeline of Hitler's steps to power.
2. Do you think that President Hindenburg underestimated Hitler?
3. Make a key words list to explain why the Enabling Act was so important.

F Life in Nazi Germany

1. Propaganda

Nazis believed in complete loyalty and obedience. One of the major tools for this was propaganda. Hitler made Joseph Goebbels Minister of Enlightenment and Propaganda.

Goebbels' job was to spread Nazi ideas and encourage all Germans to be loyal to Hitler. Goebbels (a former journalist) used his new powers to control all information that reached the German people in the following ways:

- All newspapers were censored by the government and only allowed to print stories favourable to the Nazis.
- Radio was also controlled by the government. Cheap radios were manufactured so that most Germans could afford one. Goebbels made sure that all radio plays, stories and news items were favourable to the Nazis.
- The Nazis took control of the German film industry. German films of the 1930s often showed great German heroes defeating their enemies. Cartoons were used to show Jews as weak and devious.
- Goebbels often organised mass rallies. The most spectacular was held each August in Nuremburg. At the rallies hundreds of thousands of Nazi supporters listened to choirs, sang songs and watched sporting events and firework displays.
- The Nazis used sporting events to spread their propaganda. The 1936 Berlin Olympics was used by the Nazis to suggest the superiority of the 'Aryan race'.

2. Victims of propaganda The main aim of propaganda was to provide the German people with a Nazi view of events. However, another aim was to target certain groups inside and outside Germany. These included:

- anyone who supported the terms of the Treaty of Versailles
- foreigners who criticised Hitler and the Nazis
- communists and socialists
- democrats and liberals
- Jews.

3. A police state

In July 1933 Germany became a one-party state. All other political parties were banned and people who openly criticised the Nazis were imprisoned. This policy was enforced ruthlessly by the SS (Hitler's bodyguard) and the Gestapo (secret police).

- They used terror tactics to intimidate, arrest and even kill any possible opponents.
- Enemies of the Nazis, such as liberals, socialists and communists, were often arrested and sent without trial to concentration camps.

4. Nazi control of society The Nazis took control of key parts of everyday life:

Education

Teachers had to belong to the German Teachers League and follow a Nazi curriculum.

- School textbooks were rewritten in support of Nazi ideas and history.
- Children were taught that the 'Aryan' race was superior to others.
- Outside school, parents were encouraged to allow their children to join youth groups organised by the Nazis (e.g. Hitler Youth, German Girls League), where they were indoctrinated with Nazis ideas and beliefs.

The Church

In 1933, the Catholic Church in Germany signed an agreement (Concordat) with Hitler. Both sides agreed not to interfere with each other.

The Nazis closed down a number of church organisations and set up their own 'church' called the Reich Church. It was not Christian and banned followers from using the Bible, crosses and religious symbols.

Role of women

- Hitler stated that women's role was: *Kinder, Kirche und Küche* (children, church and the kitchen).
- There were financial incentives in the Law for the Encouragement of Marriage.
- Homes for unmarried mothers were created.

The extracts below provide interesting views of how the Nazis saw the role of women.

SOURCE 9 Martha Dodd, *My years in Germany*, 1939:

Women have been deprived of all rights except that of childbirth and hard labour. They are not permitted to participate in political life – in fact Hitler's plans eventually include the deprivation of the vote; they are refused opportunities of education and self-expression; careers and professions are closed to them.

SOURCE 10 Joseph Goebbels, 1934:

Woman has the task of being beautiful and bringing children into the world, and this is by no means as coarse and old fashioned as one might think. The female bird preens herself and her mate and hatches her eggs for him.

Work

The Labour Front replaced trade unions. Workers were not allowed to leave their jobs without government permission, and strikes were made illegal.

Opposition was rare. By the late 1930s pay had increased and workers accepted the long working hours and lack of rights because of the higher pay.

Leisure

The 'Strength Through Joy' movement organised leisure activities and provided the public with sports facilities, cheap holidays and entertainments.

It also helped to plan the production of a 'people's car' (Volkswagen) cheap enough for many workers to afford. Many new motorways (autobahns) were built in the 1930s by the unemployed.

G Treatment of the Jews

Although all opponents of the Nazi regime were persecuted, it was the Jews who received the worst treatment of all.

1. Persecution

In 1933 the Nazis organised a boycott of all Jewish businesses, doctors, dentists etc. Jewish shops were marked with the star of David and the word '*Jude*'.

In education, Jewish children were intimidated at school and Germans were taught that Jews were unclean and responsible for Germany's defeat in the First World War.

In 1935 the Nuremberg Laws were introduced in Germany. Under these laws:

- Jews could no longer be German citizens.
- Marriages between Jews and Aryans were forbidden.
- Jews had to wear a yellow star on their clothing.

Kristallnacht

It is not clear how much most Germans knew about the persecution. However, in 1938 an event occurred which left nobody in any doubt.

In November 1938 a Polish Jew, Herschel Grunspan shot a German diplomat in Paris. Hitler ordered an immediate attack on Jews and their property in Germany. Between 9 and 10 November, thousands of Jewish businesses were attacked and 200 synagogues burnt down. This was called *Kristallnacht* 'the night of the broken glass'.

Violence against Jews in Germany increased. Himmler, head of the SS, began to expand the building of concentration camps.

▲ *Views and evidence*

Below are two differing views about *Kristallnacht*. The key question to be answered is, which source gives the more reliable view of the events of 9 November 1938:

SOURCE 11 Nazi press statement, 10 November 1938:

It was a spontaneous wave of anger throughout Germany as a result of the cowardly murder of Third Secretary von Rath in the German Embassy in Paris.

SOURCE 12 An American observer, 1938:

The damage was done by SS men and stormtroopers not in uniform, each group having been provided with hammers, axes, crowbars and incendiary bombs.

As with the other sources we have examined, the test for reliability depends particularly upon who wrote the source and why he/she wrote it. Source 11 gives a Nazi view of events and we have little reason to trust what it says. Source 12 is probably a more reliable view of events and it is supported by our background knowledge. However, Source 12 would be more useful (and we could be more sure about its reliability) if we knew who the observer was, and where he or she had observed the events described. In this way we would be able to cross check this description with other evidence.

3. The 'Final Solution' At the beginning of 1942, when the Second World War was at its height, Hitler ordered the extermination of all Jews in Europe. This policy of genocide became known as the 'Final Solution'.

- New extermination camps were built and older camps updated.
- Between 1942 and 1945, 4.5 million Jews were gassed in death camps such as Auschwitz, Treblinka, Dachau and Buchenwald.
- In total, the Nazis murdered over 6 million Jews.

H Opposition to the Nazis

Many Germans thought Hitler was a fine leader and genuinely supported him. Even among those who did not, many were unwilling to put their lives at risk. The Gestapo could arrest people merely on suspicion of opposing the government. People were encouraged to inform on others. Many people were imprisoned and executed without trial. Given this use of terror, together with the brainwashing techniques used by Goebbels and the youth groups, it is understandable why there was so little opposition.

However, there was some:

- Many people, including Jews, left Germany and fled to other countries. These included famous scientists, artists, writers and musicians who criticised the Nazi regime.
- Some church leaders such as the Cardinal Archbishop of Munich and the Lutheran Pastor Niemöller spoke out against Hitler. Niemöller was arrested in 1937 and spent the next eight years in concentration camps.

The Stauffenberg plot The most famous opposition plot against Hitler took place on 20 July 1944, six weeks after the allied armies had successfully landed in German-occupied France (D Day). A group of army officers led by Colonel von Stauffenberg attempted to blow up Hitler at his Prussian headquarters. The bomb killed four people but Hitler survived with damaged eardrums.

The plotters were arrested within hours, put on trial and executed.

▲ *Viewpoints and evidence*
Sources 13 and 14 show how effectively the Nazis had crushed opposition:

SOURCE 13 Emmi Bonhoeffer,opponent of Hitler:

I avoid the word resistance movement. A movement means you could move. We couldn't. In a dictatorship you can't move.... you can't work publicly for your opinion. .... you cannot develop a resistance movement when people feel better from day to day....we were stones in a torrent and the waters just crashed over us.

SOURCE 14 A former member of the Hitler Youth:

My personal feeling about concentration camps and that of all my schoolmates and my friends in the Hitler Youth was that anti-Reich elements, they were all being put there into those concentration camps, and for the first time in their lives probably they were made to work for Germany...

REVISION TASKS

1. Create your own key words summary of the methods used by the Nazis to control German society.
2. What was the Nazi view of the role of women in society?
3. Make a list of the opponents of the Nazi regime.
4. Explain why Sources 13 and 14 might be useful to an historian studying opposition to Hitler.
5. Using the information and evidence in this section, how effective do you think Nazi methods of control were?

I Nazi economic policy and foreign policy

1. The recovery of the German economy When Hitler came to power, unemployment in Germany was over 6,000,000. Hitler promised economic prosperity. If he was to remain in power therefore, it was vital that he took steps to help the German economy recover.

Hitler reduced some unemployment by creating major projects:

- Thousands of Germans found work in the organisations created by the Nazis such as the Hitler Youth. Many also took the jobs formerly occupied by Jews.
- Hundreds of thousands of German workers joined the National Labour service. New roads, hospitals and schools were built.

Rearmament

Rearmament was probably the key policy in getting Germany back to work.

- The production of arms and ammunition was significantly increased.
- The German army, air force and navy were enlarged despite restrictions imposed by the Versailles Treaty.
- Iron, steel and coal production rose rapidly as a result and made wealthy Nazi industrialists such as Krupps even richer.
- Compulsory military service was introduced in March 1935. The number of troops in the German army grew from 100,000 in 1933 to 1.4 million by 1939.

The effect of these measures was dramatic, and it is possible to see why many Germans were prepared to ignore the darker side of the Nazi regime.

- Unemployment fell from over 6 million in 1933 to about 250,000 in 1939.
- By 1938, Germany was the wealthiest country in Europe and per capita (per head) incomes of Germans equalled those of people in Britain.

Effects of a rearmament-based economy

Germany's economic recovery was fragile.

- The Nazis spent a large proportion of the country's wealth on maintaining huge numbers of people in the armed forces.
- Many of the former unemployed were in non-productive jobs (such as the army). They did not contribute to economic recovery. Administration and bureaucracy also increased significantly.
- The German balance of payments throughout the 1930s (value of imports versus exports) gave cause for concern.
- Germany's worsening relations with her neighbours caused her share of world trade to fall from 10 per cent in 1929 to 8 per cent in 1938.
- The German economy was built on the need to prepare for war and territorial expansion.

2. German territorial expansion Hitler never concealed his aims. In *Mein Kampf* (which he wrote while in prison in 1923) he outlined his plan for Germany's future. Hitler aimed to:

- Destroy the Treaty of Versailles and make Germany great again.
- Unite all the German peoples under one leader – as a result of the Treaty of Versailles many Germans in the 1930s were living within the borders of Poland, Czechoslovakia and Austria.
- Achieve 'living space' (*Lebensraum*) for the new Germany in Eastern Europe. Hitler regarded the Slav peoples of Eastern Europe, particularly Russia, as inferior. These territories were therefore ideal for conquest and occupation.

During the 1930s Hitler began to put these plans into action. They are all described in detail on pages 48–52.

REVISION TASKS

1. What evidence is there in this section to explain the lack of opposition to the Nazis in Germany during the 1930s?
2. What evidence is there in this section that Hitler's economic policy was based on getting ready for war? Note down some key words for your answer.

J Germany and the Second World War

1. German victories The war began spectacularly well for Germany.

- Within six weeks of the German invasion of Poland in September 1939, the Poles were defeated and out of the war.
- The German war machine had developed a new type of warfare – *Blitzkrieg* (lightning war). Massive air power combined with fast-moving tanks (*Panzers*) brought quick victories for the German armed forces.
- By the middle of 1940 German troops had entered Paris, and by the end of 1941, most of Europe including France, The Netherlands, Belgium, Norway, Finland and western Russia was under German occupation.

2. Turning points Despite the early successes Germany was pitted against powerful opponents.

- At the end of 1941, the USA joined the war against Germany.
- In 1942, the Germans suffered their first major defeat in Europe when 140,000 troops died in the siege of Stalingrad.
- The conquest of Europe stretched German resources and manpower to their limits. All of German industry was devoted to the war effort.
- Unlike 1939, by 1942 Germany was facing new and powerful enemies such as the USA and the USSR.

3. The defeat of Germany In the end, the combined forces of Britain, the USA and the USSR were too strong for Germany to resist. There were times when it seemed that Britain might be strangled by the German U-boats attacking supply lines in the Atlantic. Realistically, however, the enormous resources of the USA and USSR were too powerful even for Hitler's Germany.

- In 1943 Allied troops were advancing in Italy, and Russian troops were forcing the Germans to retreat.
- In June 1944, the Allies launched their invasion of Normandy and by March 1945 Allied troops had crossed the Rhine into the heartland of Germany.

The Allies also carried out massive bombing raids on German cities.

- In February 1945, 3,000 British and American bombers destroyed the German city of Dresden. In the firestorms that resulted from the bombing, it is estimated that over 100,000 people died.
- Although air power did not defeat Germany, it helped to undermine German morale and disrupt industry.

On 30 April 1945, deep in his underground bunker under the Chancellory building, Hitler and Eva Braun whom he had married the previous day, committed suicide. On 7 May 1945, Hitler's Third Reich surrendered to the Allies; the Second World War (in Europe) was over.

REVISION TASK

1. Construct a table like the one below adding each year from 1939–45. Use the information in this section to complete the table on the course of the Second World War for Germany.

	German successes	Turning points	Losses
1939			
1940			

REVISION SESSION

The aim of this revision session is for you to see how you can apply your knowledge of Germany 1918–45 to answering some source-based questions .

Examination questions

This example comes from the MEG Paper 2, 1994.

SOURCE A *An account from a British book, published in 1985, which described the economic changes in Germany during 1923.*

By December 1922 the German government had stopped reparation payments. The French decided to go and get their money. In January 1923 French troops invaded Germany's most important coal-mining and industrial area. The German government ordered workers and officials not to co-operate with the French. Now Germany had to import coal from abroad and support the workers who were resisting the French. The government's income fell and its spending rose. The German government printed more banknotes.

Study Source A. Give the name of:

a) Germany's most important coal-mining and industrial areas. *[1 mark]*

b) The country which acted with France in this invasion. *[1 mark]*

What is required? This question is testing your knowledge of events. You need to provide short answers with the correct spelling.

Ideas for your answer Explain briefly that the Ruhr was the most important industrial area in Germany and Belgium assisted French troops in the invasion in 1923.

SOURCE C *The photograph shows middle-class women selling tin cans to raise money in 1923.*

Study Source C. Give two reasons why Germany's middle classes were affected by the hyper-inflation of 1923. *[2 marks]*

What is required? This is similar to the first question. You need to give specific ways in which the middle class were affected rather than general ones.

Ideas for your answer The middle classes lost their savings and insurance policies became worthless.

Any pensions they had taken out also became worthless as prices rose to record levels.

SOURCE B *A table showing food prices (in Reichsmarks), 1918–23.*

Commodity	1918	1922	August 1923	November 1923
1 egg	0.25	180	5,000	80,000,000
500g butter	3.00	2,400	150,000	6,000,000,000
1kg bread	0.53	163	69,000	201,000,000

Study Source B. In what ways might this source be useful to an historian studying Weimar Germany? Explain your answer. [*6 marks*]

What is required? Different levels of answers will earn different marks. A simple statement (e.g. it gives useful information about inflation) will only gain 1 or 2 marks.

Examiners want you to give examples of how historians use this type of source. To aim for the higher marks (3–6 marks) you need to evaluate each of the sources thoroughly. You need to explain that whilst it might be useful it also has some limitations.

Ideas for your answer You could begin by pointing out that the table shows the dramatic increase in inflation in Germany between 1918 and 1923. The worst period of hyper-inflation occurs during the French and Belgian occupation of the Ruhr. Prices rise most dramatically during a four-month period in 1923.

It is also worth showing that you understand how an historian might use the source to show the cause and effect of hyper-inflation. For example, the source is useful particularly to economic, social or political historians. Since it shows food prices it is reasonable to suggest how the poor and middle classes were affected and how this created political instability. Remember that in November 1923 the Nazis used chaos in Bavaria to attempt a take-over in the Munich putsch.

It would also be worth speculating that hyper-inflation had occurred because the Weimar government merely printed more bank notes in order to solve its economic difficulties such as reparations payments.

SOURCE D *A middle-class housewife later recalled her experience of hyper-inflation in 1923.*

My husband set up his practice as an eye-surgeon. My own income was fixed at 30,000 marks. However, 80% of my husband's patients paid their fees three months after treatment. We were virtually without any income. My brother-in-law owned a factory and, like all businessmen, was well off. His wife and I had our babies within a few days of each other and I remember how I was lying in a borrowed iron bedstead with my baby in a borrowed cradle, while she had everything for herself and her baby in pure silk. And yet we both came from the same sort of family background.

SOURCE E *A comment on the effects of the hyper-inflation of 1923 written many years after the events described.*

As soon as factory gates opened and the workers streamed out, pay packets (often in old cigar boxes) in their hands, their wives grabbed the money and rushed to the nearest shops to buy food before prices went up again. Salaries always lagged behind. People living on fixed incomes sank into deeper and deeper poverty.

A familiar sight in the streets was of people carrying laundry baskets full of paper money. It sometimes happened that thieves stole the baskets, but tipped out the money and left it on the spot.

Study Source D and Source E. Which of these two sources gives the more reliable account of the effects of hyper-inflation in Germany in 1923? Explain your answer. *[8 marks]*

What is required? This question requires you to show a range of skills. You must show that you can understand each source, make use of each source and use your background knowledge to evaluate each source.

Simple statements about what each source contains will only achieve low marks (1–3). To reach the next level you must explain how and why the sources are different. To reach the higher level marks (6–8) you need to 'test' the reliability of each source and use the other sources or your own knowledge to cross-reference.

Usually, you do not need to choose one source as more reliable than the other but rather explain the strengths and weaknesses of each source.

Ideas for your answer It is often easier to look at each source in turn. In Source D you should be specific about the origin of the source; this is the middle-class housewife of an eye-surgeon. She is explaining how hyper-inflation affected them. Source E is written many years after the event and shows more effects of hyper-inflation. You can now 'test' each source.

1. In Source D we are told by the middle-class housewife of an eye-surgeon how inflation meant that during 1923 they lived virtually without any income. It is a personal account written after the event from memory and only shows her point of view. Your background knowledge and evidence from Sources C and B, however, support what she says; the middle class was badly affected. For high level marks you need to point out that this family suffered in particular because the husband was paid up to three months after providing treatment to his patients. During times of hyper-inflation this delay meant that when payment was settled, prices had risen so much in the meantime that the fee was practically worthless.
2. Source E is a much more general account of hyper-inflation. We are not told who wrote the extract or how long after 1923 it was written. Although from your background knowledge you will realise that paper money became practically worthless, it is difficult to rely totally on this evidence since it provides us with few clues against which to test it. Overall, therefore, you should point out that Source D is slightly more reliable since at least we know the origin of the source.

'The economic crises of 1923 brought equal suffering to all sections of the German people.'

Study all the sources. Do these sources provide reliable evidence to show this view to be true? Explain your answer carefully. *[12 marks]*

What is required? This question is the most important. You should reach a conclusion on the question and support your answer by referring to all the sources and commenting upon their value, usefulness and reliability.

Low level answers (2–3 marks) will not really comment on the usefulness or reliability of the sources. The next level of answer (4–5 marks) will have a conclusion but not be supported by evidence or examples. To reach the next level of answer (6–7 marks) you must reach a conclusion and explain which sources support your conclusion. To reach the higher level marks (8–12) you must do all of the above but also show that you understand the strengths and weaknesses of the sources.

Your aim is to produce a balanced answer.

Ideas for your answer

1. A good way to begin is to point out what your conclusion will be. In this case the sources seem to show that hyper-inflation caused suffering to some groups more than others. The middle class and poor were worst affected.
2. Source A is written by a British historian writing in 1985. He would have little reason to be biased and would have probably have looked at plenty of evidence. He seems to suggest that many groups in Germany were affected in similar ways by the economic crisis.
3. Source B shows the effect of hyper-inflation on food prices. This indicates that all people would have been affected by hyper-inflation but that the poor would have been most affected since they would spend a greater proportion of their income on food than other groups.
4. Source C is a photograph apparently showing middle-class women selling tin cans to raise money. Like any photograph, it has its problems as a source. We are not told who took the picture and for what reason, or if it is typical of this period. We do know from our background knowledge that the middle class and poor were particularly affected by hyper-inflation and often had to sell their belongings for food.
5. Source D presents the view of one person who seems to be rather bitter that one of her relatives has not suffered in the same way because of hyper-inflation. Her account, although rather biased, can be supported by your background knowledge. She seems to suggest that some middle-class people suffered more than others. She makes no mention of the poor.
6. Source E is very general and we are not told who wrote it or precisely when. It seems to suggest that the workers and people on fixed incomes suffered the most. Your background knowledge should indicate that this was true.

Conclusion: The general impression is that most of the sources suggest that hyper-inflation affected the middle class and poor equally. Some sources seem to imply that the middle class was worst affected.

SUMMARY AND REVISION PLAN

Below is a list of headings which you might find helpful. Use this as a check list to make sure you are familiar with the material featured in this chapter. Record your key words alongside each heading.

A The origins of the Weimar Republic
1. A democratic Germany
2. Problems in the new Republic
   - Opposition from the left
   - Kapp putsch
   - Other political murders

B Economic and political problems in Germany during the 1920s
1. Reparations and the invasion of the Ruhr
2. Hyper-inflation
3. Crisis under control
4. The Munich putsch

C German recovery in the 1920s under Stresemann
1. Economic recovery
2. The Locarno treaties
3. Extremist groups

D The effects of the Depression on Germany
1. Effects of the Wall Street Crash, 1929
2. Unemployment and the rise of extremism

E How the Nazis took power
1. How the Depression helped Hitler
2. The presidential election, 1932
3. Reichstag elections, July 1932
4. Fresh Reichstag elections, November 1932
5. Hitler becomes Chancellor
6. The Reichstag fire
7. Hitler takes control: the Enabling Act
8. Hitler turns on the SA

F Life in Nazi Germany
1. Propaganda
2. Victims of propaganda
3. A police state
4. Nazi control of society

G Nazi treatment of the Jews
1. Persecution
2. Kristallnacht
3. The 'Final Solution'

H Opposition to the Nazis
- exiles and church leaders
- Stauffenberg plot

I Nazi economic policy and foreign policy
1. The recovery of the German economy
   - rearmament and effects on economy
2. German territorial expansion

J Germany and the Second World War
1. German victories
2. Turning points
3. The defeat of Germany

CHAPTER 12

Russia, 1917–41

In 1917 Russia made peace with Germany and took no further part in the First World War. It was much more focused on events at home. In 1917 there were two revolutions. These were followed by two years of civil war. The communists emerged triumphant and launched a programme of reform and modernisation. The country was transformed into a modern superpower, but this cost the lives of many millions.

To answer source-based questions on Russia between 1917 and 1941, you need to be familiar with both the key content and the key themes of the period. This will help you to show your understanding of documents and other sources relating to this topic.

KEY CONTENT

You will need to have a good working knowledge of these areas:

A The collapse of the Tsarist system
B The problems of the provisional government
C The Bolshevik revolution and dictatorship
D Opposition to the Bolsheviks and the civil war
E War communism and the New Economic Policy
F The struggle to succeed Lenin
G Stalin's attempts to modernise the USSR
H Stalin's control over home and foreign policies

KEY THEMES

You will also be asked to show your understanding of some key themes:

- **The importance of the First World War**
- **Opposition to the Tsars**
- **Why the provisional government fell**
- **The supporters and opponents of Bolshevik rule**
- **How the Bolsheviks were able to win the civil war**
- **The successes and failures of war communism and the NEP**
- **How and why Stalin became leader after Lenin**
- **The causes and consequences of the measures introduced by Stalin**
- **The challenges faced by historians using first-hand evidence on Russian in this period**

Source-based questions test both your knowledge of the topic *and* your understanding of documents and other sources from the period being studied. Below is an example from MEG Paper 2, 1995.

SOURCE E *An extract from the memoirs of Lev Kopelev published in 1979. Kopelev was a Communist Party worker in the Ukraine in the 1920s and 30s. He was arrested in 1945 and spent ten years in prison.*

We were taught, when we were young, that it was our duty to denounce friends and relatives. I never believed that Bukharin and Trotsky were Gestapo agents, and I was sure that Stalin never believed it either. But I believed Stalin was right in doing these terrible things in order to make all those who opposed the Party look wrong. We were surrounded by enemies; we had to be united. Opposition leaders had to be presented as villains so that the people would hate them.

Study Source E. Give two 'enemies' which communists felt were surrounding them in the 1930s. [*6 marks*]

You can see from this question that you need to use your knowledge to look at the source in context.

- You must read and understand the events described in Source E
- You must show your background knowledge of the period by naming some of the Bolshevik's opponents hinted at (but not mentioned) in Source E.

A The collapse of Tsarist rule in Russia

1. **The Tsarist system of government** The Russian monarch was known as the Tsar. He ruled as an AUTOCRAT. He believed that God had made him Tsar and that he therefore had absolute authority to rule Russia.

The Tsar ruled with the support of the aristocracy (landowners), Church, army and the civil service.

2. **Opposition to the Tsar** There was opposition to the Tsar. In 1905 a protest by industrial workers (Bloody Sunday) broke out into a full-scale revolution. There were other protests and strikes in the years 1905–14. Probably the most important of these was the strike in the Lena goldfields in 1912.

There were several opposition groupings:

- Some middle-class Russians wanted more say in Russia's government but the Duma (parliament) was virtually powerless before 1914.
- There were also the Social Revolutionaries (SRs) who mainly represented the peasant farmers and also opposed the Bolsheviks.
- The third group was the Communists – divided into Bolsheviks and Mensheviks who disagreed with each other about tactics for overthrowing the Tsarist system.

By 1914 poor working conditions, food shortages and the opposition parties had created a very tense atmosphere in Russia.

3. **The First World War** It was the First World War which finished off the Tsarist system. Even with the protests, strikes and demonstrations of 1914 the Tsar could probably have used the army and police to keep order.

When war began in 1914 the Tsar actually gained the complete support of his people. However, war began to take its toll and by 1917 the Tsar's government was facing collapse. There were various reasons for this:

- The Russian army was not really a match for the well-equipped Germans.
- Casualties were enormous (around 9 million by 1917).
- The Tsar took personal control of the army and so took the blame for Russia's defeats.
- The Tsar's wife and her adviser Rasputin became increasingly unpopular at home.
- Food shortages began because many workers were killed in the army and the railway system could not get enough food to the cities.
- Prices rose and wages fell as goods became in short supply – this led to strikes.

4. **The February revolution** This is often called the March revolution. Confused? The explanation is simple. In 1917 Russia was using a different calendar from the West. As a result, the first Russian revolution took place in February by the Russian calendar, but March for the rest of Europe. This book will use the 'Russian' dates.

The unrest began in February 1917 with a strike at the Puetilov steelworks in Petrograd.

- Unrest and strikes spread quickly and bread queues turned into riots.
- The workers began to form councils (called soviets) and the leaders of the Duma (one of the more important of these was Kerensky) began opposing the Tsar openly.

By the end of February the troops had joined the rioters and the Tsar had no choice but to abdicate (give up power) on 3 March. The Tsar's regime was replaced by a provisional government.

B The problems of the provisional government

The provisional government of 1917 was headed at first by Prince Lvov. He was replaced by Alexander Kerensky in July of that year. Kerensky had already served in the provisional government as Justice Minister and War Minister. He was also Deputy Chairman of the Petrograd soviet (workers' council). Many people already believed the soviets were more effective as a means of government than the Duma.

1. Conditions in 1917 The provisional government was faced with pressures from outside as well as its own weaknesses. Continuing the war against the Germans made the provisional government deeply unpopular. This was made worse by continued failure and heavy casualties:

- Mutinies broke out in the army.
- There was a revolt at the Kronstadt naval base in July.
- Peasants were simply taking over the landowners' estates.
- Opposition was growing from parties like the Bolsheviks.
- The Petrograd soviet became more and more hostile to the government as it failed to solve Russia's economic problems (food supplies, prices, working conditions and wages).

2. Lenin and the Bolsheviks At the time of the February revolution, Lenin, leader of the Bolsheviks, came back from exile in Germany. His aim was to overthrow the provisional government with a second revolution of the working classes.

Lenin published his views in April 1917 in the 'April Theses'. In simple terms, he said that the Bolsheviks offered 'bread, peace, land and all power to the soviets.'

3. Kerensky, the Kornilov revolt and the Bolsheviks Alexander Kerensky began to take a grip on his opponents and Lenin was forced into hiding. However, he was then challenged by the new commander of the army, General Kornilov, who wanted to impose a strict regime and crush opponents, rather like the Tsar had done.

Kerensky asked the Bolsheviks to help him to defeat Kornilov, which they did. Kerensky was now in real trouble. He had lost the support of the army and was dependent upon the Petrograd soviet (with its strong Bolshevik influence) to run Russia.

4. The Bolshevik revolution, October 1917 (also called the November Revolution). Support for the peasants and workers' soviets grew rapidly through 1917, especially after the defeat of Kornilov. In October Lenin persuaded the Petrograd soviet to take the decision to overthrow Kerensky's government.

The Bolsheviks staged their revolution efficiently and quickly under the brilliant organisation of Leon Trotsky. Within two days Trotsky's Red Guards had seized railway stations, telegraph offices and other targets such as the Winter Palace. Kerensky fled and the Bolshevik take-over succeeded with very little bloodshed.

REVISION TASKS

1. Make a list of the opponents of the Tsar.
2. Do you agree that the First World War was the key factor in overthrowing the Tsar? Explain your answer using evidence from this section and your own reading.
3. Put the following in order of importance as factors which helped the Bolsheviks to come to power:
   a) Bolshevik strategies
   b) provisional government – policies and problems
   c) Kornilov revolt
   d) Bolshevik revolution.

C The Bolshevik revolution and dictatorship

The provisional government was replaced by the Council of the People's Commissars under Lenin. Lenin's aims were clear. He followed the theories of the political thinker Karl Marx and wanted a 'dictatorship of the proletariat' (see diagram).

This meant that the Bolshevik party would govern Russia for the good of the workers and peasants.

1. Setting up a Marxist state

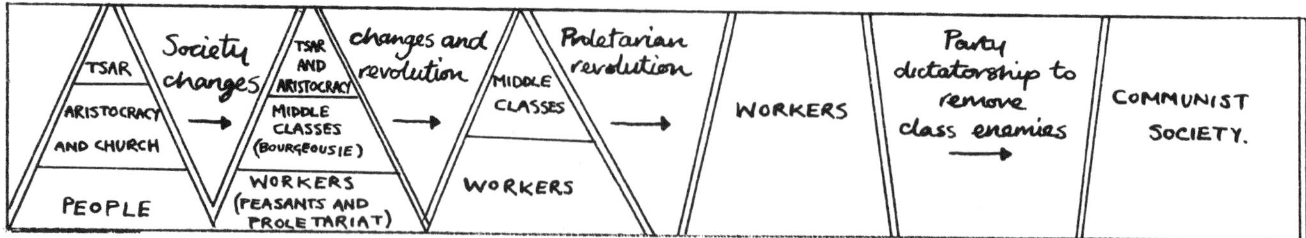

Lenin was not interested in democracy. The elections which were held late in 1917 showed that the Bolsheviks did not have the support of most Russians.

- The Constituent Assembly which met in January 1918 contained twice as many Social Revolutionaries as Bolsheviks and the SRs opposed Lenin.
- Bolshevik Red Guards closed down the Assembly. By July 1918 the Russian Congress of Soviets had agreed a new system of government for Russia (see diagram below).

The result was that Lenin effectively became a dictator, and his secret police (the Cheka) began to intimidate, imprison and murder political opponents.

2. Negotiating peace The Bolsheviks had always planned to pull out of the war with Germany. They agreed a ceasefire in December 1917. Trotsky was given the job of negotiating terms but his only real achievement was to hold the Germans up until March 1918 when the Bolsheviks were forced to sign the Treaty of Brest-Litovsk.

- Russia lost vast amounts of territory (see map below).
- Russia also lost important coal and iron resources and about one-third of its population.
- Russia also had to pay 300 million roubles compensation.

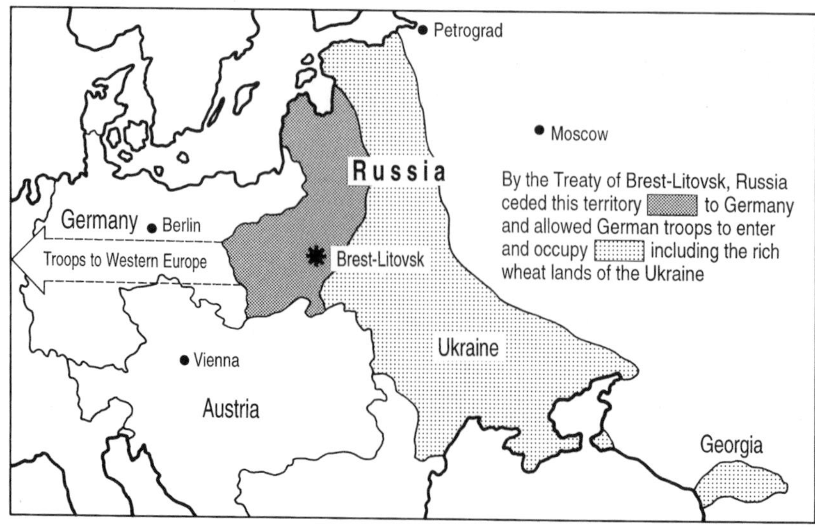

Russian losses in the Treaty of Brest-Litovsk

3. State of the land and economy

The question of land was vitally important in Russia. Farming was still by far the most important business. Lenin abolished the private ownership of land. This effectively meant that the peasants stripped the lands from landowners and the Church. In reality the countryside was in a state of chaos in the early Bolshevik days, and no government was truly in control. The Bolsheviks were strong in the towns and cities but not in the countryside.

- There was soon a problem of food shortages because Russian money was worthless and the peasants were not being paid for their produce.
- Peasants did not trust the Bolsheviks who wanted to change the way that farming was organised from individual to collective (or co-operative) farming.

▲ *Viewpoints and evidence*

Here are two viewpoints on Bolshevik rule during this period. Look at the sources below:

SOURCE 1 American writer, Leonard Schapiro, *The Communist Party of the Soviet Union*, 1963:

Bolshevik practice within a few days of 25th October was at variance with Lenin's repeated promises that when they were in power the Bolsheviks would guarantee to each political party ...facilities for publishing a newspaper. Some socialist and liberal papers, as well as the conservative papers, were closed down in the first few days.

SOURCE 2 Eugenie Fraser, *The House by the Dvina*, an historical novel, 1984:

In the town, after six months of living under our new government, conditions remain chaotic. The minds of the authorities are too occupied with establishing their doctrine and persecuting those who have opinions contrary to their own, to bother with the less important matters such as clothing and feeding hungry citizens.

Sources 1 and 2 do not present a very favourable picture of Bolshevik rule. However, Source 1 was written by an American during the Cold War (see pages 73–83). Such writings from the 1960s must be used with care as they may not be too reliable.

Source 2 is an historical novel. It is based on historical research and it fits many things you know from your background knowledge. It is here that the skills of the historian must be used to make a judgement – we must take care when using such a work as evidence.

REVISION TASKS

1. Make a key words summary of the changes brought about by the Bolsheviks after they took power. Use these headings to help you:

Government	Brest-Litovsk	Land and economy

2. What evidence can you find in this section that the Bolsheviks did not enjoy the support of the Russian people?

D Opposition to the Bolsheviks and the civil war

1. Who made up the opposition? The Bolsheviks did not have the support of all Russians when they seized power. By May 1918 they had more enemies still, especially after the losses of the Treaty of Brest-Litovsk.

By the summer of 1918 the Bolsheviks were faced with a range of opponents. The only thing uniting these opponents was their opposition to the Bolsheviks. These opponents were called the Whites, as opposed to the Bolshevik Reds. The Whites were made up of former Tsarists, Mensheviks, Social Revolutionaries and foreign powers opposed to the new regime in Russia.

2. The Bolsheviks in danger In the early stages of the war the Bolsheviks were facing several different threats:

- The Czech legion (which was made up of former prisoners of war) had seized sections of the vital Trans-Siberian railway.
- Admiral Kolchak had set up a White government in Siberia and was marching on Moscow.
- General Denikin was advancing with his army from southern Russia.
- Northern Russia was opposing the Bolsheviks led by the White General Yudenich.
- There were also risings against the Bolsheviks in Ukraine and Turkestan.
- Foreign powers supplied the Whites with arms and weapons and later landed troops to help the Whites as well. US, Japanese, French and British troops landed at Archangel, Murmansk and Vladivostok.

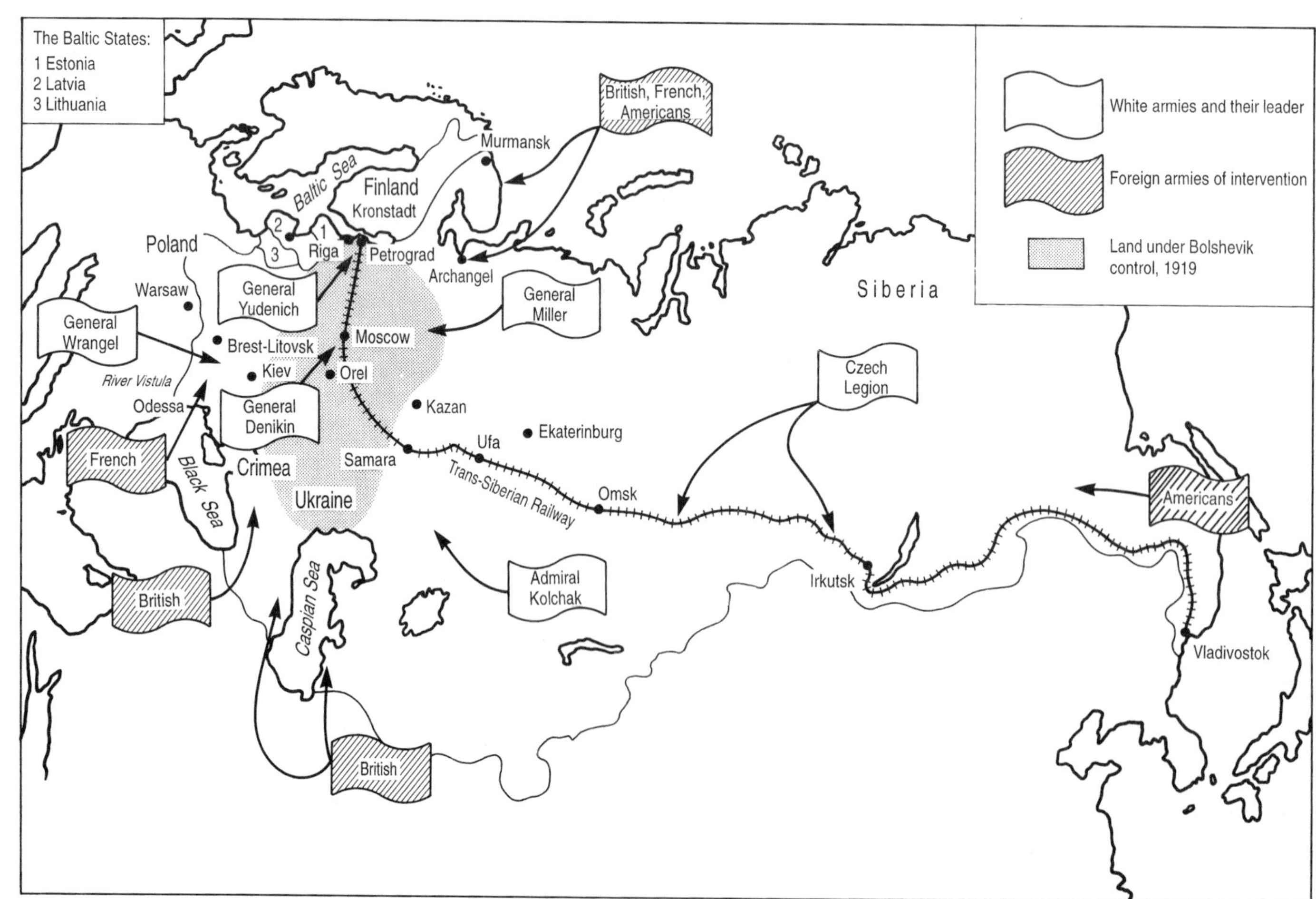

3. Bolshevik victory Despite what seemed to be overwhelming odds, the Bolsheviks won the civil war. The crucial year was 1919.

Under Trotsky's leadership the Red army defeated Kolchak and destroyed the Czech legion.

Denikin's advance on Moscow was stopped and by 1920 he was being pushed back. By late 1920 White forces were completely defeated. The Bolsheviks had won because of their own ruthless, disciplined commitment and the failings of their enemies.

The strengths of the Bolsheviks (the Reds) were:

- The Reds had large, well-organised armies under the leadership of Trotsky. They also had good communication.
- They made good use of propaganda to show that the Whites were in league with foreigners and wanted to bring back the Tsar.
- The Red Army and Cheka (secret police) kept a ruthless control over the Bolshevik territories, making sure that most people obeyed Lenin's rule.
- The Red Army was supplied by the brutal policy of war communism (see page 174) which guaranteed that the troops and towns were fed and supplied.
- The Reds controlled the major towns with their factories and industries to support the war effort.

The failings of the Whites were:

- The Whites had no aim upon which they all agreed. In some cases they disliked each other almost as much as they opposed the Reds.
- Their forces were spread across a huge area and they could not co-ordinate their attacks – they were beaten one by one.
- Their harsh treatment of people in the lands they captured led many to support the Bolsheviks against them.

▲ *Viewpoints and evidence*

The civil war period was a chaotic and confused time in Russia's history. Many records were lost or destroyed at the time; some have been tampered with since and many more are unreliable.

Look at these sources, which provide evidence on the actions of the Whites in the civil war. How useful are they in explaining why the Bolsheviks won the civil war?

SOURCE 3 M.G. Drozdovsky, *Diary of Colonel Drozdovsky*, 1923:

The mounted platoon [of Whites] entered the village, met the Bolshevik committee and put the members to death ... Then the population was ordered to deliver without pay the best cattle, pigs ... and bread for the whole detachment.

SOURCE 4 Christopher Hill, *Lenin and the Russian Revolution*, 1947:

Not infrequently the peasants said ... 'The Bolsheviks are rather unpleasant people, we do not like them, but still they are better than the White Guards.'

Sources 3 and 4 are useful in that they both suggest that the cruelty of the Whites might have helped the Bolsheviks. The primary source and the historian's view support each other. It seems then that we have some useful evidence on attitudes towards the Whites.

However, the limitations of these sources are that they do not give us any evidence about what the Bolsheviks themselves did (e.g. their organisation or even their own cruelty). They only give one part of the picture, so their utility is limited.

REVISION TASKS

1. Create your own key words summary of who the Whites were and why they opposed the Bolsheviks.
2. Explain how the Bolsheviks won the civil war (8–10 key words).

E War communism and the New Economic Policy

1. **War communism** To defeat his opponents in the civil war Lenin knew that he had to make sure that his armies were fed and equipped. To achieve this he introduced the policy of 'war communism'.

- Land and industry were nationalised – taken over by the state.
- In the factories there was severe discipline (e.g. strikers could be shot) and key items like food and coal were rationed.
- In the countryside peasants were forced to hand over their surplus produce (what they did not need themselves) to the government.
- Opposition was rooted out and destroyed by the Cheka (even the royal family was executed).

2. **The cost of the civil war and 'war communism'** By 1921 Lenin was facing a shattered and demoralised country.

- War communism had made the industrial workers poor and restless.
- War communism and war damage had led to an outbreak of famine in the countryside – millions died in 1921.

The Kronstadt mutiny of 1921 was a turning point. The Kronstadt sailors had been leading supporters of the revolution but they revolted against war communism in March 1921.

Although the Kronstadt revolt was destroyed by Trotsky and the civil war was being won, it was clear in 1921 that Lenin had to do something to improve living conditions for the Russian people. His solution was the New Economic Policy (NEP).

3. **The New Economic Policy (NEP)** Lenin introduced the NEP at the Party Congress in March 1921. Its measures were simple but controversial:

- Peasants could keep part of their surpluses to sell at a profit.
- Small factories were given back to private ownership.
- Small private businesses could be set up to trade at a profit.

Some communists saw the NEP as a betrayal but Lenin saw it as a temporary measure to keep the Russian people happy and get the economy moving. All of the major industries remained in state hands and political control (under the Cheka) remained very strict.

4. **The importance of Lenin** Lenin died in January 1924. He had brought huge changes to Russia and indeed the world:

- He had led the communist revolution.
- He had established the USSR (Union of Soviet Socialist Republics).
- He had created a powerful, disciplined Communist party by using the Cheka to purge (remove) opponents of his policies.
- The USSR had become a one-party state which was effectively a dictatorship where the Communist party controlled industry, army, police, the press – in fact almost all aspects of life.

▲ *Viewpoints and evidence*

Lenin has often had a 'good press' in history, especially when compared to Stalin. The questions which historians are now asking are:

- What kind of man was Lenin?
- Was he as ruthless as Stalin?
- Was he good or bad for Russia?

Source 5 presents two differing views from British newspapers immediately after the death of Lenin.

SOURCE 5

(i) *The Times*, 23 January, 1924:

This extraordinary man was first and foremost a professional revolutionary ... A man of iron will and inflexible ambition, he was absolutely ruthless and used human beings as mere material for his purpose.

(ii) The *Daily Herald*, 23 January, 1924:

Lenin is dead. All through Russia that news has struck as a deep personal loss. For 'Ilyitch' was loved of his own Russian people – whom he understood and loved so well – as no leader of men in our time has been loved.

For historians these are useful sources - they show the attitudes of the day very clearly. *The Times* was a conservative newspaper which opposed socialism and communism. It shows what many of its conservative readers would think of Lenin. The *Daily Herald* was also a British newspaper, but was more favourable towards socialism and communism. Again its comments reveal what many of its readers probably thought about Lenin.

However, neither source is reliable for telling us what Lenin was actually like. They each only express an opinion. We cannot therefore simply accept what they say as true without question.

REVISION TASKS

1. Write your own definition of 'war communism' using a key words list under these headings:

Reasons	How it worked	Effects

2. Now write a definition of the NEP, using the same headings.
3. If you were a Russian being interviewed by a British newspaper after Lenin's death, how would you explain the importance of Lenin to the USSR?

F The struggle to succeed Lenin

1. The candidates

Trotsky When Lenin died the most obvious candidate to take over leadership of the communists was Trotsky. He was brilliant, talented and had an outstanding 'track record' as leader of the Red Army.

Kamenev and Zinoviev They were both leading Bolsheviks. They believed in spreading revolution and both were unhappy about the NEP.

Bukharin He was more moderate. He wanted to build up the new Russia slowly and favoured keeping NEP in the short term.

Stalin He expressed no strong views – he was a hardworking administrator and few expected him to win the leadership contest.

2. Stalin succeeds

The contest was eventually won by Stalin, although it took him five years to become completely established as Lenin's successor. Stalin was able to defeat his rivals for a number of reasons.

- He had taken on many important jobs (editor of the party newspaper *Pravda*, Commissar for Nationalities, Secretary-General of the party). This gave him an important power base – he had many supporters in the ranks of the party (who owed their positions to him).
- Trotsky made himself unpopular. His ideas for spreading world revolution alarmed moderate Communists. Also, he was arrogant and offended many party members.
- The other four candidates disagreed with each other on important issues like industrialisation and the NEP.
- They all underestimated Stalin. At first Stalin sided with the others against Trotsky (who was thrown out of the Politburo in 1927). He continued to play Bukharin, Zinoviev and Kamenev off against each other by allying with one and then another, while he strengthened his own position.

By 1929 Stalin had defeated his opponents and was the dictator of the USSR.

▲ *Viewpoints and evidence*

The historical questions on this issue are clear:

- What methods did Stalin use to defeat his opponents?
- Was Stalin really just 'an eminent mediocrity' as Trotsky called him?
- Was Stalin's victory due to the incompetence of his opponents?

Sources 6 and 7 present some views from the time on Stalin.

SOURCE 6 John Reed, an American communist who lived in Russia:

He's [Stalin] not the intellectual like the other people you will meet. He's not even particularly well informed, but he knows what he wants. He's got willpower and he's going to be on top of the pile some day.

SOURCE 7 Trotsky on Stalin:

I said to Smirnov: 'Stalin will become the dictator of the USSR', 'Stalin?' he asked me with amazement, 'But he is a mediocrity, a colourless nonentity'.

'Mediocrity, yes; nonentity, no ... He is needed by all of them – the tired radicals, the bureaucrats, the NEP men, the Kulaks [wealthier peasant farmers], the upstarts ...'

Sources 6 and 7 provide us with some really interesting and useful evidence, but we must be careful. Both are first-hand accounts, or primary sources. Both also give lots of clues as to how Stalin won the contest (e.g. his determination, his supporters), which should agree with your own background knowledge.

However, Source 7 was written by Trotsky, Stalin's bitter opponent. We must be careful about accepting what he says at face value - he might be trying to give excuses for his own defeat.

REVISION TASK

1. Use a key words list to explain why Stalin succeeded in following Lenin as leader. Refer to:
   a) Stalin's opponents
   b) Stalin's qualities.

G Stalin's attempts to modernise the USSR

Stalin believed that the USSR was under threat from non-communist states. He also believed that the only way for the USSR to make itself secure was to become a modern, industrial country. His aim was to force the USSR to make 50 years progress in 10 years. There were two key aspects of Stalin's plans:

- The need to expand heavy industry (Five Year Plans)
- The need to improve food production (COLLECTIVISATION).

1. The Five Year Plans Stalin seems to have several clear reasons for industrialising the USSR:

- Security.
- To create a showpiece of success for the outside world.
- To carry out his idea of 'socialism in one country'.

In order to achieve his aims he came up with two Five Year Plans for the development of the USSR. The Five Year Plans were incredibly ambitious targets for industrial production which had to be achieved in five years.

Some targets were met (see right) but even the industries which failed to meet their targets did make huge advances.

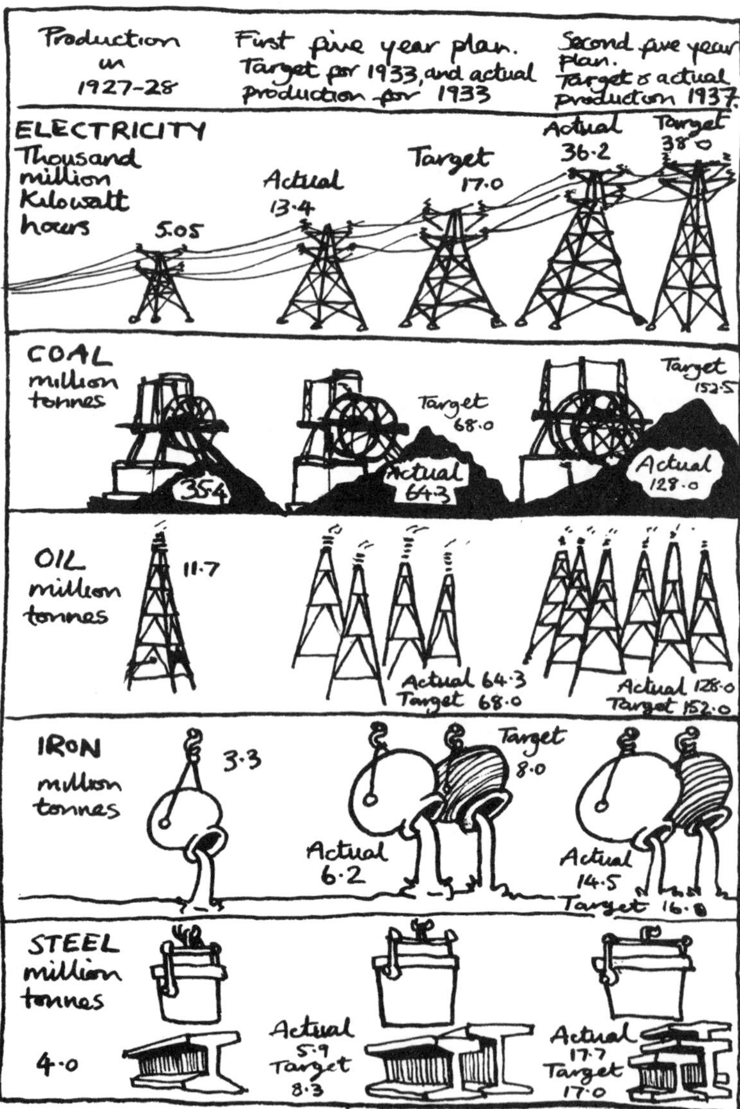

2. The effects of the Five Year Plans Historians disagree about the aims and the effects of the Five Year Plans. One thing on which all historians do agree is that the USSR was transformed.

- The main aim was achieved – by 1940 the USSR was in the 'first division' of industrial powers, along with Britain, Germany and the USA.
- Vast projects like the Belomor Canal, the Dreiper Dam, and the metalworks at Magnitogorsk were completed with amazing speed.
- Huge towns and factories were built from nothing, deep inside the USSR to protect them from invasion.
- Foreign technicians were brought in and enormous investment was put into education and training to produce skilled workers.
- Great pressure was put on workers to meet targets and to be 'Stakhanovites'. Stakhanov was a miner who managed to produce over 100 tons of coal in one shift, and was held up as a model to inspire all workers.

- The cost was high. Safety standards came second to meeting targets, discipline was harsh and many workers ended up in labour camps (gulags). All investment went into heavy industries – there were few consumer goods (clothes, luxuries).
- However, by the mid 1930s there were definite signs of improved living standards (e.g. education, welfare, housing).

▲ *Viewpoints and evidence*

Historians and contemporaries have argued long and hard on the following points:

- What were Stalin's true aims in the Five Year Plans?
- How successful were the Plans?
- What was the cost of these Plans for the people of the USSR?

SOURCE 8 Stalin on the first Five Year Plan, January 1933:

What was the fundamental task of the first Five Year Plan? The fundamental task of the first Five Year Plan was to transfer our country, with its backward technology, on to the lines of modern technology.

SOURCE 9 A female worker, Tatyana Fyodorova, remembering (in 1990) her time working on the building of the Moscow metro in 1933:

We got so dirty and we were such young things, small, slender, fragile. But we had our orders to build the metro and we wanted to do it more than anything else. We wore our miners' overalls with such style. My feet were size four and the boots were elevens. But there was such enthusiasm.

Sources 8 and 9 cover different aspects of the Five Year Plans. Source 8 gives us a view of Stalin's aims which is supported by most other information you have. This would suggest that the source is reliable on this subject. Source 9 gives the impression that the Russian people were enthusiastic about Stalin's plans, just like Stakhanov. It is, however, the view of only one individual. To make a conclusive judgement about the attitudes of the Soviet people you would need to compare this source with other evidence.

3. Farming: the need for collectivisation Stalin had made clear his ambitions to transform the USSR. The Five Year Plans could only work if Soviet agriculture could raise its production massively. There were two main reasons:

- To feed the growing population of industrial workers
- To export any surpluses to raise cash for investment in industry.

4. How it worked Most farms were smallholdings tended by peasant families. These holdings could never be efficient enough for Stalin's plans so he introduced the policy of collectivisation.

- Peasants effectively had to give up their land and join other families on very large farms.
- These new farms were supplied by the state with seed, tools, tractors and other machinery.
- Most of the produce went to the government.

The real opponents of collectivisation were the Kulaks. Kulaks were peasants who had become prosperous under the NEP and they made up a large and important part of the population of the countryside. Most refused to cooperate with the new policy, because they did not want to give up their land.

5. The effects of collectivisation The effects of collectivisation were very mixed, but this policy certainly had less claim to success than the Five Year Plans. This is what happened:

- By 1941 almost all land in the USSR was collectivised.
- A huge propaganda campaign was launched to convince peasants to modernise.
- Kulaks were murdered or put in labour camps – many killed their own animals or burnt their crops rather than let the government have them.
- Much of the countryside was devastated by struggles between Stalin's agents and the Kulaks.
- Although collectivisation was achieved, food production fell dramatically (see Source 10). In the Ukraine there was famine in the early 1930s and at the same time food was being exported.

The long-term result of this struggle was that the peasants were battered into submission and never again seriously threatened the communist regime.

▲ *Viewpoints and evidence*
The key issue surrounding collectivisation is: How successful was it?
Source 10 below gives production figures for agriculture for the years 1928 and 1933. How might these be useful?

SOURCE 10 USSR agricultural production 1928 and 1933:

Russian Livestock	***1928***	***1933***
Pigs	*26 million*	*12 million*
Sheep/Goats	*147 million*	*50 million*
Cattle	*70 million*	*38 million*

Statistics such as these are extremely useful to historians. These figures suggest that Stalin's agricultural policies were disastrous, and this is supported by other evidence you will have read. As always, however, the historian must be careful. Statistics are not always accurate or reliable, and more importantly they do not always present a complete picture. Other years may have been better or worse and this information only covers livestock, not crops. You would need to refer to your own background knowledge that grain production also dropped from 73 million in 1928 to 69 million in 1933.

REVISION TASK

1. Construct a table like the one below and use the information and evidence in this section to complete it.

	Five Year Plans	**Collectivisation**
Aims		
Methods		
Successes/failures		
Costs		

H Stalin's control over home and foreign policies

1. Opposition to Stalin Radical policies like Stalin's were bound to cause concern. Criticism within the party grew because of the human cost of Stalin's policies.

In 1934 Stalin's ally Sergei Kirov was murdered. Stalin saw this as evidence of a conspiracy and began a series of political purges (imprisonment and execution).

Historians are now fairly sure that Stalin planned Kirov's murder to give him an excuse to purge the USSR of opponents, whom Stalin saw as traitors to himself and the USSR.

2. The purges From 1934 to 1938 thousands were arrested, imprisoned, murdered or simply disappeared. They came from all areas of Soviet life.

- The Communist party: the number of party members fell from 3.5 million in 1934 to 2 million in 1935.
- Leading party members such as Zinoviev, Kamenev and Bukharin were tortured and their families threatened. Then at show trials, they 'confessed' and were executed.
- Many less important opponents (or even supporters who were not enthusiastic enough) were arrested and executed or sent to labour camps.
- In 1937 around 25,000 army officers (including the Commander of the Red Army, Marshal Tukhachevsky) were purged.

The effects of the purges were mixed. Stalin was certainly secure. His new secret police (the NKVD) ruled the population with terror. Over 8 million had been killed or sent to labour camps.

However, Stalin had weakened the USSR. Many of those purged had been skilled or educated (e.g. managers, army officers) and industrial progress slowed down. The army was seriously weakened and suffered badly against the Germans in 1941.

3. The Constitution Stalin made himself more secure still in 1936 with the USSR's new constitution. At first sight it seemed more democratic — all citizens voted for members of the Supreme Soviet. However, it had no real power and decisions were still made by Stalin and his closest supporters.

4. The culture of Stalin's USSR Stalin's USSR was disciplined and seemingly full of fear. Some real advances in industry were made, but at a cost:

- Freedom of speech was denied to Soviet citizens.
- Education improved basic standards for most Russians, but it was heavily controlled by the NKVD.

SOURCE 11 Nadezhda Mandelstam, a Russian writer:

She showed us her school textbooks where the portraits of party leaders had thick pieces of paper pasted over them as one by one they fell into disgrace – this the children had to do on instructions from their teacher ... With every new arrest, people went through their books and burned the works of disgraced leaders in their stoves.

- Artists, writers, musicians and performers had to please Stalin with their work, get out of the USSR or face being purged. Posters, radio broadcasts, the press all constantly pressed home the need for loyalty to the party and to Stalin. However, Lenin's ideals of a classless society did not seem to match the realities. High ranking party officials and the military seemed to enjoy a much higher standard of living than most Soviet citizens.

5. **Stalin's attitude to world revolution** Stalin was far too busy building socialism in one country to be concerned with Trotsky's ideas of spreading world revolution. In fact, Stalin was concerned with keeping the USSR secure, and even joined the League of Nations in 1934.

6. **Concern about fascism** Fascism was a political idea which was totally opposed to communism. Fascist governments were already in power in Italy (1924) and Germany (1933). Stalin hesitated to support the communist-backed Republicans in the Spanish Civil War (1936) and by 1939 Spain too was a fascist state. Stalin began to feel very concerned, especially when Germany and Japan signed the Anti-Comintern Pact in 1936 which placed the USSR between two powerful, hostile neighbours.

7. **The search for security** Stalin's obvious allies were Britain and France, both of whom were concerned about Hitler. However, Britain and France were just as worried about Stalin as they were about Hitler.

   The Munich crisis of 1938 (see page 50) convinced Stalin that Britain and France could not be relied upon, so in 1939 the Nazi-Soviet Non-Aggression Pact was signed (also called the Molotov-Ribbentrop Pact after the ministers who arranged it).

   Both Hitler and Stalin shocked their followers with the agreement, but each was buying time. Stalin kept his side of the agreement and even helped Hitler with supplies when the Second World War broke out. However, Hitler turned on Russia in June 1941 and the 'Great Patriotic War' began.

SOURCE 12 A British cartoonist's view of the Nazi-Soviet Pact, 1939:

REVISION TASKS

1. Why was there opposition to Stalin's policies?
2. Use a key words list to give three major effects of the purges.
3. List three ways in which freedom was restricted in Stalin's USSR.
4. If you are also studying Nazi Germany look for similarities and differences between Hitler's regime and Stalin's.
5. Do you agree that Stalin's main concern was safety from the fascist regimes? What evidence could you use to demonstrate this?
6. How useful is Source 12 to an historian studying the Nazi-Soviet Pact?

The aim of this revision session is for you to see how you can apply your knowledge of Russia 1917–41 to answering some source-based questions.

Examination questions

In this topic we shall examine a source-based question from MEG Paper 2, 1995.

SOURCE D *In a Soviet newsreel in 1937 Mikoyan, a member of the Politburo, praised the secret police.*

We can honestly say that by working to uncover spies they have saved lives and protected us from enemies, spies and Trotskyists. These enemies organise train crashes, poison the food and water of the people and infect our cattle with disease. The secret police are led by a great Bolshevik.

Study Source D.

a) State what is meant by 'Bolshevik'. [*1 mark*]

b) What was the name of the secret police? [*1 mark*]

What is required? This question is testing your knowledge of events. Examiners are looking for a short answer with the correct spelling.

Ideas for your answer

a) Explain that Bolshevik was a communist in the USSR, or a member of the Russian Communist party.

b) The secret police were known by a variety of names: MVD, NKVD, OGPU or Cheka.

SOURCE E *An extract from the memoirs of Lev Kopelev published in 1979. Kopelev was a Communist Party worker in the Ukraine in the 1920s and 30s. He was arrested in 1945 and spent ten years in prison camps.*

We were taught, when we were young, that it was our duty to denounce friends and relatives. I never believed that Bukharin and Trotsky were Gestapo agents, and I was sure that Stalin never believed it either. But I believed Stalin was right in doing these terrible things in order to make all those who opposed the Party look wrong. We were surrounded by enemies; we had to be united. Opposition leaders had to be presented as villains so that the people would hate them.

Study Source E. Give **two** 'enemies' which communists felt were 'surrounding' them in the 1930s. [*2 marks*]

What is required? The examiners want you to give specific enemies of the communists.

Ideas for your answer Enemies of the communists were fascists or capitalists. Britain and France sent forces against the Bolsheviks in 1919. Trotsky and his supporters later criticised the communist government in the USSR.

SOURCE C *A Soviet cartoon printed in 1937. It shows Trotsky washing blood from his hands.*

Study Source C. In what ways does this cartoon give a biased view of Trotsky? Explain your answer. [*6 marks*]

What is required? This answer carries 6 marks and examiners are looking for different levels of answers to award marks. A simple statement will give only 2 marks. Examiners want you to give examples of the bias in the source. You need to point out how it may be biased. To reach the top levels (5–6 marks) you should also mention the context of the source in your evaluation.

Ideas for your answer You could begin by pointing out that Trotsky is shown as washing blood from his hands as if he had committed a murder. He is shown as an ugly character, sinister and devious. It is interesting to note that Trotsky's towel is hanging on a Nazi swastika suggesting his support for fascism and Hitler. The cartoon implies Trotsky is a German agent. The cartoon also shows a smoking gun, a dagger and possibly a grenade. It seems to indicate he has carried out a murder or assassination on behalf of the Nazis. He is even washing his hands in a German helmet which suggests he is a communist traitor. The source was printed in 1937, at the height of Nazi-Soviet rivalry, and some time after Stalin had expelled Trotsky from the USSR.

SOURCE A *An extract from a letter written by the local Communist Party Secretary to the secret police in Smolensk.*

On 22 June 1936 a portrait of Trotsky was found in the home of Afanasiya Uromova. Uromova, it is said, is a corrupt member of the Kolkhoz. Vasili Ulyanov says that Uromova assaulted Ulyanov's father. I ask that Uromova be brought to trial.

SOURCE B *An extract from a novel published in 1940. The author, born in Hungary, was a journalist who had worked in the USSR writing for foreign newspapers.*

Gletkin, a member of the secret police, is explaining the Purges to a prisoner. Gletkin said: 'In my village there is now the biggest steel-rail factory in the world. In the first year, the foremen would lie down to sleep when they should have been working. So they had to be shot. In all other countries the peasants had one or two hundred years to adapt to industry and machines. Here they only had ten years. If we didn't sack them or shoot them for every little mistake no one would ever work.'

Study Sources A and B. Which of these two sources gives the more reliable explanation for the purging of ordinary people in the 1930's. Explain your answer by referring to both sources. [*8 marks*]

What is required? This question requires you to show a range of skills. You must show that you can:

- understand each source
- make use of each source
- use your background knowledge to evaluate each source.

To reach the higher level marks you need to 'test' the reliability of each source and use the other sources or your own knowledge to cross-reference. Usually, you do not need to choose one source as more reliable than the other but rather explain the strengths and weaknesses of each source.

Ideas for your answer It is often easier to look at each source in turn. In Source A you should be specific about its origin; this is a Communist Party Secretary writing to the secret police. Source B is a novel, published in 1940 by a Hungarian journalist who had worked in the USSR. You can now 'test' each source.

1. In Source A we see how a local communist party secretary asks for the arrest by the secret police of a citizen who is found with a picture of Trotsky and who is suspected of assault. The source seems to imply that the suspect is an undesirable citizen and one who supports enemies of the state such as Trotsky. Your own knowledge should suggest, however, that Trotsky was merely being used by the Soviet Government to help unite the Soviet people against potential enemies. The source therefore does not give a very reliable explanation of why ordinary citizens were persecuted.
2. Although Source B is a novel and therefore fiction, it is written by a journalist who had some knowledge of the Soviet Union. The journalist is also unlikely to be a communist and therefore unlikely to support Soviet propaganda. The source seems to give a much more reasoned view concerning the persecution of Soviet citizens. The journalist seems to have used his knowledge of the Soviet Union and events under Stalin to provide a reasonably accurate, although fictitious account of one incident. Background knowledge would also support this view. Overall, therefore, you should point out that Source B is slightly more reliable since it tends to agree with historians writing about life under Stalin.

Study all the sources. 'The purges of the 1930's only took place because Stalin feared Trotsky'.
Do these provide reliable evidence to show this view to be true? Explain your answer fully. [*12 marks*]

What is required? This question is the most important. The examiner wants you to reach a conclusion on the question and support your answer by referring to all the sources and commenting upon their value, usefulness and reliability.

Low level answers (2–3 marks) will not really comment on the usefulness or reliability of the sources. The next level of answer (4–5 marks) will have a conclusion but not be supported by evidence of examples. To reach the next level of answer (6–7 marks) you must reach a conclusion and explain which sources support your conclusion. To reach the higher level marks (8–12) you must do all of the above but also show that you understand the strengths and weaknesses of the sources. Your aim is to produce a balanced answer.

Ideas for your answer

1. A good way to begin is to point out what your conclusion will be. In this case the sources seem to show that Stalin used characters such as Trotsky to unite the Soviet people against all enemies at home and abroad.
2. Source A is written by a Communist Party Secretary. He seems to suggest that one Soviet citizen was corrupt on the basis of rumours and the fact that a picture of Trotsky was found in the suspect's home.
3. Source B is an extract from a novel and therefore a piece of fiction, in which we are told that lazy people are sacked from their jobs or even shot because the USSR needs to industrialise very quickly and cannot afford for people not to play their full part.
4. Source C is a Soviet cartoon showing the former communist hero Trotsky as a murdering Nazi agent. It is a clear attempt by the Soviet Government to unite people against potential enemies by portraying Trotsky as an enemy of communism.
5. Source D is from a Soviet newsreel in which a member of the government praises the secret police. The view expressed is one we expect from a member of the Politburo. Since Soviet cinema was controlled by the government, it presents a one-sided view of events and creates an opportunity to identify supporters of Trotsky as traitors.
6. Source E is a much more balanced view of events. The extract was not published until 1979 and shows the author reflecting on events of the 1920s and 1930s. Although a Communist Party worker who was later arrested, the author suggests that Trotsky and others were used by Stalin to help unite the Soviet people.

Conclusion: The general impression is that most of the sources indicate that Trotsky was an enemy of communism and some suggest he was working as a Nazi agent. There is little indication that Stalin feared Trotsky from the sources, but your own knowledge should suggest that Stalin was concerned about the effect the former leader of the Red Army would have on the Soviet public.

SUMMARY AND REVISION PLAN

Below is a list of headings which you might find helpful. Use this as a check list to make sure you are familiar with the material featured in this chapter. Record your key words alongside each heading.

A The collapse of the Tsarist system
1. The Tsarist system of government
2. Opposition to the Tsar
3. The First World War
4. The February revolution

B The problems of the provisional government
1. Lenin and the Bolsheviks
2. Conditions in 1917
3. Kerensky, the Kornilov revolt and the Bolsheviks
4. The Bolshevik revolution, October 1917

C The Bolshevik revolution and the dictatorship
1. Setting up the Marxist state
2. Negotiating peace
3. State of the land and economy

D Opposition to the Bolsheviks and the civil war
1. The opposition
2. The Bolsheviks in danger
3. Bolshevik victory
   - Bolshevik strengths
   - failings of the Whites

E War communism and the New Economic Policy
1. War communism
2. The cost of the civil war and war communism
3. The New Economic Policy
4. The importance of Lenin

F The struggle to succeed Lenin
1. The candidates
2. Stalin succeeds

G Stalin's attempts to modernise the USSR
1. The Five Year Plans
2. The effects of the Five Year Plans
3. Farming: the need for collectivisation
4. How it worked
5. The effects of collectivisation

H Stalin's control over home and foreign policies
1. Opposition to Stalin
2. The purges
3. The Constitution
4. The culture of Stalin's USSR
5. Stalin's attitude to world revolution
6. Concern about fascism
7. The search for security

GLOSSARY

alliances agreements made between two or more countries for a particular purpose, for example, to help each other if they are attacked

apartheid official policy of discrimination against non-white people – this affects every aspect of life such as jobs, housing, education, political power

appeasement giving in to the demands of an aggressive country as a way of keeping the peace, for example, Chamberlain's attitude to Germany in the 1930s

armistice an end to fighting in a war but not necessarily the end of the war itself, for example the armistice of 1918 ended the fighting in the First World War but the war itself did not officially end until the Treaty of Versailles was signed

autocrat a ruler who held absolute power in a country and did not have to explain his actions to anyone else, the best example was the Tsar of Russia

Bolsheviks literally translated from Russian means 'the majority', the Bolsheviks were the highly disciplined communists led by Lenin

coalitions usually means a situation where different political parties inside a country work together, either because they agree on one particular issue or because they are both opposed to some other group

collective security a way of protecting world peace and security through joint action by all nations

collectivisation the process in Stalin's USSR in the 1930s of bringing small farms together to create larger ones which were meant to be more efficient

conscription compulsory military service in the army, most countries in Europe had a system where young men spent two to three years in the army

containment a foreign policy aimed at containing the political influence or military power of another country, for example, US policy to stop the spread of communism during the Cold War

covenant a written document which lays down rules about how an organisation is going to be run

détente the relaxing of tension or hostility between nations, for example, the improvement of relations between the US and the USSR at the end of the 1960s

economic sanctions measures taken by one or more countries to restrict or stop their trade with another country

expansionism a deliberate policy followed by countries to expand the borders of their territory and gain new lands. This usually involves the use of force, for example, Japan's invasion of Manchuria in 1931

international cooperation countries working together to settle disputes – usually by peaceful means

iron curtain the guarded border which divided the communist countries of Eastern Europe and the Western democracies

isolationism a policy of not taking part in international affairs

lebensraum territory claimed by a country on the grounds that it needs more space to grow and survive, for example, Hitler's claim to lands in Eastern Europe

mandate an official order for territory to be taken under the control or protection of a certain country. Mandates are often made at the end of wars or long disputes

ostpolitik a term first used to describe Willy Brandt's attempts to improve relations with European communist countries, especially East Germany, in the 1960s and 1970s.

plebiscite vote by the people of a state or region on an important question such as union with another country

primary source a source of information which can be useful to the historian because it was produced at the time and place which the historian is examining, it can be written, recorded speech or film, or a drawing or photograph

prohibition the name given to the law in 1920s USA which made alcohol illegal

GLOSSARY

proportional representation a system of voting in which all of the votes cast in an election are counted and political parties receive seats in proportion to the number of votes they receive. This system was used in Germany after the First World War

protectionism economic policies followed by a country to protect its own industries and products from overseas competition, for example, by charging import duties on goods from abroad

radicals a term which describes people or groups (sometimes within other groups) who hold extreme political views, for example the Nazis could be described as a radical party

satellite a country or region controlled or dominated by a foreign power

secondary evidence the term given to evidence which was produced after the events which that evidence describes, the most common example is a textbook

self-determination people being allowed to choose their own government, not being ruled by a foreign power

suffragette a woman who campaigned, sometimes violently, to win the vote for women

veto the power to stop action proposed by other people or organisations